Comparing Democracies 2

Comparing Democracies 2

New Challenges in the Study
of Elections and Voting

edited by
Lawrence LeDuc • Richard G. Niemi • Pippa Norris

SAGE Publications
London • Thousand Oaks • New Delhi

First published 2002

Reprinted 2003

 SAGE Publications Ltd
6 Bonhill Street
London EC2A 4PU

SAGE Publications Inc
2455 Teller Road
Thousand Oaks, California 91320

SAGE Publications India Pvt Ltd
32, M-Block Market
Greater Kailash – I
New Delhi 110 048

British Library Cataloguing in Publication data

A catalogue record for this book is available
from the British Library

ISBN 0 7619 7222 6
ISBN 0 7619 7223 4 (pbk)

Library of Congress Control Number 2001 135327

Typeset by SIVA Math Setters, Chennai, India
Printed in Great Britain by Biddles Ltd, *www.biddles.co.uk*

Contents

List of Figures

List of Tables

Acknowledgments

The present volume builds on *Comparing Democracies* (Sage 1996), which in turn was based on a conference funded by the National Science Foundation (SES-9410345). We remain grateful to NSF for the opportunity afforded by the conference grant.

Most of the chapters in this volume are entirely new. All of the topics in the first volume, however, remain relevant, and the chapters not updated here are worth consulting. We list them here both as a way of thanking the authors and as a reference for readers:

Richard Katz, "Party Organizations and Finance"
Sylvia Bashevkin, "Interest Groups and Social Movements"
David M. Farrell, "Campaign Strategies and Tactics"
Pippa Norris, "Legislative Recruitment"
David Butler, "Polls and Elections"
Holli A. Semetko, "The Media"
Ian McAllister, "Leaders"
Helmut Norpoth, "The Economy"
Lawrence LeDuc, "Elections and Democratic Governance"

We would like to thank Allyson Marino and Jennifer McLernon for help in preparing the references and index.

We are grateful to Sage Publications—and especially to Lucy Robinson—for their support through all stages of this project.

1

Introduction: Comparing Democratic Elections

LAWRENCE LEDUC, RICHARD G. NIEMI
and PIPPA NORRIS

Elections are the lifeblood of democracy: generating public debate, shaping the policy agenda, selecting representatives, determining the composition of parliaments, and influencing the distribution of power in government. Regular opportunities to "kick the rascals out" via the ballot box remain an essential pre-condition of democracy, but as chapters in this book demonstrate, competitive elections are not sufficient by themselves to ensure a vigorous and healthy system of representative government. This also requires many other characteristics, including transparency and accountability in government, vigorous party competition and regular rotation of the parties in government and opposition, widespread respect for political rights and civil liberties (particularly for minority populations), multiple channels of political communication, extensive opportunities for citizen participation, and a vibrant civic society connecting citizens and the state.

The core challenge facing many countries in the early 21st century is that while they have created electoral democracies, maintaining the essential conditions for deepening and consolidating the full panoply of democratic institutions remains a work in progress. What Huntington (1991) termed the "third wave" of democratization has swept the globe since the early 1970s, but in recent years this tide has often faltered and even occasionally reversed, usually falling not with the bang of a dramatic military coup as in Pakistan, but with the whimper of more piecemeal steps backwards—legislative power usurped, media muzzled, corruption undermining government legitimacy, or scandal eroding public trust. Of course there is also much positive progress to report during the past decade: the development of a competitive party system in Mexico, the rise of the opposition movement that deposed Slobodan Milosevic in Yugoslavia, and the consolidation of democracy in the Czech Republic, Hungary, and Poland. During the past twenty years countries as diverse as Benin, Chile, and South Korea have all moved by leaps and bounds towards the solid establishment of political rights and civil liberties. But the modern history of democratization has proved yet another example of two steps forwards and one back, rather than the smooth and painless transition that many optimists hoped would sweep all obstacles from its path.

Nevertheless, the universe of electoral democracies and sovereign states has expanded dramatically around the globe. At the end of the nineteenth century no states could be regarded as genuine democracies if judged by the present-day standards of universal suffrage and competitive elections. A handful of the industrialized Anglo-American, Scandinavian, and West European nations possessed nascent systems of fully representative democracy, but even these continued to exclude large segments of the population by denying voting rights to women or minority groups like American blacks. By the mid-20th century, there were some 22 democracies, out of 154 nation-states, if judged by these same standards (Freedom House 1999). Another 21 nations at that time had instituted restricted democratic practices, while the remainder were ruled by a variety of non-democratic regimes, including absolute monarchies (15), totalitarian or authoritarian states (22), and countries under imperial rule as protectorates (31) or colonial territories (43).

The fall of the Berlin Wall in 1989 symbolized the end of the Cold War era, the collapse of Communism, and the rise in the number of electoral democracies in Central and Eastern Europe. But the "third wave" of democracies started earlier, in the 1970s with the fall of the Portuguese dictatorship in 1974, followed by liberalization in authoritarian regimes in southern Europe, Asia, and Latin America (Huntington 1991). The annual Freedom House (2000) survey of political rights and civil liberties provides the most comprehensive data monitoring the spread of democratization worldwide from the early 1970s to date. Utilizing Freedom House definitions, there were 42 democracies in 1972, defined as those with free and fair competitive electoral contests and meeting minimum standards of political rights and civil liberties. By the end of the 20th century, the number of such countries had doubled to 86, representing 38% of the world's population.

During the third wave the most dramatic gains were registered in many post-Communist societies; important steps were taken as well in Latin America, Asia, the Pacific, and parts of sub-Saharan Africa. Yet there has been minimal change, or even marked deterioration, in Arab States, many of which continue to be ruled by traditional monarchies or by authoritarian regimes. Considerable uncertainty clouds the future of democracy in the Andean region of Latin America, in many of the states of the former Soviet Union, and in Africa, outside of the southern cone.

Moreover, events in recent decades have challenged many of the traditional assumptions that the process of modernization would inevitably and automatically generate the necessary and sufficient conditions for a rising tide of political freedom as the shift from rural to industrialized economies expanded education and literacy, altered living standards, lifestyles, and leisure, and fostered a burgeoning middle class of professionals and managers in the service sector. Such theories of modernization were popularized in the late 1950s and early 1960s by Lerner (1958), Lipset (1959), Rostow (1961), Deutsch (1964), Bell (1973), and others. These theories suggested that factors like wealth, education, urbanization, and industrialization are the social requisites for democracy and for mass participation in the political system. The central claim, and indeed the seductive appeal, of modernization theories is that economic, cultural, and political changes go together in predictable ways, so that there are broadly similar trajectories even if particular circumstances mean that what occurs in any given society cannot be predicted exactly. This theory subsequently became unfashionable, in part because democracy initially failed to take root in many developing countries in Asia and Latin America that had experienced rapid economic development during the 1960s and 1970s. Critics also lambasted the ethnocentric assumptions of linear "progress" towards a Western model of democracy, as well as the economic determinism inherent in some earlier versions of this thesis (O'Donnell, Schmitter, and Whitehead 1987).

In recent decades the emergence of "third wave" democracies has spurred fresh interest in re-examining the association between socioeconomic development and the process of democratic transition and consolidation. As illustrated in Figure 1.1 (*top panel*), mid-1970s data suggest that there was indeed a strong and significant correlation between the level of development (measured by the standard UNDP Human Development Index combining literacy, educational enrollment, longevity, and per capita $GDP in Purchasing Power Parity) and the level of democracy (measured by the Freedom House indices of political rights and civil liberties).[1] Older democracies like Norway, Japan, and the United States were tightly clustered in the top-right corner of the graph among the most advanced and affluent industrialized economies while poorer nations, plagued by debt, disease, and illiteracy, often were deprived of fundamental human rights. There were some long-standing exceptions to this pattern among poorer democracies, such as India, Gambia, and Papua New Guinea, making the relationship far from perfect, but the regression line was nevertheless a relatively good predictor.

By the 1990s the link between economic development and democratization remained evident, but the association between these variables had greatly weakened (Figure 1.1, *bottom panel*). Today some affluent states like Kuwait and Singapore, with high levels of per capita income, are governed by non-democratic regimes that violate basic human rights. At the same time, certain poorer countries like Mali, Botswana, and Bangladesh enjoy relatively widespread freedoms, and this is particularly true of many of the developing microstates like Barbados. The scatter of countries is more widely dispersed in the 1990s than two decades earlier, suggesting that although economics strongly influences politics, it does not determine it. Other factors matter.

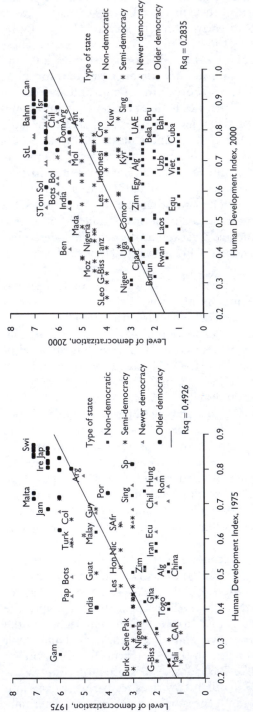

FIGURE 1.1　*Democracy and Development, mid-1970s and 2000*

NOTES AND SOURCES:

Human Development Index: The index is the standard measure of human development produced annually by the UNDP measuring longevity (life expectancy at birth), knowledge (adult literacy rate and the combined enrollment ratio) and standard of living (adjusted per capita income in Purchasing Power Parity US$). The scale ranges to a maximum value of 1. United Nations Development Programme (UNDP) (2000) *Human Development Report 2000.* New York: Oxford University Press/UNDP.

Level of democratization: Mean political rights and civil liberties (reversed seven-point scale) from Freedom House, 1999–2000. Freedom around the world. www.freedomhouse.org

Older democracies = 39 nation-states with average FH ratings of political rights and civil liberties of 2.0 or less in 1999–2000 (plus India rated at 2.5) and with at least 20 years' continuous experience of democracy (1980–2000) based on the mean FH rating 1972–1999.

Newer democracies = 43 nation-states with average FH ratings of political rights and civil liberties of 2.5 or less in 1999–2000 and with less than 20 years' continuous experience of democracy (1980–2000) based on the mean FH rating 1972–1999.

Semi-democracies = 47 nation-states with average FH ratings of political rights and civil liberties from 3.0 to 4.5 in 1999–2000.

Non-democracies = 62 nation-states with average FH ratings of political rights and civil liberties of 5.0 or more in 1999–2000.

For details see Freedom around the World. www.freedomhouse.org

One popular approach has focused on cultural attitudes and values that are thought to foster the underlying conditions for a thriving civic society (Almond and Verba 1963; Inglehart 1998; Harrison and Huntington 2001). Particular political leaders, like Nelson Mandela, Lee Kuan Yew, Vladimir Putin, and Fidel Castro, are commonly believed to play an important part in helping or hindering the transition process. Perhaps most importantly, institutional accounts emphasize that political systems have the capacity to exert an autonomous effect that may foster or prevent the consolidation of democracy. The importance of structural factors highlights the need to understand the issues covered by this book—namely, the role of electoral systems, the use of referendums and initiatives, the structure of party competition, the impact of campaign communications, and how legislative candidates are nominated and selected, along with the effects of these rules and processes on voting behavior, the structure of political cleavages, and patterns of electoral participation.

Comparing elections and voting behavior

How can we understand these issues? The rapid transformation of the political landscape in so many countries over the past thirty years has posed many intellectual challenges to the conventional understanding of elections and voting behavior. Effectively, it has changed the context of elections even as the study of voting and elections was expanding to cover a much larger set of countries and greater diversity in electoral institutions. From the 1950s to the early 1990s the study of elections focused primarily on the two-dozen or so established democracies in North America, Western Europe, Scandinavia, and the Pacific, all relatively affluent industrialized nations and market economies. The systematic analysis of voting behavior was confined to an even smaller subset of these nations that had developed a series of national election surveys (de Guchteneire, LeDuc, and Niemi 1985, 1991; Mochmann, Oedegaard, and Mauer 1998). Conceptual approaches to studying voting behavior were likewise constrained, being heavily influenced by the methodology of survey research and theoretical concepts derived from social psychology.

Beginning in the 1980s and blossoming in the 1990s, projects extended the ability of researchers to draw comparisons across countries. The 30-year series of bi-annual Eurobarometer surveys represents one such cross-national enterprise—with geographic coverage that has regularly widened with the enlargement of the European Union (http://europa.eu.int/comm/dg10/epo/eb.html). The study of elections to the European Parliament, begun systematically in 1989, has likewise fostered the growth of cross-national European research. Beyond Europe, there has been a dramatic expansion in the collection of academic survey data on public opinion, starting with the US General Social Survey in the early 1970s and spreading to annual surveys of social and political attitudes in over two-dozen new and old democracies under the umbrella of the International Social Survey Program (www.gesis.org/en/data_service/issp). The four-wave series of World Values Studies (http://wvs.isr.umich.edu/), conducted since 1980 under the direction of Ronald Inglehart, has also widened the wealth of available data, covering over 60 countries, a source that has been especially valuable in many societies that previously lacked a tradition of survey research. Further contribution along these lines has been made by the Latinobarómetro and by similar initiatives in Central and Eastern Europe, Africa, and East Asia (www.globalbarometer.org). Lastly, another resource is the Comparative Study of Electoral Systems, which began to integrate a common battery across national election studies in the mid-1990s (Mochman et al. 1998; www.umich.edu/~nes/cses/cses.htm).

The expansion of newer democracies, along with political change in many long-standing democracies, forces us to re-evaluate the study of elections. In part, the question is whether established theories and concepts of individual voting behavior are applicable beyond the confines of the countries and times in which they were developed. But the major challenge is to integrate the micro- and macro-levels—that is, to situate our understanding of individual voting choice within the *structure* of political systems, including such factors as the legal regulations governing elections, the process of political campaigning, and the pattern of party competition (Wlezien and Franklin 2002). These twin tasks underlie the work that led to the first edition of this book and to the new and revised chapters included here. Throughout, we have sought to include a wide universe of electoral democracies as well as to compare the multiple influences on voting behavior arising in different contexts.

The comparative framework

This book focuses primarily on the 58 electoral democracies listed in Table 1.1, defined as those nations with a rating of 1–3 on the 2000 Freedom House index of political rights and with a population of over three million. In addition, the Russian Federation, Turkey, and Venezuela are included, despite their lower political rights scores, because of their size and importance and their efforts to establish or maintain democratic processes. The list includes two-dozen older democracies (those with at least 20 years' continuous experience of democracy based on mean Freedom House ratings from 1980 to 2000), as well as 19 newer democracies, and 15 countries that are considered only "partly free." In total, these countries include a population of 3.2 billion out of the 5.8 billion people living around the globe at the turn of the millennium. The list excludes smaller European democracies such as Malta or Luxembourg, as well as many island microstates in the Caribbean and Pacific, some of which have a long history of stable parliamentary democracy, such as the Bahamas or Trinidad and Tobago.

TABLE 1.1   *Major Democracies of the World*

Country	Population[a] (m)	Political rights[b] 2000	5-year average	Civil liberties[b] 2000	5-year average
Argentina	36	2	2.2	3	3.0
Australia	19	1	1.0	1	1.0
Austria	8	1	1.0	1	1.0
Bangladesh	126	3	2.4	4	4.0
Belgium	10	1	1.0	2	2.0
Benin	6	2	2.0	3	3.0
Bolivia	8	1	1.4	3	3.2
Brazil	166	3	2.6	4	4.0
Bulgaria	8	2	2.0	3	2.8
Canada	30	1	1.0	1	1.0
Chile	15	2	2.2	2	2.0
Costa Rica	4	1	1.0	2	2.0
Czech Republic	10	1	1.0	2	2.0
Denmark	5	1	1.0	1	1.0
Dominican Republic	8	2	2.8	3	3.0
Ecuador	12	2	2.2	3	3.2
El Salvador	6	2	2.4	3	3.0
Finland	5	1	1.0	1	1.0
France	59	1	1.0	2	2.0
Germany	82	1	1.0	2	2.0
Greece	11	1	1.0	3	3.0
Honduras	6	3	2.6	3	3.0
Hungary	10	1	1.0	2	2.0
India	980	2	2.4	3	3.6
Ireland	4	1	1.0	1	1.0
Israel	6	1	1.0	2	2.8
Italy	58	1	1.0	2	2.0
Japan	126	1	1.0	2	2.0
Lithuania	4	1	1.0	2	2.0
Madagascar	15	2	2.0	4	4.0
Malawi	11	3	2.2	3	3.0
Mali	11	3	2.6	3	2.8
Mexico	96	3	3.4	4	3.8
Mozambique	17	3	3.0	4	4.0
Nepal	23	3	3.0	4	4.0
Netherlands	16	1	1.0	1	1.0
New Zealand	4	1	1.0	1	1.0
Nicaragua	5	3	3.0	3	3.2
Norway	4	1	1.0	1	1.0
Philippines	75	2	2.0	3	3.2
Poland	39	1	1.0	2	2.0
Portugal	10	1	1.0	1	1.0
Romania	23	2	2.4	2	2.4
Russia	148	4	3.4	5	4.2
Slovakia	5	1	1.8	2	3.0
South Africa	41	1	1.0	2	2.0
South Korea	46	2	2.0	2	2.0
Spain	40	1	1.0	2	2.0
Sweden	9	1	1.0	1	1.0

(Continued)

TABLE 1.1   *Continued*

Country	Population[a] (m)	Political rights[b] 2000	Political rights[b] 5-year average	Civil liberties[b] 2000	Civil liberties[b] 5-year average
Switzerland	7	1	1.0	1	1.0
Taiwan	22	2	2.2	2	2.2
Thailand	61	2	2.6	3	3.2
Turkey	63	4	4.2	5	5.0
Ukraine	50	3	3.0	4	4.0
United Kingdom	59	1	1.0	2	2.0
United States	270	1	1.0	1	1.0
Uruguay	3	1	1.2	2	2.0
Venezuela	23	4	2.6	4	3.2

[a]*World Bank Atlas*, 2000. Included are all countries with a population of 3 million or more that have Freedom House ratings on political rights of 1–3 in the most recent rating. The Russian Federation, Turkey, and Venezuela are included, despite their lower political rights scores, because of their size and importance and their efforts to establish or maintain democratic processes.
[b]Freedom House (http://www.freedomhouse.org/ratings/). Political rights and civil liberties are rated separately on seven-category scales—1 representing the "most free" and 7 the "least free." There is a strong correlation between the two kinds of rights; with few exceptions, countries have ratings on political rights and civil liberties that are within one point of each other.

Complete information is not available for all the countries under comparison, but wherever possible standardized reference data have been gathered in the tables appended to this chapter. Table 1.2 presents the key features of the electoral systems used in the 58 democracies under comparison. Table 1.3 documents electoral qualifications, procedures, and voter turnout in the 58 countries. Table 1.4 provides recent election results for the lower house of the national legislature and for the highest executive office where this is directly elected. The table also provides a convenient source of reference for party systems in each country, listing all political parties electing more than one member to the legislature. Sources given under each table show where updated materials can be obtained on the Internet. Further reference materials are included where relevant to specific topics in subsequent chapters.

The plan of the book

More than half of the chapters in this book have been specially commissioned for this edition; the others have been substantially revised to reflect developments since the first edition was published in 1996. Chapters are designed to offer an overview of the current state of research and a conceptual framework on the topic as well as to present some original data and analysis.

The first chapters in the book deal with the legal structure regulating elections, setting out the institutional rules of the game. In Chapter 2, André Blais and Louis Massicotte compare the role of electoral systems that define how votes are cast and seats allocated. The chapter describes the variety of systems existing around the world and then considers the political consequences of electoral laws. Once considered a largely stable phenomenon, the rise of new democracies as well as fundamental reform in established democracies like New Zealand, Italy, and Japan has revived interest in the trade-offs involved in the choice of an electoral system. In Chapter 3, Lawrence LeDuc looks at the expanding role of referendums and initiatives worldwide, the cross-national variations in the opportunities for direct democracy, and the way that voting behavior differs in elections and referendum campaigns.

The book then considers the role of parties and the news media as the key political actors linking citizens and the state, structuring voting choices, and shaping election campaigns. In Chapter 4, Peter Mair compares the role of political parties including the classification of party systems, the structure of party competition, and the relationship between electoral change and party system change. Chapter 5 (Reuven Hazan) discusses how parties choose candidates to compete in general elections, the outcome of this process, and its consequences. Chapter 6 (Pippa Norris) develops a schematic model of campaign communications and then considers how this process has evolved over time from traditional to modern and postmodern elections.

The last section of the book focuses directly on voters and elections. Chapter 7 (Mark Franklin) analyzes cross-national variations in electoral participation, suggesting that these differences can best be explained by instrumental motivations based on the costs and benefits of casting a ballot. Chapter 8 (William L. Miller and Richard G. Niemi) summarizes our understanding of electoral behavior, including the standard division between long-term factors, such as social class, ideological orientations, and psychological identifications, and short-term factors, such as issue preferences and candidate effects. But it also calls for the integration of our knowledge about voter psychology with what we know about the broader context of conditioning and constraint in shaping the choices that face voters. In Chapter 9, Russell Dalton compares the declining strength of structural cleavages like social class and religion, and considers whether these traditional anchors of party support have been displaced in recent decades by issue voting. Lastly, in Chapter 10, Larry Diamond returns to some of the themes raised in this introduction by comparing trends in democratization in major regions around the globe and then considering what we know about public support for the democratization process. The chapter reflects on the prospects for consolidating democracy and the factors needed to reform and strengthen the institutions of democratic governance.

NOTES

1. For purposes of this analysis, the Freedom House scores (see Table 1.1) are averaged and reversed, yielding a single seven-point scale running from 1 (Low) to 7 (High). All countries for which data are available are included in the analysis, regardless of population size.

TABLE 1.2 *Electoral Systems of 58 Democracies*

Country	Lower House				Upper House				Executive
	Electoral system[a]	No. of seats	No. of districts	Length of term (yr)	Electoral system[b]	No. of seats	No. of districts	Length of term (yr)	Presidential term (yr)[c]
Argentina	PR	257	24	4[d]	Plurality[d]	72	24	6[e]	4
Australia	Majority-AV	148	148	3	PR-STV	76	8	6[f]	CM
Austria	PR	183	9 + 2	4	N	64	NA	6	6
Bangladesh	Plurality	330	300	5	U	NA	NA	NA	P
Belgium	PR	150	20	4	P	71	NA	4	CM
Benin	PR	83	18	4	U	NA	NA	NA	5
Bolivia	Mixed	130	68 + 9	5	Plurality	27	9	4	5
Brazil	PR	513	27	4	Plurality	81	27	8[g]	4
Bulgaria	PR	240	31	4	U	NA	NA	NA	4
Canada	Plurality	301	301	5	N	104	NA	NA	CM
Chile	Plurality[h]	120	60	4	Plurality[h]	48	19	8[i]	6
Costa Rica	PR	57	7	4	U	NA	NA	NA	4
Czech Republic	PR	200	8	4	Plurality	81	27	6[e]	P
Denmark	PR	179	19 + 1	4	U	NA	NA	NA	CM
Dominican Republic	PR	149	30	4	Majority-Pl	30	30	4	4
Ecuador	Mixed	123	21 + 1	4	U	NA	NA	NA	4
El Salvador	PR	84	14 + 1	3	U	NA	NA	NA	5
Finland	PR	200	14	4	U	NA	NA	NA	6
France	Majority-Pl	577	577	5	N	321	NA	9[j]	7[k]
Germany	Mixed	656	328 + 1	4	N	69	NA	NA	P
Greece	PR	300	56 + 15	4	U	NA	NA	NA	P
Honduras	PR	128	18	4	U	NA	NA	NA	4
Hungary	Mixed	386	176 + 21	4	N	NA	NA	NA	P
India	Plurality	545	543	5	N	245	NA	6[e]	P
Ireland	PR-STV	166	41	5	U	60	NA	5	P
Israel	PR	120	1	4	U	NA	NA	NA	—[l]

(Continued)

TABLE 1.2 *Continued*

Country	Lower House				Upper House				Executive
	Electoral system[a]	No. of seats	No. of districts	Length of term (yr)	Electoral system[b]	No. of seats	No. of districts	Length of term (yr)	Presidential term (yr)[c]
Italy	Mixed	630	475 + 1	5	Mixed	326	232 + 1	5	P
Japan	Mixed	500	300 + 1	4	Mixed	252	126 + 1	6[f]	CM
Lithuania	Mixed	141	71 + 1	4	U	NA	NA	NA	5
Madagascar	Majority-Pl[m]	150	126	4	U	NA	NA	NA	5
Malawi	Plurality	192	192	5	U	NA	NA	NA	5
Mali	Majority-R[n]	147	55	5	U	NA	NA	NA	5
Mexico	Mixed	500	300 + 1	3	Mixed	200	32 + 1	6	6
Mozambique	PR	250	11	5	U	NA	NA	NA	5
Nepal	Plurality	205	205	5	N	60	NA	6	CM
Netherlands	PR	150	1	4	N	75	NA	6	CM
New Zealand	Mixed	120	65 + 1	3	U	NA	NA	NA	CM
Nicaragua	PR	90	17 + 1	5	U	NA	NA	NA	5
Norway	PR	165	19 + 1	4	N	41	NA	4	CM
Philippines	Mixed	222	208 + 1	3	Plurality	24	1	6	6
Poland	PR	460	52 + 1	4	PR	100	49	4	5
Portugal	PR	230	22	4	U	NA	NA	NA	5
Romania	PR	346	42	4	PR	140	42	4	4
Russia	Mixed	450	225 + 1	4	N	178	NA	4	5
Slovakia	PR	150	1	4	U	NA	NA	NA	5
South Africa	PR	400	9 + 1	5	N	90	NA	5	P
South Korea	Mixed	299	253 + 1	4	U	NA	NA	NA	5
Spain	PR	350	52	4	Mixed	252	NA	4	CM
Sweden	PR	349	29 + 1	4	U	NA	NA	NA	CM
Switzerland	PR	200	26	4	N	46	NA	4	P
Taiwan	Mixed	225	36 + 1	3	U	NA	NA	NA	4
Thailand	Mixed	500	400 + 1	4	Plurality	200	200	6	CM

(Continued)

TABLE 1.2 *Continued*

Country	Lower House				Upper House				Executive
	Electoral system[a]	No. of seats	No. of districts	Length of term (yr)	Electoral system[b]	No. of seats	No. of districts	Length of term (yr)	Presidential term (yr)[c]
Turkey	PR	550	79	5	U	NA	NA	NA	P
Ukraine	Mixed	450	225 + 1	4	U	NA	NA	NA	5
United Kingdom	Plurality	659	659	5	N	NA	NA	NA	CM
United States	Plurality	435	435	2	Plurality	100	50	6[e]	4
Uruguay	PR	99	19	5	PR	31	1	5	5
Venezuela	Mixed	165	72 + 24	5	U	NA	NA	NA	6

[a] PR = proportional representation, etc. For more detail, see Figure 2.2.

[b] For elected chambers only. N = not directly elected. U = unicameral. P = partially elected. NA = not applicable.

[c] For directly elected executives only. CM = constitutional monarchy. P = election by parliament.

[d] One-half elected every two years.

[e] One-third elected every two years.

[f] One-half elected every three years.

[g] Elected alternately every four years (1/3, 2/3).

[h] In two-member districts.

[i] One-half elected every four years.

[j] One-third renewed every three years.

[k] Will change to five years at the next election.

[l] Prime Minister is directly elected for a four-year term.

[m] With some two-member districts.

[n] In multimember constituencies.

SOURCES: Blais and Massicotte (this volume); Banks and Muller (1999); Derbyshire and Derbyshire (1999); Rose (2000); Inter-Parliamentary Union (www.ipu.org/parline); Keesing's Record of World Events; Europa World Year Book (2000)

TABLE 1.3 *Electoral Procedures and Voting Turnout in 58 Democracies*

Country	Voting age	Compulsory voting	No. of days polls are open	Work day/ rest day	Postal, proxy, or advance voting[a]	Turnout in recent election Parliamentary	Presidential[b]
Argentina	18	Yes	1	Rest	No	80.5	80.5[c]
Australia	18	Yes	1	Rest	Post, Adv (R)	96.1	NA
Austria	19	No		Rest		80.4	74.4
Bangladesh	18	No	2	Work	Post	74.0	NA
Belgium	18	Yes	1	Rest	Post, Prox (R)	90.6	NA
Benin	18	No		Work	Prox	70.1	53.4[d]
Bolivia	18	Yes		Rest	No	70.0	70.0[c]
Brazil	16	Yes		Rest	No	78.5	78.5[c]
Bulgaria	18	No		Rest	No	67.5	52.2[d]
Canada	18	No		Work	All	61.2	NA
Chile	18	Yes		Work	No	86.3	90.6[d]
Costa Rica	18	Yes	1	Rest	No	73.7	73.7[c]
Czech Republic	18	No	2	Both		73.8	NA
Denmark	18	No	1	Work	Adv	86.8	NA
Dominican Republic	18	Yes	1	Rest		65.9	76.1
Ecuador	18	Yes	1	Rest	No	64.2	71.7[f]
El Salvador	18	Yes	1	Rest		38.0	38.6
Finland	18	No	2	Both	Adv (R)	65.3	76.8[d]
France	18	No	1[e]	Rest	Prox (R)	67.9	74.8[d]
Germany	18	No	1	Rest	Post (R)	82.2	NA
Greece	18	Yes	1	Rest		75.0	NA
Honduras	18	Yes	1[e]	Rest	No	65.0	65.0[c]
Hungary	18	No		Rest	Post (R)	56.3	NA
India	21	No	5	Both	No	59.7	NA
Ireland	18	No	1	Work	Post, Adv (R)	65.9	47.4[d]
Israel	18	No	1	Work	Adv (R)	78.7	62.0[g]
Italy	18	No	2	Both	No	81.4	NA

(Continued)

TABLE 1.3 *Continued*

Country	Voting age	Compulsory voting	No. of days polls are open	Work day/ rest day	Postal, proxy, or advance voting[a]	Turnout in recent election	
						Parliamentary	Presidential[b]
Japan	20	No		Rest	Post, Adv (R)	62.5	NA
Lithuania	18	No	1	Rest	Post, Adv (R)	55.9	73.7[d]
Madagascar	18	Yes	1	Rest	No	65.9	60.9[d]
Malawi	18	No	1	Work	No	93.8	92.3[c]
Mali	18	No	1[e]	Rest	Prox (R)	21.6	28.4
Mexico	18	Yes	1	Rest	Adv (R)	64.0	64.0[c]
Mozambique	18	No	3	Both		62.8	69.5[c]
Nepal	18	No	2	Work		65.8	NA
Netherlands	18	No	1	Work	Post, Prox (R)	73.0	NA
New Zealand	18	No	1	Rest	Post, Adv	83.1	NA
Nicaragua	18	No	1	Rest		77.1	77.1[c]
Norway	18	No	2	Both	Post	78.0	NA
Philippines	18	Yes	1	Work	No	78.9	78.9[c]
Poland	18	No	1	Rest	No	47.9	61.1
Portugal	18	No	1	Rest	Post, Adv (R)	61.9	50.9
Romania	18	No	1	Work	No	56.5	50.5[f]
Russia	18	No	1	Rest		61.9	68.6
Slovak Republic	18	No	2	Both	No	84.2	74.5[d]
South Africa	18	No	1	Work		86.5	NA
South Korea	20	No	1	Work		57.2	80.6
Spain	18	No	1	Rest	Post	70.6	NA
Sweden	18	No	1	Work	All	79.7	NA
Switzerland	18	No	1	Rest	Post, Prox (RS)	43.4	NA
Taiwan	20	No	1	Rest		68.1	82.6
Thailand	20	No	1[e]	Both		70.0	NA
Turkey	18	Yes	1	Rest		87.1	NA
Ukraine	18	No	1	Rest		70.8	74.9[d]

(Continued)

TABLE 1.3 *Continued*

Country	Voting age	Compulsory voting	No. of days polls are open	Work day/ rest day	Postal, proxy, or advance voting[a]	Turnout in recent election	
						Parliamentary	Presidential[b]
United Kingdom	18	No	1	Work	Post, Prox (R)	59.4	NA
United States	18	No	1	Work	Post, Prox (RS)	51.2	51.2[h]
Uruguay	18	Yes	1	Rest	No	91.7	91.8[f]
Venezuela	18	Yes	1	Work	No	56.4	56.4[c]

[a] Postal voting denotes any type of mail-in ballot; proxy voting permits an authorized person to cast a vote on another person's behalf; advance voting refers to a poll held on any day before the regular polling date; "R" indicates that the practice is restricted to certain categories of voters (e.g. aged, infirm, etc.); "S" denotes that rules vary between states or regions.

[b] See Table 1.4 for election dates.

[c] Presidential and legislative election held concurrently.

[d] Second round.

[e] Two rounds held on separate days.

[f] Second round. First round held concurrently with parliamentary elections.

[g] Prime ministerial election.

[h] Presidential and legislative elections coincide in presidential years only.

SOURCES: Rose (2000); Banks and Muller (1999); Derbyshire and Derbyshire (1999); Massicotte, Blais, and Yoshinaka (2001); Inter-Parliamentary Union (www.ipu.org/parline); International IDEA (www.idea.intl); *Electoral Studies*

TABLE 1.4 Recent Election Results for 58 Democracies

Country	ENPP[a]	Date	Which parties formed government	Lower House No. of seats	Lower House Percentage of vote	Political parties winning seats in Lower House	Presidential Percentage of vote[b]	Presidential Date
Argentina	2.56	99 10 24	UCR/Frepaso Alliance	124	43.6	Alliance of Radical Civic Union (UCR) + Frepaso	48.5	99 10 24[c]
				101	33.7	Justicialist party (PJ)	38.1	
				12	7.6	Action for the Republic (AR)	10.1	
				3	1.7	Democratic Progressive party (PDP)		
				3	1.3	Democratic party (PD)		
				3	0.6	Republican Force (FR)		
				3	0.6	New Party Front (Frepanu)		
				2	0.5	Liberal Autonomist Pact (PAL)		
				2	0.5	Nequino People's Movement (MPN)		
				4	9.9	All others	3.3	
Australia	2.48	98 10 03	Coalition of Liberal and National parties	67	40.0	Australian Labor party (ALP)	NA	NA
				64	34.1	Liberal party (LP)		
				16	8.4	Pauline Hanson's One Nation (ON)		
					5.3	National party (NP)		
					5.1	Australian Democrats (AD)		
					2.1	Greens		
				1	5.0	All others		
Austria	3.41	99 10 03	Coalition of ÖVP and FPÖ	65	33.2	Social Democratic party (SPÖ)	63.5	98 04 19
				52	26.9	People's party (ÖVP)		
				52	26.9	Freedom party (FPÖ)		
				14	7.4	Greens		
					3.9	Liberal Forum	11.1	
					1.7	All others	25.4	
Bangladesh	2.43	96 06 12	Coalition of Awami League and JSD	176		Awami League (BAL)	NA	NA
				113		Bangladesh National party (BNP)		

(Continued)

TABLE 1.4 *Continued*

Country	ENPP[a]	Date	Which parties formed government	Lower House — No. of seats	Lower House — Percentage of vote	Political parties winning seats in Lower House	Presidential — Percentage of vote[b]	Presidential — Date
				33		Jatiyo Dal (JD)		
				3		Jamaat-I Islami (JIB)		
				1		Socialist party (JSD)		
				1		Islamic Unity Front (IOJ)		
				3		Others and independents		
Belgium	9.05	99 06 13	Coalition of VLD, PS, SP, PRL-FDF-MCC, Ecolo, and Agalev	23	14.3	Flemish-speaking Liberals (VLD)	NA	NA
				22	14.1	Flemish Christian Democrats (CVP)		
				19	10.1	French-speaking Socialists (PS)		
				18	10.1	Federation of French-speaking Liberals, Francophone Democratic Front, and Citizens Movement for Change (PRL—FDF—MCC)		
				15	9.9	Vlaams Blok (VlB)		
				14	9.6	Flemish Socialists (SP)		
				11	7.3	ECOLO		
				10	5.9	Francophone Social Christian (PSC)		
				9	7.0	AGALEV		
				8	5.6	Volksunie and ID21 (VU-ID21)		
				1	1.5	National Front (FN)		
					2.1	Vivant		
					2.5	All others		
Benin	5.93	99 03 30	Coalition of PRD, PSD, FARD, IPD, and others	27	22.7	Renaissance of Benin (PRB)		01 03 18[af]
				11	12.2	Democratic Renewal (PRD)		

(Continued)

TABLE 1.4 *Continued*

Country	ENPP[a]	Date	Which parties formed government	Lower House — No. of seats	Lower House — Percentage of vote	Political parties winning seats in Lower House	Presidential — Percentage of vote[b]	Presidential — Date
				10	5.5	Action Front for Renewal and Development (FARD)	84.1	
				9	9.3	Social Democratic party (PSD)	15.9	
				6	9.2	African Movement for Democracy (MADEP)		
				4		Impulse to Progress and Democracy (IPD)		
				4		Star Alliance (Étoile)		
				3		DUNYA		
				2		Movement for Citizens' Commitment (MERCI)		
				7		All others		
Bolivia	5.36	97 06 01	Coalition of AND, MIR, and UCS	33	22.3	Nationalist Democratic Alliance (AND)	22.3	97 06 01[c]
				26	17.7	Nationalist Revolutionary Movement (MNR)	17.7	
				25	16.7	Revolutionary Institutional Movement (MIR)	16.7	
				21	15.9	Civic Solidarity Union (UCS)	15.9	
				17	15.9	Conscience of the Fatherland (Condepa)	15.9	
				4	3.7	United Left (IU)		
				4	2.5	Free Bolivia Movement (MBL)	11.5	
					5.3	All others		

(Continued)

TABLE 1.4 *Continued*

Country	ENPP[a]	Date	Which parties formed government	Lower House			Presidential	
				No. of seats	Percentage of vote	Political parties winning seats in Lower House	Percentage of vote[b]	Date
Brazil	7.13	98 10 04	Coalition of PSDB, PFL, PMDB, PPB, and PPS	106	17.3	Liberal Front (PFL)	53.1	98 10 04[c]
				99	17.5	Brazilian Social Democratic party (PSDB)		
				82	15.2	Brazilian Democratic Movement (PMDB)		
				60	11.3	Brazilian Progressive party (PPB)		
				58	13.2	Workers' party (PT)	31.7	
				31	5.7	Labor Party of Brazil (PTB)		
				25	5.7	Democratic Labor party (PDT)		
				19		Brazilian Socialist party (PSB)		
				12		Liberal party (PL)		
				7		Communist (PCB)		
				3		Socialist People's party (PPS)	11.0	
				3		Social Democrat party (PSD)		
				2		Party of National Mobilization (PMN)		
				2		Social Christian party		
				1		Greens		
				3		All others	4.2	
Bulgaria	2.61	97 04 19[*]	ODS	134	52.2	Union of Democratic Forces (ODS)	59.7	96 11 03[*]
				58	22.0	Democratic Left (DL)	40.3	
				19	7.6	National Salvation Union (ONS)		
				14	5.6	Euro-Left Coalition (EL)		
				12	4.9	Bulgarian Business Bloc (BBB)		
					1.2	Bulgarian Communist party (BKP)		
				3	6.5	All others		

(Continued)

TABLE 1.4 Continued

Country	ENPP[a]	Date	Which parties formed government	Lower House			Presidential	
				No. of seats	Percentage of vote	Political parties winning seats in Lower House	Percentage of vote[b]	Date
Canada	2.54	00 11 27	Liberal	172	40.8	Liberal party	NA	NA
				66	25.5	Canadian Alliance		
				38	10.7	Bloc Québécois (BQ)		
				13	8.5	New Democratic party (NDP)		
				12	12.2	Progressive Conservative (PC)		
					2.3	All others		
Chile	5.18	97 12 11	Coalition of PDC and others	39	23.0	Christian Democratic party (PDC)		
				23	16.8	National Renewal party (RN)		
				17	14.4	Independent Democratic Union (UDI)	48.7	00 01 16*
				16	12.6	Party for Democracy (PPD)	51.3	
				11	11.1	Socialist party (PS)		
					6.9	Communist party (PCC)		
				6	4.7	Independents (UPC)		
				4	3.1	Radical Social Democrats (CPD)		
					2.9	Humanist party (PH)		
				1	1.2	Center Union (UCCP)		
				3	3.3	All others		
Costa Rica	2.43	98 02 01	PUSC	29	41.3	Social Christian Unity party (PUSC)	46.9	98 02 01[c]
				22	34.9	National Liberation party (PLN)	44.4	
				2	5.7	Democratic Force (FD)	3.0	
				2	3.0	Libertarian Movement (ML)		
				1	2.7	National Integration	1.5	
				1	12.4	All others	4.2	
Czech Republic	3.71	98 06 20	CCSD	74	32.3	Czech Social Democratic party (CSSD)	NA	NA
				63	27.7	Civic Democratic party (ODS)		

(Continued)

COMPARING DEMOCRATIC ELECTIONS 21

TABLE 1.4 *Continued*

Country	ENPP[a]	Date	Which parties formed government	Lower House			Presidential	
				No. of seats	Percentage of vote	Political parties winning seats in Lower House	Percentage of vote[b]	Date
				24	11.0	Communist Party of Bohemia & Moravia (KSCM)		
				20	9.0	Christian Democratic Union/Czech People's party (KDU—CSL)		
				19	8.6	Freedom Union (US)		
					3.9	Rally for the Republic/Republican (SPR—RSC)		
					3.1	Pensioners (DZJ)		
					4.4	All others		
Denmark	4.92	98 03 11	Coalition of SD and RV	63	36.0	Social Democrats (SD)	NA	NA
				42	24.0	Liberal party (V)		
				16	8.9	Conservative People's party (KF)		
				13	7.5	Socialist People's party (SF)		
				13	7.4	Danish People's party (DF)		
				8	4.3	Center Democrats (CD)		
				7	3.9	Social Liberals (RV)		
				5	2.7	Unity List (E)		
				4	2.4	Christian People's party (KrF)		
				4	2.4	Progress party (FrP)		
				4	0.5	All others		
Dominican Republic	2.32	98 05 16	PRD	83	51.4	Dominican Revolutionary party (PRD)	49.9	00 05 16
				49	30.4	Dominican Liberation party (PLD)	24.9	
				17	16.8	Social Christian Reform (PRSC)	24.6	
					1.4	All others		

(Continued)

TABLE 1.4 *Continued*

Country	ENPP[a]	Date	Which parties formed government	Lower House			Presidential	
				No. of seats	Percentage of vote	Political parties winning seats in Lower House	Percentage of vote[b]	Date
Ecuador	5.24	98 05 31	Coalition of DP and others	35	20.0	Popular Democracy/ Christian Democrat (DP—UDC)	51.3	98 07 12[xel]
				28	25.1	Social Christian party (PSC)		
				22	18.8	Roldosista party of Ecuador (PRE)	48.7	
				17	16.3	Democratic Left (ID)		
				6	9.7	New Country/Pachakutik Movement (MUPP—NP)		
				3		Alfarista Radical Front (FRA)		
				3		Conservative party (PCE)		
				2		Popular Democratic Movement (MPD)		
				7		All others		
El Salvador	3.50	00 03 12	ARENA	29	36.0	National Republican Alliance (ARENA)	51.4	99 03 07
				31	35.2	National Liberation Front (FMLN)	29.0	
				13	8.8	National Conciliation party (PCN)	3.8	
				6	7.2	Christian Democratic party (PDC)	5.7	
				3	5.4	United Democratic Centre (CDUI)	7.4	
				2	3.7	National Action party (PAN)		
					1.9	Social Christian Union (USC)		
					1.8	All others	2.7	
Finland	5.15	99 03 21	Coalition of SSDP, KOK, VAS, SFP and VIHR	51	22.9	Finnish Social Democratic party (SSDP)	51.6	00 02 06*
				48	22.4	Centre party (KESK)	48.4	
				46	21.0	National Coalition party (KOK)		
				20	10.9	Left-Wing Alliance (VAS)		

(Continued)

TABLE 1.4 *Continued*

Country	ENPP[a]	Date	Which parties formed government	Lower House No. of seats	Percentage of vote	Political parties winning seats in Lower House	Presidential Percentage of vote[b]	Date
				11	7.3	Green League (VIHR)		
				11	5.1	Swedish People's party (SFP)		
				10	4.2	Finnish Christian League (SKL)		
				3	6.2	All others		
France	3.70	97 06 01	Coalition of PS, PCF, Greens, and others	241	23.5	Socialist party (PS)	47.4	95 05 07*
				134	15.7	Rally for the Republic (RPR)	52.6	
				108	14.2	Union for French Democracy (UDF)		
				38	9.9	Communist party (PCF)		
				21	2.8	Other left-wing parties		
				14	6.6	Other right-wing parties		
				12	1.4	Radical Socialist party (PRS)		
				7	6.8	Greens		
				1	14.9	National Front (FN)		
				1	4.2	All others		
Germany	3.30	98 09 27	Coalition of SPD and Greens	298	40.9	Social Democratic party (SPD)	NA	NA
				198	28.4	Christian Democratic Union (CDU)		
				47	6.7	Christian Social Union (CSU)		
				47	6.7	Greens		
				43	6.2	Free Democratic party (FDP)		
				36	5.1	Party of Democratic Socialism (PDS)		
					1.8	Republicans		
					4.2	All others		
Greece	2.21	00 04 09	PASOK	158	43.8	Panhellenic Socialist Movement (PASOK)	NA	NA
				125	42.7	New Democracy (ND)		
				11	5.5	Communist party of Greece (KKE)		

(Continued)

TABLE 1.4 Continued

Country	ENPP[a]	Date	Which parties formed government	Lower House			Presidential	
				No. of seats	Percentage of vote	Political parties winning seats in Lower House	Percentage of vote[b]	Date
				6	3.2	Left/Progress (SIN)		
					2.7	Democratic Social Movement (DIKKI)		
					2.1	All others		
Honduras	2.20	97 11 30	PLH	67	49.7	Liberal party (PLH)	52.8	97 11 30c
				54	41.3	National party (PN)	42.7	
				5	4.2	Innovation and Social Democracy (PINU)	2.1	
				1	2.6	Democratic Unification party (PUD)	1.2	
				1	2.2	Christian Democratic party (PDCH)	1.2	
Hungary	3.45	98 05 24	Coalition of FIDESz, FKgP, and MDF	148	28.2	Federation of Young Democrats (FIDESz)	NA	NA
				134	32.3	Hungarian Socialist party (MSzP)		
				48	13.8	Independent Smallholders (FKgP)		
				24	7.9	Alliance of Free Democrats (SzDSz)		
				14	5.5	Justice and Life (MIEP)		
					4.1	Workers' party (MP)		
				17	3.1	Hungarian Democratic Forum (MDF)		
					2.6	Christian Democratic People's party (KDNP)		
					2.5	All others		
India	5.82	99 10 03	Coalition of BJP and others	183	23.8	Bharatiya Janata party (BJP)	NA	NA
				114	28.8	Congress		
				33		Communist party of India (Marxist)		
				29		Telegu Desam		
				26		Socialist party		

(Continued)

TABLE 1.4   *Continued*

Country	ENPP[a]	Date	Which parties formed government	Lower House			Presidential	
				No. of seats	Percentage of vote	Political parties winning seats in Lower House	Percentage of vote[b]	Date
				22		Janata Dal		
				15		Shiva Sena		
				14		Bahujan Samaj party		
				12		Dravida Munnetra Kazhagam		
				10		All India Anna Dravida Munnetra Kazhegam		
				10		Biju Janata Dal		
				9		All India Trinamool Congress		
				8		Nationalist Congress		
				7		Rashtriya Janata Dal		
				5		Pattali Makkal Katchi		
				5		India National Lok Dal		
				4		Jammu and Kashmir National Conference		
				4		Marumarlarchi Dravida Munnetra Kazhegam		
				3		Communist party of India		
				3		Revolutionary Socialist party		
				2		All India Forward Bloc		
				2		Muslim League Kerala		
				2		Shirumani Akali Dal		
				2		Rashtriya Lok Dal		
				2		Akhil Bharatiya Lok Tantrick Congress		
				19		Others and independents		
Ireland	2.99	97 06 06	Coalition of FF and PD	77	39.3	Fianna Fáil (FF)	58.7	97 10 30*
				54	27.9	Fine Gael (FG)	41.3	

(Continued)

TABLE 1.4 Continued

Country	ENPP[a]	Date	Which parties formed government	Lower House No. of seats	Percentage of vote	Political parties winning seats in Lower House	Presidential Percentage of vote[b]	Date
				17	10.4	Labour		
				4	4.7	Progressive Democrats (PD)		
				4	2.5	Democratic Left (DL)		
				2	2.8	Greens		
				1	2.5	Sinn Fein		
				7	9.9	Others and independents		
Israel	8.69	99 05 17	Coalition	26	20.3	Labour and allies	37.6	01 02 06[e]
				19	14.2	Likud	62.4	
				17	13.0	Shas		
				10	7.7	Meretz		
				6	5.2	Y'Israel B'alyah		
				6	5.1	Shinui Mifleget Merkaz		
				6	5.0	ha-Merkaz		
				5	4.2	ha-Miflaga ha-Datit ve ha-Leumit (NRP)		
				5	3.8	Yahadut ha Torah		
				5	3.5	United Arab list (Ra'am)		
				4	3.0	ha-Ikhud ha-Leumi		
				4	2.6	Y'Israel Beteinu		
				3	2.6	Hazit Democratit le-Shalom ve-Shivaynon (Hadash)		
				2	2.0	Al Tahammu al-Watani al-Dimuqrati		
				2	1.9	Am Ekhad		
					5.9	All others		
Italy	6.69	01 05 13	House of Freedom coalition	368	29.5	House of Freedom coalition	NA	NA
						Forza Italia		

(Continued)

TABLE 1.4 Continued

Country	ENPP[a]	Date	Which parties formed government	Lower House			Presidential	
				No. of seats	Percentage of vote	Political parties winning seats in Lower House	Percentage of vote[b]	Date
					12.0	National Alliance (AN)		
					3.9	Lega Nord		
					3.2	Christian Democratic Centre (CCD—CDU)		
					1.0	New Italian Socialist party (NPSI)		
				250		Olive Tree coalition		
					16.6	Democratic Left (PDS)		
					14.5	People's party/Democrats/Renewal Movement (PPI—SVP—RI)		
					2.1	Green Federation (VERDI)/Democratic Socialist (SDI)		
					1.7	Italian Communist party (PdCI)		
				11	5.0	Refounded Communists (RC)		
					2.2	Radical (PR)		
				1	8.3	All others		
Japan	3.43	00 06 25	Coalition of LDP, Komeito, and Ht	233	22.0	Liberal-Democratic party (LDP)	NA	NA
				127	19.6	Democratic party		
				31	10.0	Komeito		
				22	8.6	Liberal party		
				20	8.7	Communist party (JCP)		
				19	7.3	Social Democratic party		
				7	0.8	Conservative party (Ht)		
				5	0.6	Independents party		
				1	1.1	Liberal League		
				15	21.3	Others and independents		

(Continued)

TABLE 1.4 Continued

Country	ENPP[a]	Date	Which parties formed government	Lower House			Presidential	
				No. of seats	Percentage of vote	Political parties winning seats in Lower House	Percentage of vote[b]	Date
Lithuania	4.20	00 10 08	Coalition of LSS , NS, LVP, and LCS	51	31.1	Social Democratic coalition (LSS)	49.7	98 02 04*
				34	17.3	Liberal Union (LLS)	50.3	
				29	19.6	New Union (NS)		
				9	8.6	Homeland Union/Conservative (TS—LK)		
				4	4.1	Lithuanian Peasant party		
				2	2.9	Centre Union (LCS)		
				2	1.9	Polish Action (LLRA)		
				2	3.1	Lithuanian Christian Democratic party (LKDP)		
				1	1.3	Lithuanian Freedom Union (LLS)		
				1	4.2	Christian Democratic Union (KDS)		
				1	2.0	Moderate Conservative Union (NKS)		
				5	3.9	Others and independents		
Madagascar	3.94	98 05 17	Coalition of AREMA, Fanilo, AKFM-F, and others	63		Salvation of Madagascar (AREMA)	50.7	96 12 29*
				16		Fanilo		
				14		Ny Asa Vita no Ifampitsanara (AVI)	49.3	
				11		Rally for Socialism and Democracy (Rasalama)		
				6		AFFA		
				3		Movement for Madagascar Progress (MFM)		
				3		Congress for Malagasy Independence (AKFM-F)		
				34		Others and independents		

(Continued)

TABLE 1.4 Continued

Country	ENPP[a]	Date	Which parties formed government	No. of seats	Percentage of vote	Political parties winning seats in Lower House	Presidential Percentage of vote[b]	Presidential Date
Malawi	2.66	99 06 15	UDF	93	47.3	United Democratic Front (UDF)	52.4	99 06 15[c]
				66	33.8	Malawi Congress	45.2	
				29	10.6	Alliance for Democracy (AFORD)		
				4	8.3	Others and independents	2.4	
Mali	1.27	97 08 03 (f)	ADEMA	130		Alliance for Democracy in Mali (ADEMA)	95.9	97 05 04[f]
				8		National Renewal (PARENA)		
				4		Democratic Social Convention (CDS)		
				3		Union for Democracy and Development (UDD)		
				2		Party for Democracy and Progress (PDP)	4.1	
Mexico	2.66	00 07 02	PAN	218	38.2	National Action party (PAN) +	42.5	00 07 02[c]
				5		Green party (PVEM)		
				209	36.9	Institutional Revolutionary party (PRI)	36.1	
				53	18.7	Party of the Democratic Revolution	16.6	
				9		(PRD) + Labour party (PT)		
				2		Convergence for Democracy (CD)		
				2		Social Alliance party (PAS)		
				2		National Society (PSN)		
					1.9	Social Democracy (DS)	1.6	
					4.3	All others	3.2	
Mozambique	1.99	99 12 05	Frelimo	133	48.5	Mozambique Liberation Front (Frelimo)	52.3	99 12 05[c]

(Continued)

TABLE 1.4 Continued

Country	ENPP[a]	Date	Which parties formed government	Lower House			Presidential	
				No. of seats	Percentage of vote	Political parties winning seats in Lower House	Percentage of vote[b]	Date
				117	38.8	Mozambique National Resistance (Renamo)	47.7	
					2.7	Labour party (PT)		
					2.5	Liberal Democratic party (PALMO)		
					2.0	Social Democratic and Liberal party (PSLD)		
					1.6	Mozambique Opposition Union		
					1.5	Democratic Union		
					2.4	All others		
Nepal	2.48	99 05 17	NCP	110	36.3	Nepal Congress (NCP)	NA	NA
				68	30.7	Unified Marxist—Leninist (UML)		
				11	10.2	National Democratic party (RPP)		
				5	3.2	Nepal Sadbhavana		
				5	1.4	National People's Front (SJN)		
					6.4	Communist party of Nepal (CPN)		
					3.4	National Democratic—Chand (RPP—Chand)		
				6	8.4	All others		
Netherlands	4.81	98 05 06	Coalition of PvdA, VVD, and D66	45	29.0	Labour party (PvdA)	NA	NA
				38	24.7	People's party for Freedom and Democracy (VVD)		
				29	18.4	Christian Democratic Appeal (CDA)		
				14	9.0	Democrats 66 (D66)		
				11	7.3	Green Left		
				5	3.5	Socialist party		
				3	2.0	Federation for Political Reform (RPF)		

(Continued)

TABLE 1.4 *Continued*

				Lower House			Presidential	
Country	ENPP[a]	Date	Which parties formed government	No. of seats	Percentage of vote	Political parties winning seats in Lower House	Percentage of vote[b]	Date
				3	1.8	Reformed party (SGP)		
				2	1.3	Reformed Political League (GPV)		
					3.0	All others		
New Zealand	3.45	99 11 27	Coalition of NZLP and Alliance	49	38.7	Labour party (NZLP)	NA	NA
				39	30.5	National party		
				10	7.7	Alliance		
				9	7.0	Association of Consumers and Taxpayers (ACT)		
				7	5.2	Green Party of Aotearoa (GPA)		
				5	4.3	New Zealand First		
					2.4	Christian Heritage		
				—	4.2	All others		
Nicaragua	2.73	96 10 20	Coalition of AL and others	42	46.0	Liberal Alliance (AL)	51.9	96 10 20[c]
				37	36.5	Sandinista National Liberation Front (FSLN)	37.7	
				4	3.7	Nicaragua Christian Road (PCCN)	4.1	
				2	2.4	National Project (Pronal)		
				2	2.1	Conservative party (PCN)	2.3	
				—	1.3	Sandinista Renewal Movement (MRS)		
				—	1.2	Nicaragua Resistance (PRN)		
				—	0.8	Workers and Peasants Unity (Unidad)		
				—	0.7	Independent Liberal party (PLI)		
				—	0.6	UNO96		
					4.7	All others	4.0	
Norway	4.36	97 09 15	DNA	65	35.0	Labour party (DNA)	NA	NA

(Continued)

TABLE 1.4 *Continued*

Country	ENPP[a]	Date	Which parties formed government	Lower House		Political parties winning seats in Lower House	Presidential	
				No. of seats	Percentage of vote		Percentage of vote[b]	Date
				25	15.3	Progress party (FrP)		
				25	13.7	Christian People's party (KrF)		
				23	14.3	Hovre (H)		
				11	7.9	Centre party (Sp)		
				9	6.0	Socialist Left (SV)		
				6	4.5	Red Electoral Alliance (RV)		
				1	3.3	All others		
Philippines	3.05	98 05 11	LMP	110	27.1	Struggle of the Philippine Masses (LMP)	46.4	98 05 11[c]
				50	14.1	National Union of Christian Democrats/United Muslim Democrat party	17.1	
				15	4.5	Nationalist People's Coalition (NPC)	11.9	
				14	2.6	Liberal party (PL)	8.6	
				7	1.8	Struggle for a Democratic Philippines (LDP)	7.4	
				19	13.3	Other mixed lists		
				2		Others and independents	8.6	
Poland	2.95	97 09 21	AWS	201	33.8	Solidarity Electoral Action (AWS)	15.6	00 10 08
				164	27.1	Democratic Left Alliance (SLD)	53.9	
				60	13.4	Freedom Union (UW)	17.3	
				27	7.3	Polish People's party (PSL)	6.0	
				6	5.6	Movement for Reconstruction of Poland (ROP)	3.1	
					4.4	Union of Labour (UP)	1.4	
					2.7	Pensioners party (KPEIR)		

(Continued)

TABLE 1.4 Continued

Country	ENPP[a]	Date	Which parties formed government	Lower House			Presidential	
				No. of seats	Percentage of vote	Political parties winning seats in Lower House	Percentage of vote[b]	Date
Portugal	2.61	99 10 10	PS			Right of the Republic Union (UPRz)		
				2	2.3		12.7	
					3.4	All others		01 01 14
				115	44.1	Socialist party (PS)	55.8	
				81	32.3	Social Democratic party (PSD)	34.5	
				17	9.0	Unitarian Democratic Coalition (CDU)	5.1	
				15	8.3	People's party (PP)		
				2	2.4	Left Bloc (BE)	3.0	
					3.9	All others	1.6	
Romania	3.52	00 11 26	Coalition of PSDR and others	155	36.6	Social Democratic Pole (PSDR)	66.8	00 12 10[cd]
				84	19.5	Party of Great Romania (PRM)	33.2	
				31	7.0	Democratic party (PD)		
				30	6.9	National Liberal party (PNL)		
				27	6.8	Hungarian Democratic Alliance (UDMR)		
					5.0	Democratic Convention 2000 (CDR2000)		
					4.1	Alliance for Romania (ApR)		
					1.4	National Liberal party—Campeanu (PNL-C)		
					1.4	National Alliance (PAN)		
				19	11.3	All others		
Russia	5.40	99 12 19	MEDVED	113	24.3	Communist party of the Russian Federation (KPRF)	29.2	00 03 26
				72	23.3	Inter-Regional Movement (MEDVED)	52.9	
				66	13.3	Fatherland (OVR)		

(Continued)

TABLE 1.4 Continued

Country	ENPP[a]	Date	Which parties formed government	Lower House			Presidential	
				No. of seats	Percentage of vote	Political parties winning seats in Lower House	Percentage of vote[b]	Date
				29	8.5	Union of Right Forces (SPS)	5.8	
				21	5.9	Yabloko	2.7	
				17	6.0	Zhironovsky Bloc		
				7	1.2	Our Home is Russia		
				2	0.6	Support the Army—All Russia (DPA)		
				1	2.0	Pensioners' party		
					2.2	Communist Workers (KTS)		
					2.1	Women of Russia		
				2	10.6	Other parties	9.4	
				106		Independents		
Slovak Republic	4.75	98 09 26	Coalition of SDK and others	43	27.0	Movement for a Democratic Slovakia (HZDS)	42.8	99 05 29*
				42	26.3	Slovak Democratic Coalition (SDK)		
				23	14.7	Democratic Left (SDL)		
				15	9.1	Hungarian Coalition (SMK)		
				14	9.1	Slovak National party (SNS)		
				13	8.0	Party of Civic Understanding (SOP)	57.2	
					2.8	Communist party (KSS)		
					3.0	All others		
South Africa	2.15	99 06 02	ANC	266	66.4	African National Congress (ANC)	NA	NA
				38	9.6	Democratic party		
				34	8.6	Inkatha Freedom party		
				28	6.9	New National party		
				14	3.4	United Democratic Movement (UDM)		
				6	1.4	African Christian Democratic party		

(Continued)

TABLE 1.4 Continued

Country	ENPP[a]	Date	Which parties formed government	Lower House			Presidential	
				No. of seats	Percentage of vote	Political parties winning seats in Lower House	Percentage of vote[b]	Date
				3	0.8	Freedom Front (VF)		
				3	0.8	United Christian Democratic party		
				3	0.7	Pan African Congress of Azania		
				2	0.5	Federal Alliance		
				3	0.9	All others		
South Korea	2.39	00 04 13	Coalition of MD and others	133	39.0	Grand National party (HD)	38.7	97 12 18
				115	35.9	Millennium Democratic party (MD)		
				17	9.8	United Liberal Democrats (JMY)		
				2	3.7	Democratic People's party	19.2	
				1	11.6	Other parties	1.8	
				5		Independents	40.3[g]	
Spain	2.47	00 03 12	PP	183	44.6	People's party (PP)	NA	NA
				125	34.1	Socialist Workers' party (PSOE)		
				15	4.2	Convergence and Union (CiU)		
				8	5.5	United Left (IU)		
				7	1.5	Basque Nationalist party (PNV)		
				4	1.1	Canarian Coalition (CC)		
				3	1.3	Galician Nationalist party (BNG)		
				5	7.7	All others		
Sweden	4.29	98 09 21	SAP	131	36.4	Social Democratic Workers party (SAP)	NA	NA
				82	22.9	Moderate party		
				43	12.0	Left party (V)		
				42	11.8	Christian Democratic party (KD)		
				18	5.1	Centre party		
				17	4.7	Liberal People's party (FpL)		

(Continued)

TABLE 1.4 Continued

Country	ENPP[a]	Date	Which parties formed government	Lower House No. of seats	Percentage of vote	Political parties winning seats in Lower House	Presidential Percentage of vote[b]	Date
				16	4.5	Greens (MPG)		
					2.6	All others		
Switzerland	5.16	99 10 24	Coalition of SPS, FDP, CVP, and SVP	51	22.5	Social Democratic party (SPS)	NA	NA
				44	22.5	Swiss People's party (SVP)		
				43	19.9	Free Democratic party (FDP)		
				35	15.8	Christian People's party (CVP)		
				9	5.0	Green party (GPS)		
				6	2.2	Liberal party (LPS)		
				3	1.8	Protestant People's party (EVP)		
				2	1.0	Labour party (PdA)		
				2	0.9	Ticinesian League		
				1	1.8	Swiss Democrats (SD)		
				1	1.2	Federal Democratic Union (EDU)		
				3	5.4	Others and independents		
Taiwan	2.47	98 12 05	Coalition of MCT and others	123	46.4	Kuomintang (KMT)	23.1	00 03 18
				70	29.6	Democratic Progressive party (MCT)	39.3	
				11	7.1	New Party (HT)		
				2	0.7	Nationwide Democratic Non-partisan Union		
				4	3.7	Taiwan Democratic Union (DUT)		
				1	1.6	New Nation Alliance		
				1	1.4	Taiwan Independence party		
				12	9.5	Others and independents	37.6	
Thailand	3.05	01 01 29	Coalition of TRT, PCT, and PKWM	248		Thai Rak Thai (TRT)	NA	NA
				128		Democratic party (PP)		
				41		Thai Nation (PCT)		

(Continued)

TABLE 1.4 *Continued*

Country	ENPP[a]	Date	Which parties formed government	Lower House			Presidential	
				No. of seats	Percentage of vote	Political parties winning seats in Lower House	Percentage of vote[b]	Date
				36		New Aspiration (PKVM)		
				29		National Development (PCP)		
				12		Justice and Freedom (PST)		
				6		All others		
Turkey	4.87	99 04 18	Coalition of DSP, MHP, and AnaP	136	22.3	Democratic Left (DSP)	NA	NA
				129	18.1	National Movement (MHP)		
				111	15.5	Virtue party		
				86	13.3	Motherland party (AnaP)		
				85	12.1	True Path (DYP)		
					8.9	Republican People's party (CHP)		
					4.7	Democratic People's party (HADEP)		
				3	5.1	Others and independents		
Ukraine	6.58	98 03 29	Coalition of Independents and others	113	24.7	Communist party (KPU)	37.8	99 11 14*
				46	9.4	People's Movement (Rukh)		
				44	8.5	Socialist party/Peasant's party (SPU-SelPU)		
				28	5.0	People's Democratic party (NDPU)		
				26	4.0	Social Democratic party (SDPU)		
				23	4.7	All-Ukraine Association (Hromada)		
				19	5.5	Green party (PZU)		
				16	4.0	Progressive Socialist party (PSP)		
				10	3.7	Agrarian party (APU)		
					3.1	Reforms and Order (RiP)		
					3.1	Workers of Ukraine (TU)		
					2.7	National Front (NF)		
					1.9	Labour party/Liberal party (PP-LP)		

(Continued)

TABLE 1.4 *Continued*

Country	ENPP[a]	Date	Which parties formed government	Lower House			Presidential	
				No. of seats	Percentage of vote	Political parties winning seats in Lower House	Percentage of vote[b]	Date
					1.7	Forward Ukraine (VU)		
					1.3	Christian Democratic party (KDPU)		
					1.2	Democratic Bloc (VDBP)		
				21		Others		
				104		Independents	56.3[h]	NA
United Kingdom	2.13	01 06 07	Labour	413	40.7	Labour party	NA	NA
				166	31.7	Conservative party		
				52	18.3	Liberal Democrats		
				6	0.8	Ulster Unionist party		
				5	1.8	Scottish National party (SNP)		
				5	0.7	Democratic Unionists (DUP)		
				4	0.7	Plaid Cymru		
				4	0.7	Sinn Fein		
				3	0.6	Social Democratic and Labour party (SDLP)		
				1	1.5	UK Independence party		
					2.5	All others		
United States	2.02	00 11 07	Republicans	221	47.9	Republicans	48.1[i]	00 11 07[c]
				212	47.9	Democrats	48.3	
					4.2	All others	3.6	
				2		Independents		
Uruguay	3.14	99 10 31	Coalition of PC and PN	40	38.5	Progressive Encounter (EP)	45.9	99 11 28[*d]
				32	31.3	Colorado party (PC)	54.1	
				22	21.3	National party—Blanco (PN)		

(Continued)

TABLE 1.4 *Continued*

Country	ENPP[a]	Date	Which parties formed government	No. of seats	Percentage of vote	Political parties winning seats in Lower House	Percentage of vote[b]	Date
							Lower House →	**Presidential**
Venezuela	3.74	00 07 30	Coalition of MVR and other parties	4	4.4	New Space (NE)		
				1	4.5	All others		
				76		Movement for the Fifth Republic (MVR)	59.5	00 07 30[c]
				29		Democratic Action (AD)	37.5	
				21		Socialist Movement (MAS)		
				7		Project Venezuela (Proven)		
				5		Social Christian party (Copei)		
				5		Justicia (PJ)		
				4		Radical Cause (LCR)		
				3		Conive		
				3		Lapy		
				4		Misc. alliances		
				8		All others	3.0	

[a]ENPP = Effective number of parties in parliament. Calculated by the editors using the formula in Laakso and Taagepera (1979).

[b]Second round percentages are shown (denoted by asterisk*) where there is more than one round.

[c]Presidential and legislative election held concurrently.

[d]Several parties boycotted these elections.

[e]First round held concurrently with parliamentary elections.

[f]Prime ministerial election.

[g]Kim Dae Jung was elected as the joint candidate of the two main opposition parties.

[h]Leonid Kuchma stood as an independent but was supported by a coalition of non-Communist parties.

[i]George W. Bush (Republican) was elected by a majority of the electoral votes.

SOURCES: Keesing's Record of World Events; Electoral Studies; European Journal of Political Research Political Data Handbook; Inter-Parliamentary Union (www.ipu.org/parline); Agorà (www.agora.stm.it/elections); Banks and Muller (1999); government sites

2

Electoral Systems

ANDRÉ BLAIS and LOUIS MASSICOTTE

Electoral rules have fascinated politicians and political scientists for decades, because they are commonly assumed to condition the chances of success of competing parties or candidates. This chapter covers one important set of electoral rules, namely the electoral system, which defines how votes are cast and seats allocated. Other sets of rules, such as those concerning the use of referenda, the control of election spending, and the regulation of political broadcasting, are dealt with in other chapters.

We first document the great diversity of electoral systems presently existing among democracies. This raises the question of whether electoral systems matter, of what concrete impact they have on political life. The second section thus examines the political consequences of electoral laws. Once these consequences are known, we are in a position to tackle the crucial normative question of which is the best electoral system. The third section of the chapter reviews the debate and identifies the major tradeoffs involved in the choice of an electoral system.

Diversity of electoral systems

Even scholars specialized in the field are amazed by the diversity and complexity of contemporary electoral systems. The rules that govern how votes are cast and seats allocated differ markedly from one country to another.

Selecting an electoral system is not a purely technical decision. It may have huge consequences for the operation of the political system. As discussed in the following section of the chapter, applying two different formulas to the same distribution of votes will produce quite different outcomes in terms of members elected for each party.

To give a concrete example, let us look at the critical British election of 1983, the first election in a major nation where voters were passing judgment on the record of a neo-conservative government. As the ruling Tories were reelected with more seats than in the previous election, many observers concluded that Mrs Thatcher's policies had been strongly endorsed. The fact is, however, that the actual vote for the Tories decreased slightly between 1979 and 1983, and the outcome of the election would have been quite different if Britain had had proportional representation.

The first necessary step for an understanding of the consequences of an electoral system is to have a good grasp of the kinds of electoral systems that exist. Hence the need for classification. We provide a summary of the rules that apply to direct legislative and presidential elections.

Typologies of electoral systems can be based on the *electoral formula*, which determines how votes are to be counted in order to allocate seats, on *district magnitude*, which refers to the number of seats per district, or on *ballot structure*, which defines how voters express their choice (Rae 1967; Blais 1988). Emphasis on district magnitude ignores the fact that multi-member districts produce very different outcomes depending on the electoral formula used, while grounding a typology on the ballot structure similarly leads one to overlook that the two systems providing for ordinal ballots (the alternative vote and the single transferable vote) have different consequences. We follow the classical approach and describe electoral formulas first, while taking into account district magnitude and ballot structure. Other typologies exist (Martin 1997; Reynolds and Reilly 1997). We do not pretend to summarize all possible systems, just the existing ones. Experience teaches that electoral engineers are quite imaginative folks.

There are three basic electoral formulas, corresponding to as many criteria of legitimacy as to what is required to be elected. Supporters of *plurality* are satisfied when a candidate gets more votes than each individual opponent, while others feel that one should be declared the winner only if he or she can muster more than half of the vote, that is, a *majority*. Advocates of *proportional representation* (PR) feel that political parties should be represented in parliament in exact (or nearly exact) proportion to the vote they polled. *Mixed systems* combine PR with either plurality or majority.

It is convenient to examine electoral formulas in chronological order (from the oldest to the more recent) and in the order of their complexity (from the simplest in its application to the most sophisticated). While plurality in English parliamentary elections dates back to the Middle Ages and majority began to be applied to legislative elections in the early 19th century, PR was imagined during the first half of the 19th century and began to be used for national legislative elections at the end of that century.

Before the First World War, Joseph Barthélemy (1912) confidently predicted that the day would come when proportional representation would become as widespread and unchallenged as universal suffrage. So far he has not been vindicated. The proportion of democratic countries using PR has remained more or less constant since the early 1920s, hovering around 60%. The only significant trend is the increasing popularity, lately, of mixed systems, where different formulas are used simultaneously in the same election.

Figures 2.1 and 2.2 outline, in some detail, the electoral systems that exist in the 58 countries covered in this book, for presidential and legislative (first chamber) elections.[1] Readers are advised to refer to those figures for a better understanding of the typology offered in this chapter.

Plurality systems

Plurality, also known as *first-past-the-post* (FPTP), outperforms all other options in terms of its pristine simplicity. To be elected, a candidate needs simply to have more votes than any other challenger.

The plurality rule is usually applied in single-member districts: indeed, this is so often the case that we sometimes forget or overlook that it can be used in multimember districts as well. For example, in US presidential elections, members of the Electoral College are elected within each state on a winner-take-all basis (also known as the *bloc vote*), as the party slate which gets the highest number of votes in the state gets all the votes of that state in the Electoral College.[2] Under the plurality rule, even when voters cast as many individual votes as there are members to be elected (and thus can split their ballot between parties if they wish), party cohesion usually allows the majority party to sweep all, or almost all, seats.[3]

As the bloc vote normally results in the elimination of minority parties within each district, variants were imagined in the 19th century in order to allow for some minority representation within multimember districts using the plurality rule. One is the now-extinct *cumulative vote*, used in the State of Illinois until 1980, whereby voters were granted as many votes as there were members to be elected but were allowed to cumulate two or more votes on a single candidate: it was expected that supporters of the minority party in each district would focus their voting power on a single candidate to enhance their chances of securing at least one seat. The *limited vote*, still used for elections to the Spanish Senate, aims at a similar objective, though by the different device of granting each voter *fewer* votes than there are members to be elected (for example, most Spanish provinces elect four Senators, with each elector casting up to three votes for different candidates): here the expectation is that the majority party will not be able to carry all seats if the minority party presents a single candidate. A variant of the limited vote is the *single nontransferable vote* (SNTV) used in Japan until 1994 and still used for electing most legislators in Taiwan, where electors cast a single vote in a district electing between three and five members.

Cruder procedures for ensuring minority representation while keeping the plurality rule were common in Latin America before PR was introduced, and they still can be found. Post-Pinochet Chile has two-member districts, where the leading party gets both seats only if it polls twice as much as the party that came second.[4] Otherwise, one seat goes to each of the two leading parties. In the now directly elected Senate of Argentina, two seats in each province go to the leading party while the third goes to the party that came second in the popular vote.

Out of the 58 democracies covered by this book, six use the plurality rule for presidential elections (Figure 2.1) and nine for legislative elections (Figure 2.2).

Other countries have provided for presidential election systems that incorporate the plurality rule with some qualifications. In Argentina, which did away with the electoral college in 1994, the candidate with a plurality of the vote is elected, provided that plurality is equal to at least 45% of the vote, or exceeds 40% of the vote coupled with a lead of at least 10 points over the strongest challenger. If not, a runoff is held. Costa Rica requires a plurality representing at least 40% of the vote. Failing that, a runoff election is held. In recent years, Ecuador and Nicaragua have enacted complex arrangements of that kind.[5]

Majority systems

With majority systems, we cross a small step towards greater complexity. Requiring a majority without further specification opens the possibility of having no winner at all if there is a single-round election, or to have a succession of indecisive ballots if no candidate is eliminated following each round. These problems are solved through one of the following three variants. In *majority-runoff* systems, a majority is required on the first ballot. If no candidate obtains a majority, a second and final ballot, known in the US as a runoff, is held between the two candidates who received the highest number of votes in the first round.[6]

This is the system utilized in 19 of the 32 countries with direct presidential elections (Figure 2.1) (Blais, Massicotte, and Dobrzynska 1997); Mali uses the same method for legislative elections (Figure 2.2). In *majority-plurality* systems (used for French legislative elections), there is no such drastic reduction in the number of contestants on the second ballot (though a threshold may be imposed for candidates to stand at the second ballot)[7] and the winner is the candidate who gets a plurality of the vote. While one normally must have stood as a candidate on the first ballot to be allowed to compete at the second, there are past instances of major countries imposing no such requirement.[8]

As both formulas require the holding of a second round if no majority is reached on the first one, the *alternative vote* emerged as a less costly option whereby voters, instead of casting a vote for a single candidate, rank candidates in order of preference. First preferences are initially counted, and candidates winning a majority of these are declared elected. Second and lower preferences are taken into account only if no candidate secures a majority of first preferences. The candidate who received the smallest number of first preferences is eliminated, and second preferences expressed on his or her ballots are counted and "transferred" to other contestants. If this

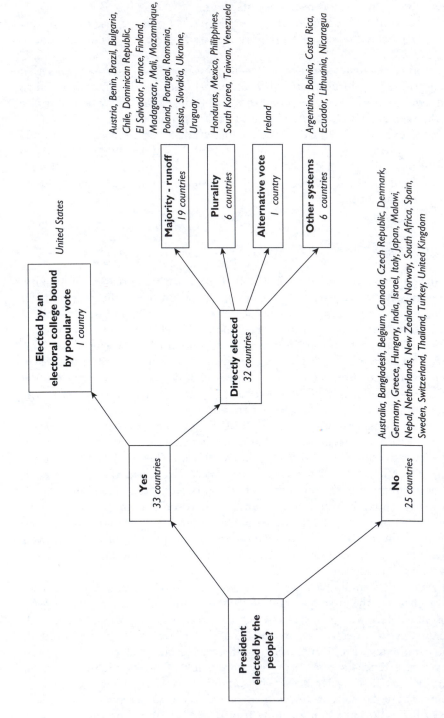

FIGURE 2.1   A Typology of Electoral Systems (presidential)

operation produces a winner, the contest is over. If not, the weakest candidate then remaining is eliminated and subsequent preferences on his or her ballots (which then means third preferences on transferred ballots and second preferences on untransferred ballots) are similarly transferred, and so on until eliminations and transfers produce a majority for one of the remaining candidates. As in all other majority systems, transfers may result in the final victory of a candidate who did not get the highest number of first preferences. The alternative vote is used in Ireland for presidential elections (Figure 2.1) and in Australia for elections to the House of Representatives (Figure 2.2).

Proportional representation

By definition, PR can be used only in multimember districts, for it is obviously impossible to distribute a single seat among many parties, except on a chronological basis, an option that no legislator to our knowledge has adopted.

There are two major types of PR systems. With 29 countries, the *list system* is by far the most widely used type among the countries surveyed (Figure 2.2). The other type, the *single transferable vote*, is in force only in Ireland.

List systems

Devising a PR list system involves making five major decisions as to districting, formula, tiers, thresholds, and preferences for candidates. There are many different ways of combining these variables, which explains why no PR systems are exactly alike.

DISTRICTS   The first choice concerns district magnitude. One option, which is the most conducive to accuracy of representation, is to have the whole country as a single electoral district. Israel, the Netherlands, and Slovakia all have a single national constituency electing 120, 150, and 150 members respectively (Figure 2.2).

The vast majority (26) of PR countries covered in this book have opted for smaller districts, the boundaries of which generally correspond to administrative subdivisions. For example, the 350 members of the Spanish Congress of Deputies are elected in 52 electoral districts: each of the 50 provinces constitutes an electoral district, as well as the African enclaves of Ceuta and Melilla. The latter two are single-member districts in view of their small population. The number of seats in the provinces ranges from three in Soria to 34 in Madrid. The resulting small district magnitude has repeatedly allowed the largest party to get a majority of seats with a plurality of votes: in 2000, the Popular Party won 183 seats out of 350 with 44.5% of the vote.

THE ELECTORAL FORMULA   A second choice involves the method by which seats will be distributed *within each district*. The two basic options are

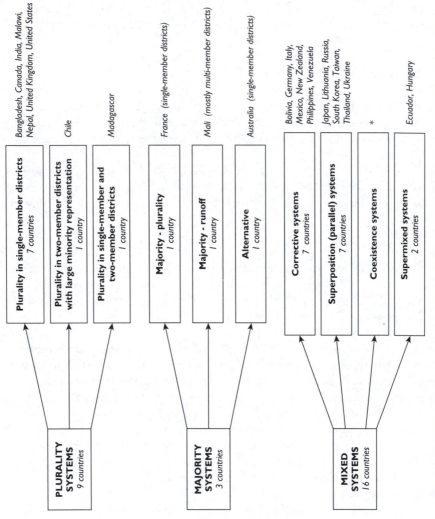

PLURALITY SYSTEMS *9 countries*

Plurality in single-member districts *7 countries* → *Bangladesh, Canada, India, Malawi, Nepal, United Kingdom, United States*

Plurality in two-member districts with large minority representation *1 country* → *Chile*

Plurality in single-member and two-member districts *1 country* → *Madagascar*

MAJORITY SYSTEMS *3 countries*

Majority - plurality *1 country* → *France (single-member districts)*

Majority - runoff *1 country* → *Mali (mostly multi-member districts)*

Alternative *1 country* → *Australia (single-member districts)*

MIXED SYSTEMS *16 countries*

Corrective systems *7 countries* → *Bolivia, Germany, Italy, Mexico, New Zealand, Philippines, Venezuela*

Superposition (parallel) systems *7 countries* → *Japan, Lithuania, Russia, South Korea, Taiwan, Thailand, Ukraine*

Coexistence systems → *

Supermixed systems *2 countries* → *Ecuador, Hungary*

* No example of a directly elected first chamber among democracies surveyed. Exists for the indirectly elected French Senate.

FIGURE 2.2   *A Typology of Electoral Systems (Legislative)*

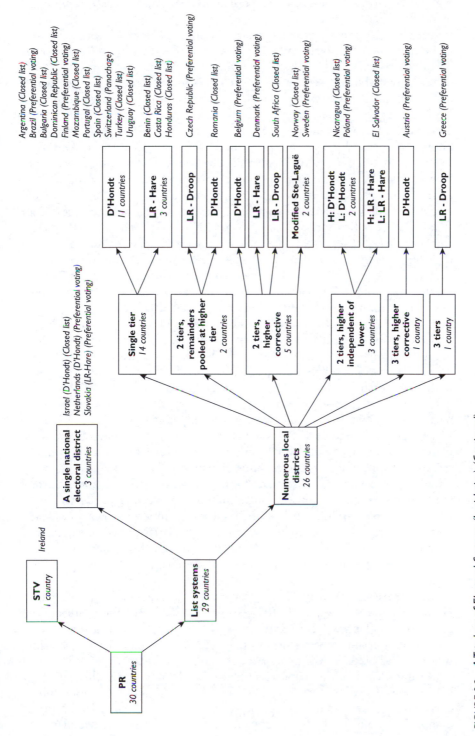

FIGURE 2.2 A Typology of Electoral Systems (Legislative) (Continued)

highest averages methods, which use a divisor, and *largest remainders* methods, which use quotas.

Highest averages methods require the number of votes for each party to be divided successively by a series of divisors: seats are allotted to the parties that secured the highest resulting quotients, up to the total number of seats available. There are three such methods currently in use[9] which differ by the sequence of divisors. The most widely known and used (18 countries; see Figure 2.2) is the *D'Hondt* formula, which uses divisors 1, 2, 3, 4, etc.[10] The logical alternative is the *"pure" Sainte-Laguë* formula (also known as the odd-integer number rule), where divisors are instead 1, 3, 5, 7, etc. In this pure form (which can be found in the mixed system of New Zealand), Sainte-Laguë normally produces a highly proportional distribution of seats, a feature which may explain why a *"modified" Sainte-Laguë* formula was devised, the single difference being that the first divisor is raised to 1.4 (instead of 1), a move which makes it more difficult for smaller parties to get a seat. The modified Sainte-Laguë formula is used in Denmark (in local districts), Norway, and Sweden. Of the three highest averages methods, D'Hondt is acknowledged to produce a bonus for larger parties and pure Sainte-Laguë the most likely to produce a proportional outcome, with modified Sainte-Laguë falling in-between.

Table 2.1 shows how seats would be allocated in a 12-member district under each of the three methods among the six following parties: Blues, 57,000 votes; Whites, 26,000 votes; Reds, 25,950 votes; Greens, 12,000 votes; Yellows, 6,010 votes; Pinks, 3,050 votes, for a total of 130,010 votes. In this case, each formula produces a slightly different outcome. The strongest party, the Blues, are better off under D'Hondt, while the second weakest party, the Yellows, manage to secure a seat only under pure Sainte-Laguë.

Largest remainders (LR) systems involve two successive operations. First, the number of votes for each party is divided by a quota, and the resulting whole number corresponds to the number of seats each party initially gets. Second, seats still unallocated are awarded to parties that had the largest surpluses of unused votes (known as remainders) following division.[11] The only variations within the largest remainders system concern the computation of the quota. The total number of votes polled in the district may be divided either by the number of members to be elected (a *Hare quota*) or by the number of members to be elected *plus one* (a *Droop quota*).[12]

LR-Hare is used in Benin, Costa Rica, Denmark, El Salvador, Honduras, and Slovakia, and LR-Droop in the Czech Republic, Greece, and South Africa (Figure 2.2).[13] Raising the divisor by one unit gives a lower quota. As a result, fewer seats normally remain unalloted after division, which slightly reduces the proportionality of the outcome.

Table 2.2 uses the same example as in Table 2.1 to illustrate how LR-Hare and LR-Droop work. The first step is to obtain a quota, which corresponds to the total number of votes (130,010) divided by 12 in the case of Hare and by 13 for Droop. Each party's votes are divided by the

TABLE 2.1   *Distribution of Seats by the Three Highest Averages Methods*

Votes	Blues 57,000	Whites 26,000	Reds 25,950	Greens 12,000	Yellows 6,010	Pinks 3,050
			D'Hondt formula			
÷						
1	57,000 A	26,000 C	25,950 D	12,000 I	6,010	3,050
2	28,500 B	13,000 G	12,975 H	6,000		
3	19,000 E	8,667 L	8,650			
4	14,250 F	6,500				
5	11,400 J					
6	9,500 K					
7	8,143					
Seats won	6	3	2	1	0	0
			Modified Sainte-Laguë formula			
÷						
1.4	40,714 A	18,571 C	18,536 D	8,571 H	4,293	2,179
3	19,000 B	8,667 F	8,650 G	4,000		
5	11,400 E	5,200 K	5,190 L			
7	8,143 I	3,714	3,707			
9	6,333 J					
11	5,182					
Seats won	5	3	3	1	0	0
			Pure Sainte-Laguë formula			
÷						
1	57,000 A	26,000 B	25,950 C	12,000 E	6,010 K	3,050
3	19,000 D	8,667 G	8,650 H	4,000	2,000	
5	11,400 F	5,200 L	5,190			
7	8,143 I	3,714				
9	6,333 J					
11	5,182					
Seats won	5	3	2	1	1	0

NOTE: The letters indicate the order in which seats are awarded to parties in a 12-member district.

quota (10,834 for Hare and 10,001 for Droop), and unallotted seats go to the parties with the largest remainders. LR-Hare yields more proportional results than LR-Droop (in our example, they are identical to those obtained under pure Sainte-Laguë).

TIERS   While most PR countries covered in our book have settled for a single tier of districts (whether national or local), quite a few have added a second tier of distribution, generally in order to reduce distortions resulting from the allocation of seats in the first tier (see Figure 2.2). There can be two or even three tiers. Belgium has 20 *arrondissements* while its ten provinces serve as higher tiers. The Greeks have been the fondest practitioners of multiple tiers, and currently have 56 local districts, 13 regional districts and a single national one.

The distribution of seats at the higher tier can proceed in three basic ways. The first approach, now found in the Czech Republic and Romania,

TABLE 2.2 *Distribution of Seats by the Two Largest Remainders Methods*

	Votes	Quota	Dividend	Seats won
	Hare quota			
	Quota = (130,010 ÷ 12) = 10,834			
Blues	57,000 ÷ 10,834 =	5,260		5
Whites	26,000 ÷ 10,834 =	2,400	(x)[a]	3
Reds	25,950 ÷ 10,834 =	2,395		2
Greens	12,000 ÷ 10,834 =	1,110		1
Yellows	6,010 ÷ 10,834 =	550	(x)[a]	1
Pinks	3,050 ÷ 10,834 =	280		0
Total			10 (2)[b]	12
	Droop quota			
	Quota = (130,010 ÷ 13) = 10,001			
Blues	57,000 ÷ 10,001 =	5,699	(x)[a]	6
Whites	26,000 ÷ 10,001 =	2,660	(x)[a]	3
Reds	25,950 ÷ 10,001 =	2,595		2
Greens	12,000 ÷ 10,001 =	1,200		1
Yellows	6,010 ÷ 10,001 =	601		0
Pinks	3,050 ÷ 10,001 =	305		0
Total			10 (2)[b]	12

[a]Seats going to the parties with largest remainders.
[b]Total number of seats allocated through largest remainders.

necessitates a pooling at the higher level of remainders from local districts. In the lower tier (that is, in the basic electoral districts), party votes are divided by the quota. The higher tier is where the seats unallocated in each district following division by the quota are grouped and distributed among parties on the basis of the collected remainders from each district. This procedure normally works to the advantage of the smaller parties insofar as it allows them to offset the wastage effect produced by the dispersion of their vote in local districts.

One implication of this technique is that the number of seats that are allocated at the higher tier(s) are not predetermined by the law. Indeed it may vary from one election to the next, depending on the extent of party fractionalization—the more fractionalized the electorate in districts, the smaller the number of seats awarded at this initial stage—and on the quota used. As noted above, a Hare quota normally results in a smaller number of seats being allotted at the lower level than a Droop quota.

The second approach uses the higher tier as a corrective. In this case, a fixed number of seats are reserved for correcting at the higher level the distortion between votes and seats generated by the use of local districts with small magnitudes. Sweden, for example, is divided into 28 basic districts which together elect 310 members. There are also 39 seats to be awarded at the national level in order to correct imbalances. The distribution of those 39 seats involves the following operations. First, the total number of seats, this is 349 (310 + 39) is distributed among parties on the basis of their total vote as if Sweden were a single national constituency. Next, the resulting seat allotment is compared with the actual distribution of 310 district seats. Whenever a party wins fewer seats in districts than it would be entitled to under the national computation, it gets the difference as national seats. Thus imbalances created at the district level are corrected at the national level. This kind of corrective higher tier is used in Austria, Denmark, Sweden, Norway, and South Africa. Belgium's *apparentement provincial*, through different procedures (which do not provide for a fixed number of corrective seats), also has a corrective effect.

A third option is for members elected at the higher level to be selected independently of members elected in basic districts. Poland has 391 members elected in 52 districts under the D'Hondt rule. There is also a national constituency where 69 seats are distributed on the basis of national party totals under the D'Hondt method, bringing the total size of the legislature to 460. This kind of arrangement also prevails in Nicaragua and El Salvador.

Multiple tiers normally reduce distortions, provided there is no threshold that prevents smaller parties from getting national seats. If such thresholds exist, a higher tier can serve to give a bonus to larger parties.

THRESHOLDS   This brings us to a fourth dimension of PR, namely the existence in most PR countries of legal thresholds of exclusion. Politicians are rarely willing to follow a principle up to its full logical conclusion. As previous paragraphs make clear, there are plenty of ways, even in PR systems, to grant a "bonus" to stronger parties at the expense of the weakest. While the effect of other techniques for dampening proportionality, like the D'Hondt rule or low district magnitude, is subtle and difficult to gauge except for trained electoral engineers, a threshold flatly states that political parties that fail to secure a given percentage of the vote, either in districts or nationally, are deprived of parliamentary representation or at least of some of the seats they would otherwise be entitled to.

Thresholds are fairly common. Only ten countries having list systems of PR do not impose any, while 19 do (Figure 2.3). Eight have local thresholds, seven have national thresholds, while Greece, Poland, Romania, and Sweden combine local and national thresholds. In addition, many mixed systems also impose thresholds for the PR tier. The law may require a fixed percentage of the national or district vote, or a certain number of votes or seats at the district level, to be entitled to seats at the national level. In Eastern Europe, higher thresholds are sometimes imposed upon coalitions. The best-known threshold is the German rule, which excludes from the Bundestag any party which fails to obtain 5% of the national vote or to elect three members in single-member districts. Turkey goes the farthest, by demanding 10% of the national vote to secure a local seat, followed by Poland with a national threshold of 7% for national seats.[14] All other countries require 5% or less of national or regional vote.

Thresholds send a clear and frank message that marginal parties are not considered suitable players in the parliamentary arena. As there is

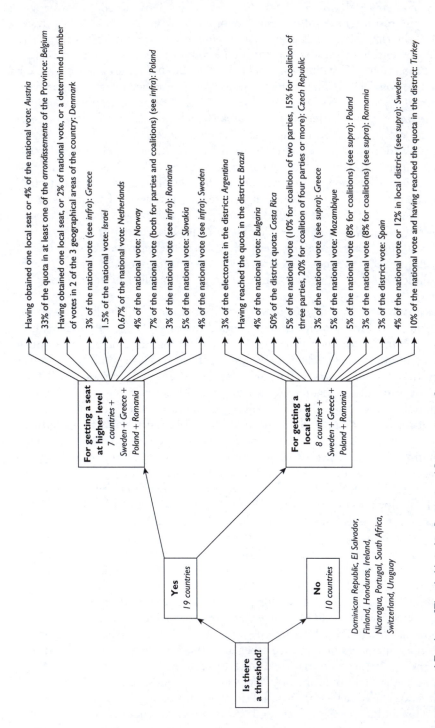

Is there a threshold?

Yes
19 countries

No
10 countries

Dominican Republic, El Salvador, Finland, Honduras, Ireland, Nicaragua, Portugal, South Africa, Switzerland, Uruguay

For getting a seat at higher level
7 countries + Sweden + Greece + Poland + Romania

Having obtained one local seat or 4% of the national vote: Austria

33% of the quota in at least one of the *arrondissements* of the Province: Belgium

Having obtained one local seat, or 2% of national vote, or a determined number of votes in 2 of the 3 geographical areas of the country: Denmark

3% of the national vote (see *infra*): Greece

1.5% of the national vote: Israel

0.67% of the national vote: Netherlands

4% of the national vote: Norway

7% of the national vote (both for parties and coalitions) (see *infra*): Poland

3% of the national vote (see *infra*): Romania

5% of the national vote: Slovakia

4% of the national vote (see *infra*): Sweden

For getting a local seat
8 countries + Sweden + Greece + Poland + Romania

3% of the electorate in the district: Argentina

Having reached the quota in the district: Brazil

4% of the national vote: Bulgaria

50% of the district quota: Costa Rica

5% of the national vote (10% for coalition of two parties, 15% for coalition of three parties, 20% for coalition of four parties or more): Czech Republic

3% of the national vote (see *supra*): Greece

5% of the national vote: Mozambique

5% of the national vote (8% for coalitions) (see *supra*): Poland

3% of the national vote (8% for coalitions) (see *supra*): Romania

3% of the district vote: Spain

4% of the national vote or 12% in local district (see *supra*): Sweden

10% of the national vote and having reached the quota in the district: Turkey

FIGURE 2.3   *A Typology of Thresholds in List Proportional Representation Systems*

no logical reason to opt for a threshold of 1% rather than 10%, such thresholds are more vulnerable to constitutional and political challenges. When numerous parties fail by a hairbreadth to reach the threshold, the total number of voters unrepresented may be quite high. An extreme case is the Russian Duma election of 1995, where as many as 40 parties failed to cross the 5% threshold: their combined vote added to 49.5% of all the votes cast.

SELECTION OF CANDIDATES   Plurality and majority systems result in the election of an *individual*, while in PR *seats* are distributed. This highlights the fact that the chief preoccupation of proponents of PR is that each *party* gets a number of seats corresponding to the number of votes it polled. If election contests nowadays are basically fights between party organizations, PR certainly is the system that pushes this logic to its ultimate conclusion.

This can be seen by the prevalence in PR countries of the *closed list*, whereby voters are not allowed to express any preference for individual candidates and members are elected in the order specified on the party list. No less than 17 of our PR countries follow that method (see Figure 2.2), while Poland uses it for its higher tier. In 11 PR systems, including the lower tier in Poland, voters may express a preference for one or more candidates within the party list they voted for. This can be done in various ways: voters may vote for a party and mark the name of one of its candidates (Belgium), or they may mark the name of a single candidate and have this vote counted as a party vote (Finland). These preferences increase the likelihood that the sequence of candidates on a party list be altered according to the voters' wishes, though in practice this rarely occurs. *Panachage*, to be found in Switzerland, is the system which grants voters the highest degree of freedom, as they have as many votes as there are seats to be distributed in the district and may freely distribute those votes among candidates irrespective of the party they stand for.

The single transferable vote

List systems of PR are frequently vilified for granting parties too much control over the selection of legislators. The single transferable vote (STV) is advocated as a form of PR that does away with party lists, thus giving voters more freedom. As in list systems, members are elected in multimember districts. However, candidates are grouped on a single ballot, to be rank ordered by voters as in the alternative vote. There is no obligation for voters to express preferences for the candidates of a single party, which makes it an instance of panachage.

Only first preference votes are initially counted. A Droop quota is computed for the district. Candidates whose first preference votes are equal to or higher than the quota are elected. Surplus votes cast for the winners (that is, the number of votes in excess of the quota) are transferred to the other remaining candidates on the basis of second preferences. When all winners' surpluses have been transferred and seats remain unallotted, the weakest candidates are eliminated and their votes are similarly transferred to remaining candidates, until all seats are filled.

While this system has been warmly advocated for over a century in Anglo-American circles, Ireland is the single country covered in this book to use it for elections to the first chamber, while Australian Senators are also elected by STV (Bowler and Grofman 2000).

Mixed systems

It is technically possible to mix together different electoral systems in order to devise a hybrid, or "mixed" system. Not all scholars agree on the meaning of that expression (Massicotte and Blais 1999; Shugart and Wattenberg 2001). We define a mixed system as a system where different formulas (plurality and PR, majority and PR) are used simultaneously in a single election.[15] Before the 1990s, mixed systems were often dismissed as eccentricities, transitional formulas, or instances of sheer manipulation doomed to disappear. It may be time to revise such generalizations, as 16 of our countries (including Germany, Japan, Italy, and Russia) have mixed systems. The Scottish Parliament and the Welsh National Assembly are also elected under mixed systems, as well as 13 of Germany's 16 Länder assemblies.

There are at least three ways of mixing PR with either the plurality or majority rule.[16] The simplest way (which we propose to call coexistence) is to apply PR in some parts of the national territory, and either plurality or majority everywhere else. In French Senate elections, a majority-plurality system is used in departments having one or two seats, while PR prevails in departments where three Senators or more are to be elected (about 70% of all seats).[17]

A second type of mixed system involves having two tiers of members (some elected by PR, the others elected by plurality or majority) through-out the country. Following the 1994 electoral reform, Japan offers an example of this kind of mixed system, which we call superposition or parallel. Three hundred members of the House of Representatives are elected in single-member constituencies under first-past-the-post. The other 200 (180 since 2000) are elected in 11 regional constituencies by proportional representation. The Russian system is of the same broad type, except that PR members account for half of the total and are elected in a single national constituency. Taiwan combines 125 members elected by the single nontransferable vote in 27 constituencies, with 36 members elected nationally by PR.

In the Japanese and Russian systems, PR seats are not distributed so as to correct party distortions created by the operation of the plurality rule in single-member districts. Each tier is elected independently of the other. The German system is the best example of a third type of mixed system, where PR seats are distributed in a corrective way, so as to compensate weaker parties that did poorly in single-member seats and to produce a parliament where each party gets its fair share of seats. Thus the Bundestag includes 328 members elected by plurality in single-member districts, plus 328 PR seats in a single national constituency. Electors cast two votes, first for a candidate in their single-member district, second for a party.

The allocation of seats requires first the distribution, on the basis of second or "party" votes cast by electors, of 656 seats by proportional representation (LR-Hare method). The results of such computation are compared with the actual distribution of the 328 constituency seats among parties. The other 328 seats are then awarded so as to make the final distribution of 656 seats fully proportional. In 1993, New Zealanders opted for a formula close to the German one. The Italian system of 1994 reaches the same corrective goal through more complex procedures.[18] Mexico provides for PR seats so as to ensure the presence of some opposition members in its Chamber of Deputies, while the ruling party normally sweeps the vast majority of single-member districts. All these cases mix plurality with some form of PR.

Hungary's system provides one of the most byzantine mixes ever tried. Broadly speaking, it is a superposition system, as 176 members are elected by majority in single-member districts while 152 members are elected by PR D'Hondt in 20 regional districts. However, a further 58 national seats are allocated at the national level with a corrective effect, since they are to be distributed by PR on the basis of *votes cast for candidates defeated at the other two levels.*

A country may use the same system for elections at all levels, but it may also resort to different formulas for different levels. France, for example, uses majority-runoff for presidential elections, majority-plurality in single-member districts for legislative and departmental elections, majority-plurality in multimember districts for senatorial elections in smaller departments and for municipal elections in smaller municipalities, PR D'Hondt in a nationwide district for European elections and in larger departments for senatorial elections. Larger municipalities elect councillors, generally in a single constituency, through a unique procedure: half the seats are allotted to the list that secures an absolute majority of the vote on the first ballot (or a simple plurality on the second), while the other half is distributed among all lists (including the leading one) under PR D'Hondt. A variant of that original formula (which we propose to call *fusion*) is now used for regional elections. In countries with directly elected second chambers, it is quite common for the latter to be elected under a system entirely different from the one used for electing the first chamber (Massicotte 2000).

Political circumstances sometimes produce intricate arrangements. In Malta, where STV prevails, the Labour Party got in 1981 a majority of seats while the other party had obtained more than 50% of the vote. Public outrage resulted in a "safety net" mechanism guaranteeing that if this kind of scenario occurred again, the aggrieved party would have its representation increased so as to obtain a majority. Since then, the safety net has come into operation twice (Hirczy de Mino and Lane 2000).

Electoral systems tend to be relatively stable. Some countries, like the United States, Britain, and Canada, have clung to the same system since their origins. Others, like most continental European countries, once switched from majority or plurality to PR, and never changed again. A few countries, like France and Greece, have altered their systems repeatedly, from plurality or majority to PR, and back and forth afterwards. The 1990s, however, have witnessed major electoral reforms in Japan, Italy, and New Zealand. Disillusion with politicians seems to have been a major factor behind these changes, two of which (the exception is Japan) were driven from outside parliament by a disgusted citizenry through referendums (Dunleavy and Margetts 1995; McKean and Scheiner 2000). The outcomes have not always met all the expectations.

Political consequences of electoral systems

We may distinguish two types of consequences: those that take place before the vote and those that occur after. Following Duverger (1951), we may call the former *psychological* and the latter *mechanical*. Mechanical effects are those that directly follow from electoral rules. Psychological effects pertain to how parties and voters react to these rules: they may change their behavior because of their expectations about the mechanical effects of electoral systems and about how other actors will react. Psychological effects affect the vote, mechanical effects affect the outcome of the election, given the vote (Blais and Carty 1991).[19]

The psychological effect

Electoral rules can affect the behavior of parties and voters. Concerning parties, two questions may be raised. First, does the number of parties contesting an election depend on electoral rules? Katz (1997) looks at more than 800 elections held in 75 countries over more than a century and compares the actual number of parties running in different systems. The average number is nine in PR and single-member majority systems and six in single-member plurality ones. Elites thus refrain from forming new parties in plurality systems because they know it is more difficult for small parties to win seats. On the other hand, there are almost as many parties running in majority as in PR elections. This underlines the fact that majority elections are quite different from plurality ones, a point to which we return below.

Party leaders respond to the incentives created by electoral rules. The response, however, is not automatic. This is clearly illustrated by Gunther's (1989) thorough analysis of the impact of the electoral law on party elites in Spain. As noted above, this country has a PR system, but it contains many features that make it strikingly unproportional. The system should serve as a deterrent to schisms and an inducement to mergers among parties.

Yet, little of this has happened, partly because party leaders miscalculate their likely level of support and partly because the maximization of parliamentary representation in the short run is less important than other political objectives. Gunther's analysis is a useful reminder that electoral rules only create incentives, they do not determine behavior. Over the long haul, however, these incentives do leave their imprint.

A second question is whether electoral rules affect party strategies. The question is examined by Katz (1980), who shows that PR and large district magnitude tend to make parties more ideologically oriented, whereas party cohesion tends to be weaker when voters are allowed to express preferences among candidates within the same party. In the latter case, as Katz explains, candidates must mount an independent campaign, and that weakens party attachments.

Turning to voters, the question that has attracted the most attention is the presence or absence of strategic or tactical voting in plurality systems.[20] Suppose there are three candidates in an election: A, B, and C. Consider voters who prefer C, then B, then A, and know C is not popular and has very little chance of winning. These voters have the choice of voting for their most-preferred candidate or of voting strategically for their second-preferred, because that candidate has a better chance of defeating their least-liked candidate (Cox 1997).

A number of studies have looked at how candidate viability affects the vote in plurality elections. Black (1978) and Cain (1978) have shown that the propensity to vote for a second choice is related to the closeness of the race (as indicated by the actual outcome of the election) in a district. Abramson et al. (1992) go a step further and show that the vote in American primaries reflects both preferences and perceptions of candidates' viability. Blais and Nadeau (1996), Alvarez and Nagler (2000), and Blais et al. (2001) refine the analysis and estimate how many voters cast a strategic vote, that is, would have voted for another party if they had not factored in their perceptions of the various parties' chances of winning in their constituency. The standard estimate is around 5%, which indicates that strategic voting exists but also that it is not a widespread phenomenon.

This raises the question as to whether strategic considerations play a role in PR or majority elections. We would expect thresholds in PR systems to induce some degree of strategic voting. If a voter's most preferred party is expected to have fewer votes than the required threshold, he/she has to choose between voting for that party even though it has little or no chance of being represented in parliament and supporting another party that is likely to meet that threshold. The only piece of evidence we have on this is provided by Gunther (1989), who shows that sympathizers of small parties are less likely to vote for those parties in smaller districts, with high effective thresholds.[21] An even more intriguing question, which has not been examined in the literature, is whether voters in PR systems hesitate to vote for parties that are perceived to have no chance of being part of the government.

In two-ballot majority elections, the issue is whether voters express their pure preferences on the first ballot, knowing that they will be able to have another say in the second ballot. There is little doubt that the vote on the first ballot does not merely reflect preferences, that strategic considerations play a role. In the French legislative election of 1978, for instance, a substantial number of RPR supporters voted UDF in those constituencies where the UDF had won in the previous election and was thus more likely to defeat the Left (Capdevielle, Dupoirier, and Ysmal 1988: 29).[22] We should also note an intriguing pattern identified by Parodi (1978): the electoral coalition that gets more votes on the first ballot tends to lose votes on the second. The exact reason why this occurs has not been elucidated.[23] It is an interesting case of voters reacting to the collective signal given on the first ballot.

The mechanical effect

The electoral law determines how votes are to be translated into seats. The most direct issue regarding the mechanical impact of electoral systems thus pertains to the relationship between the proportion of votes a party gets and the proportion of seats it wins in the legislature. Two subsidiary questions concern the outcome of the election: the number of parties that get represented in the legislature, and the presence or absence of a parliamentary majority.

Votes and seats

Rae's seminal book (1967) is the starting point. Rae regressed seat shares against vote shares under PR and under plurality/majority formulas. He finds the regression coefficient to be 1.07 for PR and 1.20 for plurality/majority. All systems give an advantage to stronger parties but that bias is much less pronounced in PR systems. The average bonus to the strongest party is eight percentage points in plurality/majority systems, and only one point under PR.

Unfortunately, that specific line of inquiry has not been pursued in a cross-national perspective. Some studies have looked at specific countries and refined the analysis by incorporating other factors such as the concentration of the vote (Sankoff and Mellos 1972, 1973) and the relative performance of parties in constituencies of different sizes (Spafford 1970), but we do not have updated and revised estimates of the basic seat/vote relationship in various types of electoral systems.

Taagepera (1986) proposed a radically new perspective to the issue. His starting point was the cube law of plurality elections, formulated at the beginning of the century, according to which the ratio of seats won by two parties equals the cube of the ratio of their votes. Taagepera showed that the most appropriate exponential is not necessarily three but rather the logarithm of the total number of votes divided by the logarithm of the total number of seats. He extended the model to PR elections, in which case the exponential depends on district magnitude as well as on total numbers of votes and seats.

Taagepera's work constitutes a major improvement. It is elegant and has the great advantage of proposing a model that can be applied to all electoral systems. For plurality elections, Taagepera is very persuasive in showing that his model outperforms the cube law. It is not clear, however, that it does a better job than the models proposed by Spafford or Sankoff and Mellos. We still lack a systematic comparative evaluation of these various approaches.

With respect to PR elections, Taagepera and Shugart (1989: ch. 11) stress the decisive impact of district magnitude. Rae (1967) had already shown that district magnitude strongly affects the degree of proportionality of PR. He did not, however, take into account the presence of supradistrict adjustment seats or legal thresholds. Taagepera and Shugart devise a complex procedure for computing a measure of effective magnitude that incorporates all these elements.

The number of parties in parliament

Duverger (1951) claimed that the plurality rule favors a two-party system while the majority rule (with second ballot) and proportional representation are conducive to multipartyism. He also argued that only the relationship between plurality rule and a two-party system approached a true sociological law. Riker (1986) concluded that Duverger was basically right. There is an association, but only a probabilistic one, between proportional representation and multipartyism. In Riker's view, the relationship between plurality and a two-party system is much stronger. He points to only two exceptions, India and Canada, and proposes a revised law accounting for these two exceptions. This is not very compelling, however, as the number of cases supporting the law is very small[24] and as Britain can hardly be characterized as a two-party system, at least as far as the distribution of votes is concerned.

This raises the question of how to count parties. One simple method is to count the number of parties represented in the legislature. Unfortunately, no study has compared electoral systems on that criterion. Attention has focussed on measuring the "effective" number of parties, which weights parties according to their electoral strength.

The most popular measure is the one proposed by Laakso and Taagepera (1979), where the effective number of parties equals 1 divided by the sum of squared vote shares. Molinar (1991) proposes an index giving special weight to the largest party. As Lijphart (1994a: 69) shows, both measures have their merits and limits, and they yield similar results in most instances.

Lijphart (1994a) compares the effective number of parliamentary parties in various systems. The average is 2.0 in plurality, 2.8 in majority, and 3.6 in PR systems. Within PR systems, the only important factor is the effective threshold. Within the sample examined by Lijphart, the effective threshold varies from 1% to 13%; the number of effective parties is reduced by 1 when the threshold is over 8%.

Finally, Ordeshook and Shvetsova (1994) and Neto and Cox (1997) look at how electoral systems mediate the impact of ethnic heterogeneity on the number of parties. These two studies show that "the effective number of parties appears to depend on the product of social heterogeneity and electoral permissiveness, rather than being an additive function of these two factors" (Cox 1997: 221).

Is there a parliamentary majority?

The ultimate objective of an election is to determine who will govern. A crucial question in parliamentary systems is whether the election allows the formation of a single-party majority government. Clearly, parliamentary majorities are infrequent in PR systems. Blais and Carty (1987), in their study of 510 elections in 20 countries over almost a century, reported that 10% of PR elections produced such a majority. Lijphart (1994a), who examined elections in 27 countries between 1945 and 1990, found a majority in 20% of the cases. He also showed that the probability of a one-party majority government in a PR system hinges very much on the effective threshold. It is about nil when that threshold is very small but reaches 30% when the effective threshold is 10%, as in Spain.

Parliamentary majorities, either natural or manufactured,[25] are much more frequent in plurality elections. Blais and Carty (1987) and Lijphart (1994a), who look at different sets of countries and periods, report that in their samples the proportion of plurality elections that produced one-party majority governments is respectively 69 and 93%.

What about majority elections? Lijphart (1994a) examines France and Australia; he finds a parliamentary majority in half of the cases. The same proportion is reported by Blais and Carty (1987), who consider many more cases. The latter study includes, however, multimember majority systems; the proportion drops to 27% when these are excluded. On this criterion, the single-member majority system is closer to PR than to plurality.

In plurality systems, one-party majorities are normally won by parties that secure a plurality or a majority of the votes. It is possible, however, for a party that comes second in terms of votes to obtain a majority of the seats. This was the case, for example, in two successive elections (1978 and 1981) in New Zealand. This may occur for two reasons. Seats carried by the winning party tend to come from less populated districts, and/or votes for the losing party are too highly concentrated (and wasted) in some districts (Taylor and Johnston 1979; Massicotte and Bernard 1985; Grofman, Koetzle, and Brunell 1997).[26]

The debate over electoral systems

Which is the best electoral system? Analysts and practitioners have debated the issue for more than a century. The debate has touched upon every dimension of electoral systems, the ballot, the constituency, and the formula. As we have seen in the first section of this chapter, there is a wide range of options available, especially if we take account of the possibility of combining these options in various ways.

The debate has focussed mainly on the choice of an electoral formula, and it is thus logical to start with that dimension. We then turn to the debate over the constituency and the ballot. Our review is confined to the most important arguments advanced to support or oppose a given option.[27]

As we show, a good case can be made for almost any electoral system. This is so because there are alternative visions of democracy, and because electoral systems are meant to accomplish not one but many objectives, which entail tradeoffs.[28] That the debate remains unsettled may account for the recent popularity of mixed systems.

The formula

The dominant debate in the literature has been between plurality and PR systems. The basic argument in favor of the plurality rule is that it produces one-party majority government, while PR is advocated because it produces broad and fair representation.

Why is one-party majority government such a good thing, according to proponents of the plurality rule? For two main reasons. The first is stability. One-party majority governments are believed to be more stable and government stability is perceived to enhance political stability. There is little doubt that one-party majority governments are more stable than coalition governments typically found in PR systems. At the same time, it must be acknowledged that most coalition governments in PR systems are reasonably stable (Laver and Schofield 1990: ch. 6). The most difficult question concerns the relationship between government and political stability. The jury is still out on this question. Powell (1982) finds no relationship, while Blais and Dion (1990) note that among non-industrialized countries democracy breaks down more often in PR systems with low government stability. Lijphart (1994b, 1999) argues that PR countries in fact perform better than plurality/majority countries on crucial indicators like economic growth, the incidence of strikes, and political violence. He points out that too many arguments against PR are drawn from specific cases like Italy or Israel. More research is needed on this important topic in order to sort out the specific impact of electoral systems versus other factors such as presidentialism (Stepan and Skach 1993).

The second virtue that is claimed for one-party majority government is accountability. Accountability stems from decisiveness. An election is decisive when it has a direct and immediate impact on the formation of government (Powell 1989; Strøm 1990: 72–4; Powell and Whitten 1993). It is easier for voters in a plurality system to get rid of a government they do not like; they just throw the rascals out and replace them with a new government. In a PR system, the fate of a government is decided only partly and indirectly by voters. A party may lose support but still remain a member of a coalition government, as the composition of the government depends on deals among the parties. In this sense, one-party majority governments are more accountable than their coalition counterparts. A serious drawback, however, is that there is no guarantee in a single-member plurality system that the party with the most votes overall will actually form the government, as approximately one plurality election out of ten held since 1944 resulted in a plurality of seats for a party that was lagging behind in the popular vote.[29]

For advocates of proportional representation, the two key words are fairness and responsiveness. Almost by definition, PR is fair since it is intended to give each party a share of seats more or less equal to its share of votes. That principle is of course qualified by the use of small districts and/or legal thresholds. Moreover, the distribution of seats in the legislature may be fair, but the distribution of cabinet seats in government is surely much less fair.[30] Nevertheless, it cannot be disputed that PR leads to fairer representation than the plurality rule.

Proportional representation also allows for a greater diversity of view-points to be expressed in the legislature and in government, as more parties are represented in both. Parties in plurality systems must of course be sensitive to different perspectives if they want to attract enough votes to win, but the mere fact that more parties get to argue their positions in a PR system should make governments more aware and concerned about the diversity of opinions. And there is indeed evidence of greater congruence between the median ideological position in the legislature and the median ideological position of the electorate in PR systems (Powell 2000; Powell and Vanberg 2000).

Proportional representation is especially advocated for societies with deep ethnic or linguistic cleavages. The argument is that in such societies it is imperative that minority groups be fairly represented within political parties, in parliament and in cabinet, and that only under PR can that goal be achieved (see Cairns 1968; Lijphart 1977; Sisk 1995). Critics reply that PR can induce the formation of narrow ethnic parties that appeal to ethnic cleavages in order to maximize support (Tsebelis 1990). They also point out that there is no evidence that minority groups are more supportive of the system in PR countries (Norris 2000a).

The choice between plurality and PR is thus mostly about what is deemed to be more important: accountability and (perhaps) stability on the one hand, fairness and responsiveness on the other hand.

There is a third option: majority rule. The arguments in favor of majority rule have not been as systematically articulated.[31] There are, we believe, two basic reasons for advocating it. First, the majority principle is at the very heart of democracy. In a direct democracy, the majority wins and in a representative democracy, most decisions are made by legislators through the majority rule. It would thus seem natural to apply the same logic to the selection of representatives.

The second argument in favor of majority rule is that it offers a reasonable degree of both responsiveness and accountability. It allows the presence of many parties, fewer than does PR but more than the plurality rule. It often leads to the formation of coalition governments, but the process of coalition-building tends to be more open than under PR. Coalitions are more likely to be formed before the election, or at least before the second ballot, so electors have an opportunity to pass judgment. Compared with the situation under PR, voters have a more direct say in which coalition will form the government, and parties and governments are more accountable, though less than under the plurality rule. The majority rule should thus appeal to those who wish to obtain a mixture of responsiveness and accountability. The majority rule is, however, much less satisfactory with respect to fairness. In fact, it is in majority systems that disproportionality between seat shares and vote shares can be the greatest.[32]

The constituency

The main debate here is about the virtues and vices of single- and multi-member districts. That debate overlaps, to some extent, the one over plurality and PR systems, as the latter entail multimember districts (MMDs) and the former (as well as majority systems) usually resort to single-member districts (SMDs).

Supporters of single-member districts claim that SMDs give voters a closer relationship with their representatives and maximize accountability, as district representatives can be held responsible for defending constituency interests. That responsibility is diluted among many representatives in multi-member districts. Representatives have to work in a smaller district, which presumably facilitates contacts with constituents. Some formerly PR countries (Germany, Bolivia, Venezuela) have switched to corrective mixed systems so as to guarantee that a substantial portion of the membership of the Assembly would be drawn from single-member districts while not impairing the fairness of party representation.

Single-member districts have at least one important drawback. They have to be altered periodically in order to maintain populations of relatively equal size. This may result in artificial units of no particular relevance to citizens and raises all the problems involved in designing and redesigning districts (Butler and Cain 1992). Multimember districts need not be of the same size. They can be made to correspond to sociological or administrative boundaries and are thus more congruent for voters (Niemi, Powell, and Bicknell 1986). Their boundaries can remain intact even if their population increases or decreases as it is possible to simply adjust the number of members to be elected in the district.

The alleged advantage of multimember districts is that they ensure a better representation of various groups, especially minority ones. There is much evidence, in particular, that women tend to be better represented in multimember districts, as parties strive for an overall balance (Rule 1992; Rule and Norris 1992), although the Jenkins report in Britain has concluded that this evidence was not overwhelming (Jenkins 1998). The consequences of MMDs are less certain, however, for groups that are territorially concentrated. In the United States, in particular, blacks and Hispanics do better under SMDs (Rule 1992; Welch and Herrick 1992; Davidson and Grofman 1994), especially since the Votings Right Act encourages the creation of districts where racial minorities predominate.

The choice between single- and multimember districts is thus one of competing values, mainly the advantage of having accountable individual representatives versus the benefit of having a more representative and responsive legislature.

The ballot

How voters are allowed to express their preferences depends to a great extent on the kind of electoral formula that is used. Consequently, the debate over voting procedures takes different forms in plurality, majority, and PR systems. Before reviewing these debates, one general observation should be made. Everything else being equal, it seems likely that the more information the ballot reveals about voters' preferences, the more accurate the representation of preferences is likely to be. Thus a system that allows voters to express degrees of preferences is arguably preferable to one that does not. At the same time, however, such a system may be less simple for voters, and there may be a tradeoff between simplicity and the amount of information that voters are asked to provide.

The ballot in plurality systems: one or many votes?
In single-member plurality systems,[33] voters are typically asked to indicate which candidate they prefer. There are other possibilities: voters can be asked to rank order the candidates or to vote for as many candidates as they approve of. The latter approach, approval voting, has been advocated by Brams and Fishburn (1982).

There are two major reasons for supporting approval voting. First, it provides voters greater flexibility in expressing their preferences; voters are not forced to choose only one candidate. It thus yields a more accurate measure of preferences, without undue complexity. Second, it ensures the candidate with greatest overall support is elected. It makes it impossible, in particular, for an extremist to squeeze in as the winner when there are two moderate candidates, something that can occur in a standard plurality election.

The main objection to approval voting is that it may increase the number of parties and reduce the probability of a one-party majority government. The reason is that when voters have to vote for one candidate in a plurality election, they are induced to vote strategically for parties that have a chance of winning and not to support parties that appear to be weak.

While strategic voting may well occur under approval voting (Niemi 1984), the incentive for voters not to support weak candidates is not as strong: they may vote for both their preferred weak candidate and their second choice. As a consequence, more parties are likely to get votes and seats, and one-party majority government is likely to be less frequent.

For those who are firm believers in the virtues of one-party majority government, then, approval voting is not likely to be very popular. When such considerations are not crucial, for the election of a president for instance, it has greater appeal. Approval voting can also be used for majority and PR elections, where it does not have the same disadvantage (one-party majority governments are unlikely anyway).

Majority rule: the alternative vote versus multiple ballots

Under majority rule, a candidate must obtain more than 50% of the votes to win. It is possible that no candidate meets that condition and that no one is elected. As noted earlier in this chapter, there are two ways to proceed when this occurs. The first is to resort to multiple ballots. The second approach is to have voters rank order the candidates (the alternative vote).

The case for the alternative vote is that it provides richer information about voters' preferences; it conveys information about how they react to each candidate. The procedure is somewhat more complex for voters but it is less costly as they vote only once. The case for two ballots is that it allows voters to reconsider their choice and to compare more systematically the two or three "serious" candidates that remain on the second ballot. Citizens are also faced with a simpler task, simply to choose one candidate on each ballot.

PR systems: can voters express their preferences among candidates?

The basic principle of proportional representation is that seats should be distributed among *parties* according to their vote shares. This assumes that people vote for parties or lists of candidates. The problem with closed list PR is that voters are not allowed to express preferences among individual candidates. Critics claim that this is an important shortcoming. Proponents reply that it is preferences among parties that really matter. The bottom line here is the importance to be attached to the representation of opinions about candidates versus those about parties. It is possible, however, to allow voters to express their opinions about candidates in a PR system, through either *panachage* or preferential voting in a list system or the single transferable vote (see earlier).

The single transferable vote allows voters to rank order candidates and thus grants them maximum freedom to express their preferences. It is a more complex procedure but it provides richer information about voters' preferences. It has two drawbacks. First, it can be applied only if there are relatively few members to be elected in each district: otherwise there would be too many candidates to be rank ordered by voters. But small districts entail a lower degree of proportionality in party representation. Second, it induces candidates of the same parties to compete against each other, hindering party cohesion (Katz 1980). The single transferable vote is thus an appealing option only for those who are willing to accept only a modest degree of proportionality and relatively uncohesive parties.

The other approach is to keep the list system but to allow voters to indicate their opinions about candidates through panachage or preferential voting. This is a simpler procedure and it can be used in large districts, thus ensuring a high degree of proportionality in party representation. However, *panachage* and preferential voting have the same detrimental effects on party unity. They entail the coexistence of two simultaneous contests, one among parties and one among candidates within the same party.

The debate over electoral systems highlights the role of competing values and tradeoffs in deciding which rules best serve democracy. At least two basic questions need to be addressed. First, which preferences should be represented? The issue is the relative importance to be attached to preferences about parties and candidates. The case for list PR, in particular, rests very much on the assumption that top priority should be given to parties. The greater the importance given to individual candidates, the less appealing list PR becomes. Second, which is the best way to ensure that those elected follow public opinion? One approach is to focus on the make-up of legislatures and of governments. The assumption is that representatives are more likely to be in accordance with public opinion if they resemble those they represent. This is the fundamental belief underlying support for PR. A second view is to focus on legislators' and governments' incentives. The assumption is that representatives will follow public opinion if they think they will not be reelected if they do not and that we should devise a system that makes it easy to get rid of a government that does not do a good job. This is the reasoning of advocates of the plurality rule.

Because of these competing values, it is impossible to characterize any electoral system as inherently better than the others. As Katz (1997) has forcefully argued, the choice of electoral institutions very much depends on one's conception of democracy. This may be one reason why mixed systems have become more popular recently.

NOTES

We thank the Social Sciences and Humanities Research Council of Canada for financial support, and Agnieszka Dobrzynska for research assistance.
1. Data for this chapter are drawn from Blais and Massicotte (1997), Blais, Massicotte, and Dobrzynska (1997) and Massicotte and Blais (1999). The main sources were the databank maintained by the Inter-Parliamentary Union (Internet site http://www.ipu.org), *Keesing's Record of World Events*, Blaustein and Flanz (n.d.), and the Political Database of the Americas maintained by Georgetown University (Internet site http://www.georgetown.edu/LatAmerPolitical/Constitutions/

constitutions.html). We also relied on the electoral laws of many countries as well as on many other sources, all of which are listed in our contributions cited above.

2. However, in two states (Maine since 1969, and Nebraska since 1991), the procedure for allocating electoral votes is more complex. Two votes are allocated to the candidate winning the state. The remaining votes are allocated to the winner in each congressional district, a modification that might allow the candidate who is trailing on a statewide basis to secure a few votes. Up to, and including, the 2000 election, this feature has failed to produce a split electoral vote in either state.

3. For an analysis of US state legislative elections, see Niemi, Hill, and Grofman (1985).

4. Some analysts (see, especially, Jones 1995a; Cox 1997) characterize the Chilean system, also used for part of the Ecuador and Madagascar legislatures, as PR D'Hondt. It is true that the system works exactly as PR D'Hondt would. It is also true, however, that none of these laws (except Madagascar's) refers to PR, or D'Hondt, or highest averages. Furthermore, the rule that applies in the great majority of instances is simple plurality: the two leading parties each get one seat. It seems to us that a system in which only two parties can get elected can hardly be described as PR.

5. In Nicaragua, a runoff is held unless the leading candidate has at least 40% of the vote, or at least 35% of the vote with a 5-point lead over the main challenger. In Ecuador, under the 1998 Constitution, no runoff is held if the leading candidate gets 40% of the vote and a 10-point lead over the main challenger.

6. Majority-runoff is used for elections to the US House of Representatives in the states of Georgia and Louisiana, which elect a total of 18 members (out of 435).

7. The threshold for standing at the second ballot in French legislative elections is now 12.5% of the electorate.

8. The examples are German presidential elections under the Weimar Republic and French legislative elections in the 1930s (Lakeman 1974). A particularly interesting instance occurred in Germany at the 1925 election: the candidate of the rightist parties, Karl Jarres, withdrew after the first ballot in favor of Field-Marshal von Hindenburg, who had not stood at the first ballot. Hindenburg won.

9. There is a fourth highest average method, known as the Imperiali rule. In Belgian municipal elections (the only occasion where this method is used), the divisors are 1, 1.5, 2, 2.5 etc. This rule works strongly in favor of larger parties (van den Bergh 1955). This Imperiali system, named after a Belgian Senator, should not be confused with the Imperiali quota formerly used in Italian legislative elections.

10. Under D'Hondt, each seat is awarded to the party that would have the highest average vote per seat if it received this seat This is the purest application of the principle of highest average.

11. Largest remainders and highest averages methods are normally considered mutually exclusive. However, in South Africa, the first five seats unalloted after division are distributed to the parties with the largest remainders, while the D'Hondt highest averages method is used for the remaining seats.

12. Strictly speaking, this should be called a *Hagenbach–Bischoff quota* rather than a Droop quota, as the latter is a Hagenbach–Bischoff quota increased by one. The difference is so minute that Lijphart (1994a) has proposed to select the shortest name to refer to these two quotas. A few Latin American countries resort to a so-called "double quota" system, whereby the first quota serves as a threshold, while the second is used for allocating seats among the parties that crossed the threshold. We classify those systems on the basis of the second quota.

13. We leave aside the Imperiali quota, where the total number of votes is divided by the number of seats *plus two*. This method was used in a single country (Italy) and was dropped in 1993.
14. In Turkey, in districts returning at least five members, the party getting the most votes is awarded a bonus seat, with the rest of the seats awarded under D'Hondt. The system not only disadvantages weak parties, but also advantages the strongest of all.
15. Geographical conditions may necessitate, in a country where PR is the rule, the election of a handful of members in single-member constituencies. This occurs in Finland, Spain, and Switzerland. In our view, such cases should not be considered as instances of mixed systems, a label that should be used only when the proportion of members elected under a different system is more than 5% of the total.
16. For a thorough overview of all the options, see Massicotte and Blais (1999).
17. Until July 2000, the French Electoral Code provided that PR would prevail in departments electing five Senators or more, while majority-plurality was to be used in departments having four seats or less. This meant that only one-third of Senators were elected by PR.
18. Three-quarters (475) of members of the Chamber of Deputies are elected by plurality in single-member districts, while the other 155 are elected by straight PR in a single national constituency and subsequently reallocated between 26 regional constituencies. However, PR seats are allocated to parties not on the basis of their total vote, but on the basis of "amended" party totals that include only votes cast for candidates defeated in single-member districts and for winning candidates in excess of what they needed to win, that is, a plurality of one over their strongest opponent. In other words, only votes wasted at the local level are considered for PR purposes, with the result that parties that do poorly in single-member districts get some correction under PR.
19. We focus, as does the literature, on legislative elections held in parliamentary systems. There have been few studies of the impact of electoral rules on presidential elections (see, however, Shugart and Carey 1992; Jones 1995b; Shugart 1995). Little attention has been given to potential interaction effects between electoral systems and other institutional variables. It is quite possible, for instance, that the consequences of electoral rules are quite different in parliamentary and presidential systems.
20. We leave aside the question of whether proportional representation fosters voter turnout, which is examined in Chapter 7.
21. The *legal* threshold is the minimum number of votes a party needs under the law to be entitled to seats. In small districts, however, a party may cross the legal threshold without winning any seat. The *effective* threshold is the minimum number of votes a party must actually garner in order to win at least one seat. That effective threshold is not a specific number but a range between the so-called thresholds of inclusion and exclusion. The former is the minimum vote that *may* earn a party a seat under the most favorable conditions, and the latter is the minimum vote that *guarantees* a party a vote even under the most unfavorable conditions. For three parties competing in a three-member district with the D'Hondt formula, the threshold of inclusion is 20% since it is possible for a party to win a seat with that percentage if the other two parties split the rest of the vote evenly, each receiving 40% of the vote. The threshold of exclusion is 25% since by exceeding that percentage by only one vote a party wins a seat even in the most unfavorable condition of another party garnering all other votes, that is, almost 75%. The effective threshold is assumed to be the midpoint between the lower and higher thresholds. For a lucid exposition, see Lijphart (1994a: 25–9).
22. We should note that strategic voting is inferred here from the non-concordance of party identification and vote. This inflates the amount of strategic voting

since voters may vote for a party that is not the one they feel attached to because of the issues of the campaign, party leaders, or local candidates. The fact that the number of parties does not tend to diminish over time in France suggests that strategic voting on the first ballot is limited.

23. A similar pattern seems to take place in plurality elections. In Canada and the United States the frontrunner at the beginning of a campaign tends to lose votes during the campaign (Johnston et al. 1992; Campbell 2000). It could be that the frontrunner is more attacked by other parties and gets closer scrutiny from the media, and that this induces some voters to reconsider their support for that party.

24. Furthermore, one of the few cases supporting the law, the United States, has other institutional features—presidentialism and primaries—that could account for the presence of a two-party system.

25. A natural majority occurs when a party gets a majority of both votes and seats. A manufactured majority is one where a party obtains a majority of seats without having a majority of votes.

26. An analogous result can occur under special rules such as those governing the election of the US president. In 2000, George Bush won the US presidential election while trailing Al Gore by about 500,000 votes nationwide.

27. For a more elaborate review, see Blais (1991) and Dunleavy and Margetts (1995).

28. For a cogent exposition of the tradeoffs see Dunleavy and Margetts (1995), and Katz (1997).

29. This assessment is based on an analysis of national elections held in Britain, New Zealand, and Canada as well as provincial elections in the latter country.

30. This problem is sometimes solved by a requirement that the executive mirrors party strength in the legislature (as in a few Austrian *Länder*) or by a decision to build government coalitions including more parties than is mathematically necessary to command a majority in the legislature (as in Switzerland).

31. See, however, Fisichella (1984) and Blais (1993). There is also a debate over the merits and limits of the plurality and majority rule for presidential elections. The majority rule ensures that the elected candidate has strong support. Its main drawback is that it induces many candidates to run in the first election (Shugart and Carey 1992: 215–6).

32. It is in France, for instance, that the index of proportionality tends to be the lowest (Rose 1984: 75). This occurs, however, because only first-ballot votes are taken into account.

33. We confine ourselves here to single-member plurality systems and do not consider the single nontransferable or limited vote. Lijphart, Pintor, and Sone (1986) show that in their consequences these systems lie somewhere between single-member plurality and proportional representation.

3

Referendums and Initiatives: The Politics of Direct Democracy

LAWRENCE LEDUC

Even in many of the older established democracies, citizens frequently express dissatisfaction with the quality of their democracy. Periodic elections alone cannot always guarantee sufficient choice or accountability, and elected officials are sometimes seen as unresponsive and "out of touch," even in countries with long established and seemingly well functioning electoral regimes. Citizens of the European Union have become increasingly concerned with what has come to be known as the "democratic deficit," as they have seen power over many areas of political life pass from their elected national governments to the more remote centralized institutions of the new Europe. Nor are elections always the best mechanism for resolving contentious policies, or embarking on a program of fundamental political change. For these and other reasons, interest has arisen in many countries in alternative electoral institutions which promise to enhance the quality of democracy. In particular, the referendum, a long-established but sparingly used method of deciding important or contentious political issues, has found new favor in many parts of the world (Figure 3.1).

The growing appeal of direct democracy

A number of countries and jurisdictions which previously had no provision in law for the conduct of referendums have adopted new initiative or referendum legislation, or have held "ad hoc" referendums on particular issues. Britain, whose parliamentary institutions once seemed inconsistent with institutions of direct democracy, has conducted referendums on Northern Ireland (1973, 1998), membership in the European Community (1975), Scottish and Welsh devolution (1979, 1997), and London local government reform (1998) and now appears likely to hold further votes on European monetary union and perhaps national electoral reform. Other European

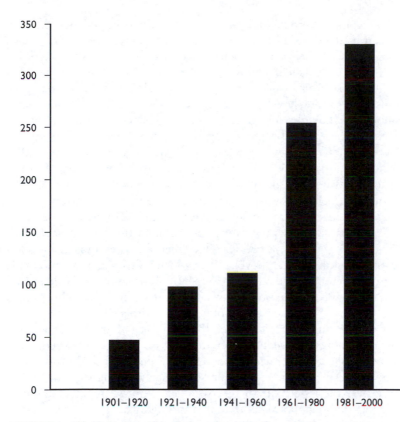

FIGURE 3.1   *Worldwide Use of the Referendum in the Twentieth Century*
Figures are for national referendums only.
SOURCE: Butler and Ranny (1994: 4–6), updated by the author. See also University of
Geneva Center for the Study of Direct Democracy (http://c2d.unige.ch/)

countries such as Ireland and Denmark, which have long had referendum
provisions in their national constitutions or on the statute books, seem to be
using these mechanisms more frequently. Ireland, for example, has conducted referendums on a number of European Union related issues (1972,
1987, 1992, 1998), on the contentious issues of divorce (1986, 1995) and
abortion (1983, 1992), and on the Northern Ireland peace agreement (1998),
as well as on various other constitutional questions. While the referendum
device may not be capable of resolving all of democracy's problems, it seems
to respond to at least some of the concerns of both governments and citizens
in contemporary democratic societies. This new interest in the old institutions
of direct democracy appears to reflect the mood of the times.

    In theoretical terms, representative democracy and direct democracy are
sometimes presented as opposing versions of the democratic vision (Budge
1996; Setälä 1999). Citizens in a democracy either delegate power to elected
representatives or retain it for themselves. In practice, however, many nations
seem able to combine elements of *both* direct and representative democracy

in their political institutions, and have merely shifted the balance more in one direction or the other in order to address the concerns of their citizens or the objectives of their governments. Nations such as Switzerland for example, the country which perhaps comes closest today to putting into practice the ideals of direct democracy, have not abandoned representative institutions even as they have come to make greater use of referendums. In Europe more generally, the emergence of the new challenges of the European Union has also been met by increasing use of the referendum in several member countries (Gallagher and Uleri 1996). But this does not mean that the representative institutions of these countries are under threat. Rather, these nations have increasingly sought ways to combine some of the elements of direct democracy with their existing political institutions.

Evidence of the extent to which the referendum has found a place in the political life of many representative democracies over the past 25 years may be seen in Table 3.1. Of the 58 nations which met our criteria for inclusion in earlier tables (see Chapter 1 above), 39 conducted at least one nationwide referendum between 1975 and 2000. A number of countries such as Switzerland, Ireland, or Italy utilized the referendum with greater frequency, while others like Brazil, Canada, or Norway did so only to deal with a single, very specific, issue of national importance. Among the minority of major democratic nations which conducted *no* national referendums over this 25-year period are such well established democracies as the United States, Germany, India, and Japan. This suggests that the referendum, although growing substantially in importance over the latter part of the twentieth century, is not ubiquitous. Some countries whose political cultures are thoroughly democratic manage to live happily without it, a few use it extensively, and others have integrated it by varying degrees into their national political life.

The numbers shown in Figure 3.1 or Table 3.1 do not include referendums or initiatives conducted at the sub-national level. In the United States, institutions of direct democracy are employed in many states and localities, even though the United States has never held a *national* referendum. All states except Delaware provide for amendments to their state constitutions to be submitted to a popular vote, and most also permit the legislature to place other types of issues on the ballot. Twenty-four have provisions for citizen initiatives. Several western states such as California, Oregon, Colorado, and North Dakota use instruments of direct democracy extensively, and the frequency of usage of such procedures in those states has increased dramatically in recent years. While some scholars have seen these trends as a positive development for the quality of American democracy, others have viewed them with alarm (Broder 2000). Following a period of gradual decline in the post-war period, the use of initiative and referendum procedures in the American states exploded during the 1980s and 1990s (Magleby 1988, 1994). On the day of the November 2000 presidential election in the United States, more than 200 separate issues were also on the ballot in 41 states.[1] The acceptance which these processes have found at the sub-national level in the United States provides a laboratory rivalled only by Switzerland in which political scientists

TABLE 3.1   *Frequency of National Referendums in 39 Democracies, 1975–2000*

Country	Number of referendums	Number of items on ballots	Country	Number of referendums	Number of items on ballots
Switzerland	72	222	Slovak Republic	2	5
Ireland	12	16	Venezuela	2	3
Italy	11	46	Austria	2	2
New Zealand	10	11	France	2	2
Uruguay	8	10	Portugal	2	2
Lithuania	7	17	Romania	2	2
Philippines	6	12	South Africa	2	2
Denmark	6	6	Sweden	2	2
Ecuador	5	34	Brazil	1	2
Australia	4	13	Argentina	1	1
Chile	4	4	Benin	1	1
Madagascar	4	4	Canada	1	1
Poland	3	8	Finland	1	1
Russia	3	7	Malawi	1	1
Ukraine	3	7	Mali	1	1
Hungary	3	6	Nepal	1	1
Bangladesh	3	3	Norway	1	1
South Korea	3	3	Taiwan	1	1
Spain	3	3	United Kingdom	1	1
Turkey	3	3			

can gain a better understanding of the form and functioning of the institutions of direct democracy in the world today.

Variations in form and practice

While the term *referendum* is commonly used as a synonym for *all* institutions of direct democracy, it should be recognized that such usage does not adequately differentiate among the several types of legal frameworks within which a direct vote of the people on a public issue might take place (Figure 3.2). Strictly speaking, the term "referendum" applies when a vote is initiated by a governing body such as a legislature, with the result of that vote being legally binding on the body that authorized it. But such votes are not *always* binding on the authorities that initiate them. In an older form of usage, these might have been called *plebiscites*. Today they are generally referred to as *consultative referendums* (Suksi 1993). The 1994 votes in Finland, Norway, and Sweden on membership in the European Union were not legally binding on the governments that conducted them, but similar votes in Ireland and Denmark on EC membership in 1972 were binding. A number of other issues in Ireland have gone to mandatory referendums because they involved changes in constitutional provisions. But legally binding or not, governments in a modern democracy would be ill advised to ignore a formal vote of their citizens on an important public issue. Hence, this distinction in practice may not be as important as it once seemed to be.

Votes that come about through a petition of citizens rather than by the action of a government or legislature are more properly called *initiatives* or *citizen-initiated referendums*. In a number of countries, citizens themselves can bring about a vote on a public issue by meeting statutory or constitutional provisions for a minimum number of signatures, and thus force a vote on a proposal whether the government wishes it or not. Most Swiss referendums come about in this manner, and the results of these are always legally binding. Many US state propositions also reach the ballot by this method. In 1993, New Zealand adopted new provisions for citizen-initiated referendums, and The Netherlands is currently considering such legislation. Britain, on the other hand, has no provision for citizen-initiated referendums, and the results of the several votes there which have taken place in recent years would be properly considered consultative rather than binding under current rules.

Italy employs what is sometimes called the *abrogative* referendum or popular veto, in which citizens may, by petition, force a public vote on a law which has already been adopted by the legislature. Thus, referendums may be used in some instances by governments to consult the people and in others by the people themselves to challenge or bypass the government. In several countries, more than one of these routes to a referendum is possible. Switzerland, for example, does not use consultative referendums initiated by the government, but all of the other types are found there. Under the newly adopted New Zealand provisions, a vote of the people on any issue may be triggered either by citizen initiative or by parliament.

Organizing and conducting referendums and initiatives

Referendums arise under a variety of legal forms, but they don't just "happen." The origin of any referendum is nearly always found in a conscious political decision taken by a party, organization, or group. Even in the case of citizen-initiated referendums, the undertaking generally requires the political and financial resources of a well organized group in order to collect the thousands of signatures needed to get a proposed measure onto the ballot. In most countries, it will be the governing party or parties that is in the best strategic position to organize a referendum. Sometimes the decision to hold a referendum will be made because the governing parties have concluded that a particular political agenda requires demonstrated public support in order to carry it through. No British government today, for example, would risk joining the European Monetary Union without obtaining public approval in a referendum, even though such a course is not legally required. Similarly, none of the governments of the Nordic countries in 1994 was willing to undertake the historic decision to join the European Union without the concurrence of their citizens (Jenssen, Pesonen, and Gilljam 1998).

The reasons why a governing party or coalition might opt for a referendum strategy are many and varied. Morel (1993) notes that divisions *within*

	REFERENDUM		INITIATIVE	
	Constitutional (binding)	**Consultative** (non-binding)	**Abrogative**	**Citizens' Initiative**
	A vote that is required in order to effect a change in the constitution or basic law, altering the form of political institutions, or to ratify international treaties	A vote on any subject initiated by the government or legislature	A procedure to force a vote on a law already passed by the legislature. Generally initiated by petition of citizens, or sometimes by a legislative minority	A referendum on any subject which is brought about by petition of citizens. The number of signatures required varies widely. Results may be binding, but can also be subject to review by the courts or legislature
	• Australia • Denmark • Ireland • Switzerland	• Britain • Canada • Finland • Sweden	• Austria • Italy • Sweden • Switzerland	• New Zealand • Switzerland • Many US states

FIGURE 3.2 *Forms and Variations of the Referendum*

a party on a sensitive issue are one of the most common reasons. By consulting the electorate, party leaders may hope to quell dissent within the party on a divisive issue. The decision by the British Labour party to hold a referendum on the issue of British EC membership shortly after coming to power in 1974 provides one good example of this strategy. The Swedish and Austrian referendums on the divisive issue of nuclear power provide another illustration of circumstances in which a popular vote was used to prevent a difficult issue from tearing the party apart. A referendum may also be part of some larger political objective. The 1997 Scottish and Welsh devolution referendums, together with the 1998 referendum on local government in London, were clearly part of the Blair government's wider constitutional agenda, which also includes Northern Ireland, restructuring of the House of Lords, and electoral reform.

The campaign which takes place following the call of a referendum is as important to the outcome as is that of an election, perhaps even *more* important. Over the course of a referendum campaign, public opinion can shift dramatically. The dynamics of a referendum campaign can often be harder to anticipate than those of an election, and the breadth of participation of the electorate cannot always be assumed. It follows, therefore, that the outcome of many referendums is not easily predictable, even in some cases where the distribution of public opinion on the issue of the referendum is well known. The short-term perceptions of the referendum question on the part of voters, the images that they hold of the groups and individuals involved, or their reactions to the campaign discourse, can be as important to the voting decision as their opinions or beliefs on the issue itself. It might be expected that the subject matter of a referendum will be related in a variety of ways to its potential for volatility. Clearly, the more directly that the referendum issue involves core political beliefs, the easier it will be for voters to find their own positions on the issue. Likewise, the more partisan the context in which a referendum comes about, the more likely that party identification will play a role in the outcome. However, these same linkages ought to have some bearing also on the decision to hold a referendum in the first place. A party that can find other ways of dealing with a complex political issue may not need to hold a referendum in order to pursue its agenda. Likewise, there is no point in a governing party taking the decision to hold a referendum that it expects to *lose*.

When a governing party opts for a referendum strategy, it generally does so in the expectation that its position on a particular issue will be sustained. Even in those instances where a party is internally divided, it is generally possible to discern the preferred outcome of those who planned and organized the referendum strategy. Harold Wilson saw the 1975 referendum as a means of maintaining British membership in the European Community, even though some in his party continued to oppose it. Similarly, Felipe Gonzalez used the 1986 Spanish referendum on NATO membership as a means of defusing opposition to NATO membership within his own governing party. But such strategies can easily fail. The volatility and uncertainty of a referendum campaign can place at risk even the most carefully thought out referendum strategy. François Mitterrand may not have fully anticipated the high degree of political risk involved in putting the Maastricht treaty to a referendum in 1992, believing as he did that the treaty would be readily endorsed by French voters (Morel 1996). Neither did Canadian political leaders, having committed themselves to a referendum following the 1992 constitutional agreement, anticipate that the electorate would decisively reject their carefully balanced package of reforms (LeDuc and Pammett 1995; Johnston et al. 1996). While the strategy which lies behind calling the referendum may be clear, the outcome of the venture, once undertaken, becomes much more uncertain.

Referendum campaigns generally tend to follow one of three distinctive patterns (LeDuc 2000). The type of referendum campaign that is *least* like that of an election is one in which there is little partisan, issue, or ideological basis from which voters might tend to form an opinion. Lacking such information, they take more time to come to a decision, and that decision becomes highly unpredictable. In this dynamic, which might be termed *opinion formation*, voters cannot be expected to have fully developed opinions on an issue that has not previously been a subject of political debate. In instances such as these, voters clearly need the campaign in order to come to a conclusion about the issue on which they are being asked to render a decision. Only through the various information sources available to them over the course of the campaign will voters be able to form opinions on new and perhaps unfamiliar political questions which are presented to them. As Zaller (1992) notes, this is a process by which voters systematically convert information from various sources into an opinion. Some referendums fitting such a profile are those that involve multiple issues, complex international treaties, or large packages of constitutional provisions. Some of these cases are also ones in which elites may take strong positions at the beginning of the campaign, to which the voters slowly begin to react. The 1988 Australian and 1992 Canadian constitutional referendums seem to conform to this pattern, with elite-driven projects being decisively rejected once the voters had learned enough about them (Hughes 1994; Johnston et al. 1996). In such circumstances, the degree of change in opinion over the course of even a short campaign is potentially large, because there is little in the way of stable social or political attitudes which might anchor opinions on the issue of the referendum.

By contrast, where an issue is a familiar one in the political arena, or where parties take clearly competing positions, voting decisions are easier and tend to be made earlier in the campaign. Here, opinion is much firmer and less subject to rapid change or sudden reversal. Voters have strong cues based on partisanship or ideology, and are receptive to arguments presented by familiar and trusted political leaders. In such a campaign, much of the attention is directed toward wavering or "undecided" voters, in the knowledge that a swing of only a few percentage points might make the crucial difference in the outcome. Anticipating an *uphill struggle*, the party initiating the referendum knows that it can count on the votes of its core supporters. It knows also where the additional votes may lie that it needs in order to secure a majority, and that it can win these only through an effective campaign. The government of Felipe Gonzalez was successful in mobilizing partisan voters to support his NATO position in the 1986 Spanish referendum, and the Swedish government successfully overcame opposition to EU entry in the 1994 referendum. A similar strategy, however, failed in the case of the Norwegian EU referendums of 1972 and 1994, as it did also in the 1995 Quebec sovereignty referendum. In all of these cases, the vote was extremely close and might conceivably have gone either way.

As Tonsgaard (1992) has argued, the extent to which basic values and beliefs are linked to the referendum issue in the public debate, and the relative strength and stability of those beliefs, is a key starting point for any theoretical understanding of referendum voting. For some voters, opinions on Quebec sovereignty or on European integration might indeed reflect strongly held fundamental beliefs about the nation or a sense of political community. For others, however, such attitudes might be less the product of deeply held beliefs than a more transient opinion based on the persuasive arguments of an advertising campaign, apprehensions about the state of the economy, or judgments about the relative credibility of those delivering the message. Particularly in those instances where the issue(s) of the referendum are entirely new to the voter, the learning process of the campaign becomes critical to the determination of the outcome. Bowler and Donovan (1998) note that voters draw upon a variety of sources in forming opinions about the sometimes complex and confusing initiatives which appear on many US state ballots. Among the most frequently mentioned sources of such information are campaign pamphlets, newspaper and television editorials, and direct mailings from various campaign organizations. Voters in such situations take "cues" from these and other sources. Learning that the prominent consumer advocate, Ralph Nader, backed a proposal on auto insurance and opposed several competing proposals put forward by business groups was instrumental in shaping opinion on five insurance propositions which appeared together on a 1988 California ballot (Lupia 1994). Similarly, knowledge that the tobacco industry was behind a 1994 California proposition to loosen local smoking restrictions led to its defeat (Bowler and Donovan 1998).

Figure 3.3 provides a 'conceptual map' on which a number of the variables that are familiar from the study of elections might be rearranged to fit the more widely varying context of referendum voting. The more closely a referendum comes to involving elements at the left-hand side of the diagram, the more limited the effects of the campaign should be. As one moves toward the right-hand side of the diagram, the greater the potential for volatility and the more inherently unpredictable the outcome. Thus, following Tonsgaard's (1992) schematic, a referendum which involves a cleavage or ideological issue, and/or in which political parties take well known and predictably opposite

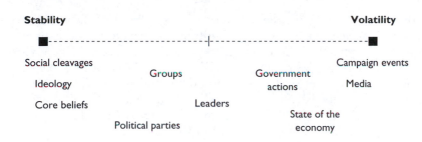

FIGURE 3.3   *Elements Leading Towards Stability or Volatility in Referendum Voting*

positions, ought to see the least volatility. One which involves a new or previously undiscussed issue, or in which parties line up in a non-traditional manner, is more likely to promote some of the short-term variables toward the right-hand side of the diagram.

Referendums such as the 1980 vote on nuclear power in Sweden, or the Irish referendums on divorce and abortion, provide good examples of the kinds of issues on which a significant part of the electorate could be expected to have strong predispositions. But a different dynamic can develop when a referendum on a well known issue begins to take on a new and unanticipated direction over the course of the campaign. Often this occurs when opposition groups are successful in "changing the subject" of a referendum, or in "raising doubts" about the true motives of those behind a particular proposal. Darcy and Laver (1990) documented this type of campaign in their study of the 1986 Irish divorce referendum, coining the term *opinion reversal* to describe the dynamic which ensued in that instance. Prior to that campaign, public opinion polls had shown substantial support for a change in the laws governing divorce, and there was initially little organized opposition to the government's reform proposal. But the campaign took on an unexpected direction when non-party groups became involved and began to refocus the debate in terms of the rights of women and the integrity of family life. Support for the proposed change in the divorce law plunged rapidly. Within a few months after the referendum, public opinion polls in Ireland had returned to a "normal" reading on the issue of divorce. But the rapid shift in the nature of the discourse over a short campaign had been enough to defeat the amendment. The 1986 Irish divorce referendum might have seen less volatility had it been fought solely along religious or partisan lines, as many at the time had expected. But the dramatic reversal which took place in voter sentiment during that contest was attributable in part to the success of certain campaign actors in redefining the issue for the voters, persuading them to view the matter as something *other* than a traditional cleavage issue.

Raising doubts about the motives of those behind the referendum, or changing the subject of the debate in mid-course, can be a highly effective campaign tactic. In the 1999 Australian republic referendum, public opinion polls indicated that a majority of Australians favoured ending the monarchy, both before *and* after the referendum.[2] But opponents of the change were successful during that campaign in shifting the debate to the issue of an elected vs. appointed president, thereby dividing potential YES voters. Many Australian voters became persuaded during the campaign to view the choice in terms of an elected or appointed presidency rather than one of maintaining or abolishing the monarchy. Persuaded that the "politician's republic" deserved to be defeated, many republicans who might otherwise have supported the YES side voted NO (McAllister 2000).

Figure 3.4 represents an estimate of the magnitude of opinion change in a number of referendum campaigns obtained by comparing the outcome of a referendum with the result which would have been predicted by a public opinion poll taken one or two months before voting day.[3] The pattern shown by these examples conforms roughly to the theoretical expectations suggested in Figure 3.3. Referendums on issues which have been debated extensively in political arenas *other* than that of the campaign, or in which there were strong linkages to the positions taken by political parties, generally display less volatility. Those involving new issues, or areas of political debate in which the mass public is not highly engaged, tend to show greater movement in public opinion over the duration of the campaign, often culminating in an outcome which would *not* have been accurately predicted by pre-campaign polls.

Referendums and elections: how do they differ?

A referendum presents a different set of choices to the voter than does an election. In a referendum, unlike an election, no political parties or candidate names appear on the ballot. Yet some referendums are highly partisan contests nevertheless. Where the positions of parties on an issue are well known, or where the referendum debate follows clearly understood ideological lines, voting behavior may tend to conform to relatively predictable patterns. In such situations, voting choice may be driven by partisan or ideological cues, or by familiarity with one or more of the issues in a long-standing political debate. But the 1994 Nordic referendums on European Union membership, or the 1992 Canadian constitutional referendum, found political parties who regularly oppose each other in elections campaigning together on the same side of an issue, thus providing mixed cues to their electorates. In some other instances, parties that might normally have provided their supporters with reliable voting cues were themselves internally divided. In the 1992 Maastricht referendum in France, for example, or the 1980 Swedish nuclear power referendum, prominent figures from the same political party were found actively campaigning on opposite sides of the issue.

Voting choice in referendums can also become entangled with other short-term political factors, above and beyond the issue appearing on the referendum ballot. In this respect, referendums may take on some of

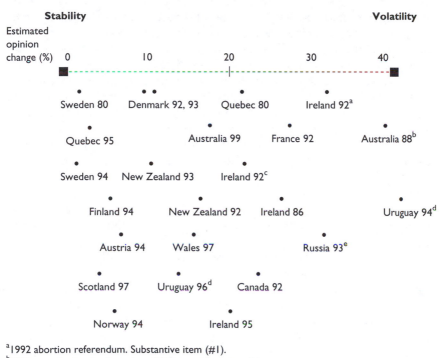

[a] 1992 abortion referendum. Substantive item (#1).
[b] 1988 constitutional referendum. "Rights and Freedoms" item.
[c] 1992 referendum on the Maastricht treaty.
[d] 1994 and 1996 Uruguayan referendums on electoral reform.
[e] 1993 referendum. Q2 (support government policies).

FIGURE 3.4   *Categorizing Selected Referendum Campaigns by Degree of Volatility*

the characteristics of "second order" elections (van der Eijk, Franklin, and Marsh 1995; Heath and Taylor 1999b). Examining the 1992 Danish and French referendums on the Maastricht treaty, Franklin, van der Eijk, and Marsh (1995) argued that shifting attitudes toward domestic political actors, or the relative popularity or unpopularity of the government of the day, can sometimes provide a more plausible explanation of shifts in voter sentiment than feelings about the referendum issue itself. Others have similarly argued that short-term variables such as the state of the economy may also play a role in determining the outcome of some referendums (Clarke and Kornberg 1994, 1996).

Another question that arises in comparing referendum and election voting behavior is that of voter turnout. Evidence suggests that turnout can vary much more widely in referendums than it does in national elections. In Switzerland, where referendums are commonplace events, turnout is generally well below 50%, and can sometimes be much lower (Kobach 1993a). It can, however, rise to higher levels when a particular issue engages wide voter interest or when an intense campaign is waged by interested groups.[4] Butler and Ranney (1994) found that turnout over a large number of referendum cases in various nations averaged 15 percentage points lower than that found in general elections in the same countries. Cronin (1989) found a comparable rate of "drop-off" (the difference between voting on the candidate and proposition sections of the ballot) in American state referendums. However, there is no reason to believe that turnout in referendums is *necessarily* lower than that found in elections. As is seen in Table 3.2, the turnout in some of the more important European referendums has been comparable to that found in national elections. There are also a number of instances where a referendum held to coincide with a general election assures a higher turnout.[5] But clearly, a referendum held separately on a less salient issue runs the risk of lower voter participation. The 1980 Swedish nuclear power referendum (76%), and the 1992 Uruguayan referendum on privatization of state industries (77%) registered turnout below that of the most nearly comparable election, a clear contrast with other referendums held in those countries on higher profile issues (Table 3.2).

The wider variations in turnout found in referendums also suggest a greater potential for volatility. The electorate taking part in a referendum is not always the same one that participates in elections. In examining California state propositions, Bowler and Donovan (1998) found considerable variation in participation across 190 votes over a 14-year period. Accounting for this variation were some factors specific to the proposition itself (type of measure, ballot position), some external to it (presidential election, state primary), and others relating to specific characteristics of the campaign (for example, spending, advertising). However, Jenssen, Pesonen, and Gilljam (1998) found generally that the same factors that predict participation in elections also correlate with referendum voting. Where parties fail to mobilize their supporters on behalf of an issue, or where non-party groups succeed in mobilizing *theirs*, the outcome of a referendum can be more directly subject to a differential turnout effect. Since the turnout in referendums generally appears to vary more widely than in elections, the potential for turnout effects in a referendum will often be greater than that typically found in elections.

As noted earlier, we would expect that in those instances where the issues of the referendum are entirely new to the voter, the learning process of the campaign will be more critical for deciding how to vote and therefore also more important in determining the outcome. When voters clearly need the campaign in order to form an opinion on the issue(s) of the referendum, we might expect individual voting decisions to be made later, when more information about the issue has become available. Conversely, where voters are able to make up their minds on the basis of clear partisan or ideological cues, or where there is a high degree of prior familiarity with the issue(s) of the referendum, we might expect voting decisions to be made earlier. The timing of the vote decision therefore is a useful indicator of the extent to which the characteristics of the referendum vote decision vary from that typically found in an election.

TABLE 3.2 *Selected Turnout Comparisons—Referendums and General Elections (percentages)*

Country	Year, election or referendum	Turnout
Australia	1998 federal election	95
	1999 republic referendum	95
Canada	1992 constitutional referendum	75
	1993 federal election	70
Denmark	1992 Maastricht treaty referendum	83
	1993 Edinburgh agreement	86
	1998 general election	87
	2000 European currency referendum	89
France	1992 Maastricht treaty referendum	70
	1993 national assembly election	69
Ireland	1992 parliamentary election	69
	1992 abortion laws	65
	1995 divorce amendment	62
Norway	1993 general election	76
	1994 EU referendum	89
Sweden	1994 EU referendum	83
	1994 general election	87
Switzerland	1993 (March) casino gambling, gasoline taxes, animal experiments	51
	1994 (June) citizenship, culture, UN peacekeeping participation	46
	1995 federal election	42
Uruguay	1994 general election	89
	1996 constitutional referendum	86

SOURCES: Butler and Ranney (1994); University of Geneva Center for the Study of Direct Democracy (http://c2d.unige. ch/); International IDEA (www.idea.int/)

Survey data on reported time of vote decision are available for some of the referendums used as examples throughout this chapter. Table 3.3 presents data for ten cases where surveys were conducted.[6] The 1992 Canadian constitutional referendum provides a fairly extreme example, because that referendum could not have been anticipated in advance and voters could not have been expected to have had a high degree of prior knowledge of the content of a complex constitutional agreement which had been negotiated in closed sessions. Not surprisingly therefore, nearly two-thirds of those voting in that referendum made their decision over the course of the campaign, a substantial number of those as late as the final week. By contrast, voters in the 1995 Quebec sovereignty referendum were able to come to a decision much more quickly on the issue, because the subject matter of that referendum was well known, and the campaign provided strongly reinforcing partisan cues for most voters. While the campaign was still important to the outcome, in part because of the closeness of the result, fewer voters needed additional information in order to reach a decision. Three-quarters of the Quebec electorate had already made up their minds how to vote at the time that the referendum was called.

TABLE 3.3   *Reported Time of Vote Decision in Ten Referendums (percentages)*

Country	Year	Long before	At call	During campaign	Final week
Quebec[a]	1995	70	5	14	11
Finland[b]	1994	62	—	16	22
France[c]	1992	60	—	20	20
Norway[b]	1994	59	—	24	17
Sweden[b]	1994	58	—	17	25
Quebec[d]	1980	49	19	27	5
Australia[e]	1999	42	19	20	19
Scotland[f]	1997	40	21	16	24
Wales[f]	1997	32	20	16	33
Canada[g]	1992	—	38	33	29

[a] 1995 Carleton ISSP Study.
[b] Comparative Nordic Referendums Study (Pesonen 1998).
[c] SOFRES/Le Figaro (Franklin, van der Eijk, and Marsh 1995).
[d] 1980 Canadian National Election Study. Quebec referendum wave.
[e] 1999 Australian Constitutional Referendum Study.
[f] 1997 CREST surveys.
[g] 1992 Carleton Referendum Study.

The 1994 European Union membership referendums in the Nordic countries provide examples which fall between these two extremes, as does the 1992 French referendum on the Maastricht treaty. In these four cases, more than half of all voters surveyed reported having made their decision how to vote "long before" the campaign had begun. The balance decided how they would vote over the course of the campaign, dividing roughly evenly between those reporting that they made their decision in the final week and those deciding earlier in the campaign. Voters in the EU referendums may have had a high degree of knowledge of the underlying issue but would still have needed the campaign in order to assess the specific arguments about the accession agreements which were being put forward. In Sweden, divisions among the governing Social Democrats spilled over into the campaign, with the government actively supporting the YES side but some of its own partisans campaigning against it under the umbrella group *Social Democrats Against the EU*. These circumstances present a quite different picture than the 1995 Quebec case, where parties with well known and strongly held positions on the sovereignty issue were putting forward familiar arguments right from the beginning and mobilizing their traditional supporters in support of a cause to which they could be expected to have a strong prior commitment.

The positions which political parties take, either in the evolution of the referendum issue or during the campaign itself, often provide important information cues to voters. Where these are present, voters are often able to find their own positions fairly quickly. When they are absent, other short-term elements tend to become more powerful, or well known groups, organizations, or individuals may intervene to provide voters with the kinds of "short cuts" that political parties might otherwise provide (Lupia 1992, 1994; Bowler and Donovan 1998). Ideology can provide a similar type of anchor for some types of issues put to a referendum. Where voters are easily able to locate an issue on a left–right spectrum, they might more easily form their own opinions on the issue, particularly in those countries where party politics arrays itself along clearly understood ideological lines.

Listhaug, Holmberg, and Sänkiaho (1998) concluded that partisanship played an important role in voting in the 1994 EU referendums in all of the three Nordic countries, but also found that the strength of this relationship varied significantly both between countries and between parties. Several of the parties which campaigned for a YES vote in all three countries were able to deliver high percentages of their supporters. The voting patterns found in Sweden in the 1994 referendum, however, were somewhat different than in the other two countries, in part reflecting the deep divisions among the governing Social Democrats. The correlation with ideology was significantly stronger in Sweden than was found in Norway or Finland (Aardal et al. 1998). In spite of these divisions, the Social Democrats were able to win back about half of their supporters to the YES side over the course of the campaign, perhaps making the difference between victory and defeat for the proposal.[7]

The 1999 Australian referendum on the monarchy presents a case involving an entirely different type of issue, on which linkages to partisanship were fairly weak. This issue was also not primarily an ideological one for most voters. Nevertheless, some fairly clear partisan voting patterns were in evidence, at least on the central issue of the referendum involving replacement of the monarchy. Sixty per cent of Labor partisans voted YES on that issue compared to only 34% of Liberals and 24% of National voters (McAllister 2000). On the second question of the referendum involving adoption of a controversial constitutional preamble, there was little pattern, with majorities in all party groups ultimately voting NO on that item.[8] In general, however, the partisan patterns that did exist reflect the effectiveness of the campaign strategies followed by the NO side more than the existence of an underlying party/issue cleavage. Had the referendum itself been either a straight party fight or a contest driven entirely by public opinion on the underlying issues, the outcome might very well have been different. In reality, it was neither of these. Rather, it was a contest in which campaign tactics mattered a great deal, and in which short-term movement in public opinion was sufficient to overcome, at least temporarily, partisan, ideological, or issue cleavages that may have existed prior to the beginning of the referendum campaign.

Conclusion: referendums and elections

The referendums discussed in this chapter represent a range of different electoral contexts, surely wider and more diverse than would be found in comparing several elections within the same set of countries. There are, of course, many similarities between the factors that affect voting behavior in elections and those which determine the outcome of referendums— situations, for instance, in which familiar party, ideological, and issue variables matter a great deal in the determination of voting behavior. But, as empirical analyses of referendum voting in a number of countries have demonstrated, the nature of the referendum issue, the positioning of the parties, and the involvement of other non-party organizations or groups can range a great deal more widely than the variation typically found in elections. Such variation is found not only between countries employing the referendum device, but also among different referendums in the *same* countries. In those few polities where referendums are commonplace events, this variation in electoral context is more readily observed. The Irish referendums on divorce, abortion, several European issues, and other constitutional matters, for example, display a number of distinctive patterns with respect to voting turnout, the positioning of the parties, the dynamic of the campaign, and the outcome of the vote. In countries where referendums are more exotic events, we tend naturally to apply the more familiar electoral models. But these models work best when the cleavages around which the referendum is fought are the most similar to those found in elections. In Quebec, for example, there is little doubt that any future sovereignty referendum will be contested along lines that have by now become a familiar characteristic of party politics in that province. As the "European" issue becomes a potentially more important element of ordinary electoral politics in some of the EU countries, we may begin to see a similar kind of convergence between voting patterns in national elections and those in referendums on issues dealing with various aspects of European integration, if and when these occur. But one would not predict that such patterns will be found in *all* referendums, particularly those where the issue involved is relatively untested in the electoral arena, or where systemic factors produce wide variations in voting turnout or campaign organization. Constitutional referendums in Canada or Australia, for example, have been among the most unpredictable of all types of electoral contests, subject to wide swings in public opinion and considerable uncertainty as to which short-term factors may ultimately prove most decisive to the outcome. If electoral events of this kind should become less rare in the future, our ability to develop models of voting behavior which are more suited to them than those derived solely from elections may be further enhanced. Theories of direct democracy tend to presume that referendum voters are always "issue" voters. But the research to date on referendum voting, like that on elections, teaches us that attitudes toward issues are only one of the variables affecting voting choice, and not always the most important one in determining outcomes.

NOTES

Material for this chapter was compiled as part of the Comparative Referendums Project at the University of Toronto. The support of the Social Sciences and Humanities Research Council of Canada (grant no. 410-98-4161) for this research is gratefully acknowledged. I also wish to thank Michael Harvey, Josh Koziebrocki, and Helder Marcos for their work on this project.
1. Initiative and Referendum Institute. (http://www.iandrinstitute.org)
2. The proposal put to Australian voters in the 1999 referendum was: "To alter the constitution to establish the Commonwealth of Australia as a republic, with the Queen and Governor General being replaced by a President appointed by a two-thirds majority of the members of the Commonwealth Parliament."
3. The poll chosen was as close to the beginning of the campaign as possible. For a more detailed discussion of this exercise, involving a larger number of referendum cases, see LeDuc (2000).
4. For example, turnout in the 1992 referendum on Swiss membership in the European Economic Area was 78%. The average turnout for all Swiss referendums since 1960 (43%) is about 11 percentage points lower than that for all federal parliamentary elections over the same period (Kobach 1993a; Franklin, this volume, Chapter 7). In more recent years, however, the difference has narrowed because turnout in Swiss parliamentary elections has declined.
5. The 1992 referendum in Ireland on abortion took place at the time of the general election of that year, although referendums in Ireland do not necessarily coincide with elections. The second New Zealand referendum on electoral reform, held in 1993, also took place at the same time as an election. The turnout of 83% in that referendum provides a significant contrast with the turnout in New Zealand's first referendum on this issue, which was held a year earlier and drew only 55% turnout.
6. The categories found in the surveys do not always coincide perfectly with the labels employed in Table 3.3. In the CREST surveys in Scotland and Wales, for example, the categories were: *before the general election* (i.e., 1 May 1997); *between the general election and the referendum*; *in the month before; in the week before*. The category *when the referendum was called* was not used in the SOFRES or the Nordic countries surveys, but the other categories utilized in those instances were similar to those shown in the table.
7. The vote in Sweden on EU membership in the 1994 referendum was 52% YES, 47% NO. The remaining 1% of the ballots were recorded as blank.
8. Forty-five per cent voted YES on the republic proposal (see note 2), and 55% voted NO. On the preamble item, the vote was 39% YES, 61% NO. Neither item carried a majority in any of the states.

4

Comparing Party Systems

PETER MAIR

The comparison of party systems has always formed an essential component of the more generalized comparison of democratic political systems. On the one hand, by noting the number of parties in competition in any given polity, and by taking at least some account of the manner in which these parties interact with one another, it has proved possible to gain a reasonably valuable insight into the ways in which these polities differ from one another. On the other hand, following a more normative imperative, it has often proved tempting to trace the source of problems of the legitimacy and stability of democratic regimes back to the character of their party systems. For both reasons, an understanding of the nature and character of a country's party system has always been accorded priority in cross-national comparative analysis, even if the criteria by which party systems are compared have often been subject to debate.

This chapter begins with a review of the principal existing approaches to the classification of party systems, pointing to both their limits and possibilities when applied within comparative analysis. It then goes on, in the second section of the chapter, to underline the importance of understanding the structure of competition in any given party system, since in many ways the very notion of a party system is centred on the assumption that there exists a stable structure of competition. As is shown here, structures of competition can be seen to be either closed (and predictable) or open (and unpredictable), depending on the patterns of alternation in government, the degree of innovation or persistence in processes of government formation, and the range of parties gaining access to government. Given the overall concern of this volume, the emphasis in the third section is on the need to distinguish between processes of electoral change on the one hand, and changes in party systems and the structures of competition on the other, a distinction which also allows us to conceive of situations in which electoral change is the consequence rather than the cause of party system change.

Approaches to the classification of party systems: a review

The most traditional and most widely accepted criterion for classifying party systems is also the most simple: the number of parties in competition. Moreover, the most conventional distinction involved here also proves appealingly straightforward: that between a two-party system on the one hand, and a multiparty system (that is, more than two parties) on the other (see Duverger 1954). When first promoted as the principal means of distinguishing between party systems, this mode of categorization was seen as tapping into a more fundamental distinction between more or less stable and consensual democracies, which were those normally associated with the two-party type, as opposed to more or less unstable and conflictual democracies, which were those associated with the multiparty type. Thus, and particularly in early applications, two-party systems, which were typically characteristic of the United Kingdom and the United States, and which invariably involved single-party government, were assumed to enhance accountability, alternation in government, and moderate, centre-seeking competition. Multiparty systems, on the other hand, which usually required coalition administrations, and which were typically characteristic of countries such as France or Italy, prevented voters from gaining a direct voice in the formation of governments, did not necessarily facilitate alternation in government, and sometimes favoured extremist, ideological confrontations between narrowly based political parties. And although this simple association of party system types and political stability and efficacy was later challenged by research into the experiences of some of the smaller European democracies in particular, which boasted both a multiplicity of parties and a strong commitment to consensual government (e.g., Daalder 1983), the traditional categorization of two-party versus multiparty has nevertheless continued to command a great deal of support within the literature on comparative politics.[1]

This simple distinction is, of course, far from being the only possible approach, and since Duverger a number of attempts have been made to develop more sensitive and discriminating criteria (see Table 4.1). In the conclusion to his classic *Oppositions* volume, for example, Robert Dahl (1966) sought to move away from an almost exclusive concern with simply the numbers of parties, and built an alternative classification based around the competitive strategy adopted by the opposing parties, distinguishing between competitive, co-operative, and coalescent strategies, and distinguishing further between opposition in the electoral arena and opposition in the parliamentary arena (see also Laver 1989). This led Dahl to elaborate a four-fold typology, distinguishing between strictly competitive systems, co-operative–competitive systems, coalescent–competitive systems, and strictly coalescent systems. Shortly after this, in what proved subsequently a very influential study, Jean Blondel (1968) developed a typology which took account not only of the numbers of parties in competition, but also

TABLE 4.1   *Types of Party Systems*

Author	Principal criteria for classification	Principal types of party system identified
Duverger (1954)	Numbers of parties	Two-party systems
		Multiparty systems
Dahl (1966)	Competitiveness of opposition	Strictly competitive
		Co-operative–competitive
		Coalescent–competitive
		Strictly coalescent
Blondel (1968)	Numbers of parties	Two-party systems
	Relative size of parties	Two-and-a-half-party systems
		Multiparty systems with one dominant party
		Multiparty systems without dominant party
Rokkan (1968)	Numbers of parties	The British-German
	Likelihood of single-party majorities	"1 vs. 1 + 1" system
		The Scandinavian
	Distribution of minority party strengths	"1 vs. 3–4" system
		Even multiparty systems: "1 vs. 1 vs. 1 + 2–3"
Sartori (1976)	Numbers of parties	Two-party systems
	Ideological distance	Moderate pluralism
		Polarized pluralism
		Predominant-party systems

their relative size (and, in a later refinement, their "place on the ideological spectrum"), distinguishing four types: two-party systems, two-and-a-half-party systems, multiparty systems with a dominant party and multiparty systems without a dominant party. In practice, however, this new approach did little more than improve the traditional two-party versus multiparty distinction by disaggregating the otherwise overloaded multiparty category. Stein Rokkan's (1968) contemporaneous attempt to classify the party systems of the smaller European democracies also did little more than disaggregate the multiparty category, in this case by taking account of the likelihood of single party majorities (akin to Blondel's dominant party) and the degree to which there was a fragmentation of minority party strengths. Using these criteria, Rokkan developed a three-fold distinction involving a "British-German" type system, in which the system was dominated by the competition between two major parties, with a third, minor party also in contention; a "Scandinavian"-type system in which one big party regularly confronted a more or less formalized alliance between three or four smaller parties; and an "even" multiparty system in which competition was dominated by three or more parties of equivalent size.

Counting the numbers of parties—or what he referred to as the "format" of the party system—is also an essential component of the more comprehensive typology which was later developed by Sartori (1976: 117–323).[2] But although Sartori's approach underlined the relevance of party numbers, it also went much beyond this by including as a second principal criterion the ideological distance that separated the parties in the system. In fact, Sartori's typology, which was explicitly concerned with the interactions between the parties in any given system—what he refers to as the "mechanics" of the system—and which was therefore explicitly concerned with differential patterns of competition, drew on the combination of these two criteria. Party systems could therefore be classified according to the number of parties in the system, in which there was a distinction between formats with two parties, those with up to five parties (limited pluralism) and those with six parties or more (extreme pluralism); and according to the ideological distance separating the extreme parties in the system, which would either be small (moderate) or large (polarized). The two criteria were not wholly independent, however, in that, as Sartori also argued, the format of the system, that is the number of parties, contained mechanical predispositions (that is, it could affect the degree of polarization), such that extreme pluralism could lead to polarization. The combination of both criteria then yielded three principal types of party system—two-party systems, characterized by an evidently limited format and a small ideological distance (for example, the United Kingdom); moderate pluralism, characterized by limited pluralism and a relatively small ideological distance (such as Denmark); and, which was the most important for the typology, polarized pluralism, characterized by extreme pluralism and a large ideological distance (examples being Italy in the 1960s and 1970s, and Chile prior to the 1973 coup). In addition, Sartori also allowed for the existence of a "predominant-party system," a system in which one particular party, such as, most notably, Congress in India or the Liberal Democrats in Japan prior to the 1990s, consistently (that is, over at least four legislatures) won a majority of parliamentary seats.[3]

There are a number of reasons why Sartori's typology can be regarded as the most important of those briefly reviewed here. In the first place, it is the most comprehensive of all the available typologies, both in terms of the care with which it is developed, as well as in terms of the way in which it is applied to empirical cases. Second, notwithstanding the continued appeal of the simple two-party/multiparty distinction, Sartori's typology has subsequently been employed in a variety of sophisticated national and cross-national studies, yielding a degree of insight into the functioning of party systems which is incomparably better than that developed by any of the alternative typologies (e.g., Bartolini 1984; Bille 1990). Third, it underlines the influence exerted by systemic properties, and by the party system, on electoral behavior and electoral outcomes. More than any of the other typologies, it therefore allows the party system to operate as an independent variable, constraining or even directing electoral preferences. This last aspect is particularly important in this context, and I will return to it at a later stage. Finally, as noted, it is a typology that is explicitly concerned with patterns of competition and with the interactions between parties, and in this sense it is much more directly concerned with the functioning of the party *system* itself. Indeed, Sartori's definition of a party system, formulated in his 1976 volume, still stands as the most precise and complete definition within the literature:

> Parties make for a "system", then, only when they are parts (in the plural); and a party system is precisely the *system of interactions* resulting from inter-party competition. That is, the system in question bears on the relatedness of parties to each other, on how each party is a function (in the mathematical sense) of the other parties and reacts, competitively or otherwise, to the other parties. (Sartori 1976: 44)

At the same time, however, and some 25 years after the publication of Sartori's seminal volume, questions can be raised regarding the continued utility and discriminating capacity of the typology, not least because of what is now a potential overcrowding in the moderate pluralism category and a virtual emptying of the alternative types. For example, and this criticism can also be levelled against the traditional Duverger classification, it is now relatively difficult to find clear-cut examples of the classic two-party system. The United States, which is often cited as an almost pure two-party model, can also be understood as a "four-party" system, in which a presidential two-party system co-exists with a separate congressional two-party system, or even as having 50 two-party systems, each functioning separately in each of the 50 states (e.g., Katz and Kolodny 1994). The United Kingdom, which was also always seen as the paramount case of a two-party system, recently, albeit temporarily, fulfilled Sartori's conditions for a predominant party system, with the Conservative party consistently winning majorities in the 1979, 1983, 1987, and 1992 Westminster elections. Against this, of course, it might be argued that a number of newer democracies are beginning to approximate the two-party model, and that this could restore the relevance of the category as a whole. Since becoming full democracies in the 1970s, for example, Greece, Portugal, and Spain have all tended to drift increasingly towards a two-party format with alternating single-party governments. The Czech Republic may yet go in a similar direction, in that the two biggest Czech parties, the Civic Democrats and the Social Democrats, currently commanding some two-thirds of the seats in parliament, are together pushing for a reform of the electoral system which would effectively strengthen their own position and weaken that of their smaller opponents. Costa Rica, one of the most well established Latin American democracies, also reflects a two-party format, with the two biggest parties, the Christian-Social Unity party and the National Liberation party together winning more than 75% of the vote and some 90% of the seats in the 1998 Assembly elections. The purest two-party system is that found in Malta, one of the world's smallest democracies, where the two main parties together poll almost exactly 100% of the vote. With this handful of exceptions, however, the two-party category is almost complete.

At the other extreme, and particularly given the recent decline and/or eclipse of traditional communist parties, it has also become difficult to find an unambiguous example of polarized pluralism. Sartori's criteria for this latter system had been very carefully elaborated (1976: 131–73), and depended crucially on there being a "maximum spread of [ideological] opinion" (p. 135), *bilateral* oppositions (p. 134), and hence, necessarily so, on there being a relevant anti-system party, that is, a party which "undermines the legitimacy of the regime it opposes" (p. 133) at *each* end of the political spectrum. It follows from this that should *either* of these anti-system alternatives become irrelevant or disappear, there would then occur an attenuation of the spread of opinion and thus a reduction in the degree of polarization, so forcing the case out of the category. This is now certainly the case in France, for example, where the fading anti-system party of the left, the Communist party (PCF), was sufficiently legitimated to be admitted to government office as long ago as 1981; and, more recently, in Italy, where the Communist party (PCI) divided into the unequivocally moderate Democratic Left (DS) and the smaller, more radical, but certainly no longer anti-system alternative of the Communist Refoundation (RC). In addition, with the advent of the former neo-fascist National Alliance (AN) to office in the Berlusconi government of 1994, Italy can also be seen to have shed its anti-system alternative of the right. This is not to suggest that anti-system oppositions have everywhere ceased to exist; on the contrary, despite the eclipse of the traditional anti-system parties of the communist and fascist variety, a number of European party systems are now confronted with the rise of new parties, particularly on the right, which might well be seen as anti-system in orientation, such as the National Front in France or the Vlaams Blok in Belgium (Betz 1994; Ignazi 1992, 1994; Mudde 2000). But even if these parties do reflect an extreme of opinion on the right-wing side of the political spectrum, they tend not to be counter-balanced by an equivalent anti-system extreme on the left, and hence, by definition, the poles are no longer "two poles apart" (Sartori 1976: 135). In short, if two-party systems in a strict sense are thin on the ground, and if examples of polarized pluralism are also increasingly hard to find, then, perforce, most systems tend to crowd into the category of moderate pluralism,[4] which clearly reduces the discriminating power of the typology.

Party systems and the structure of competition

That said, Sartori's approach remains particularly useful and important in that, unlike the alternative approaches, it helps to focus attention directly on what is perhaps the most important aspect of party systems, and on what distinguishes most clearly between different party systems: *the structure of inter-party competition*, and especially *the competition for government*. To be sure, it might be argued that this is in fact the core variable underlying each of the other established classifications of party systems. Duverger's (1954) classic distinction between two-party systems and multi-party systems, for example, is obviously based on the numbers of parties in competition, but it can also be seen as differentiating systems in which two major parties compete with one another over the question of which will form a (single-party) government from those in which government usually involves some form of shifting coalition. In a similar vein, Rokkan's (1968) distinction between the British-German, Scandinavian, and even the multi-party types, though ostensibly, and within his own terms, "purely numerical," is really an attempt to tap into the different patterns of coalition formation. But while some notion of the competition for government may well have informed these earlier classifications, they certainly did not confront the issue directly. Indeed, among alternative approaches, it is really only Dahl's (1966) distinctions that come anywhere close to addressing the question of government formation as a key defining feature, even though within his particular analysis this takes second place to the more central question involved in identifying differences in party strategies in different competitive arenas.

Building from Sartori, then, how might we best understand those differential patterns in the competition for government that can be seen to define the character of party systems? What is important here is that we not only have a set of criteria which can distinguish between differential patterns of competition for government, but that we also have something that is sensitive to shifts over time. That is, we need criteria which can be used to categorize party systems in different polities, and which, at the same time, can allow us to see when party systems change. This involves not only placing competition for government at the heart of the definition of party systems, but also involves adopting a more dynamic perspective that can move away from the rather static categories that have tended to dominate the literature to date.

Seen from this perspective, there are three factors that can be considered relevant. In the first place, there is the question of the prevailing mode of government alternation, since it is the competition between potential teams of governors which lies at the core of any party system. Second, there is the question of stability or consistency in the governing alternatives, and the extent to which competition for government takes on a familiar, and hence predictable character. Finally, there is the simple question of who governs, and the extent to which access to government is either open to a wide range of diverse parties or limited simply to a smaller subset. Let us now look at each of these factors in turn and at how they serve to shape the logic of any given party system.[5]

Alternation in government

There are three conceivable patterns of alternation which need to be considered here. The first, and most obvious pattern might be termed *wholesale alternation*, in which incumbents are wholly displaced by a former opposition. In other words, all of the parties in government at time t are removed from office and are replaced at time *t* + *1* by a new government made up of a party or coalition of parties which were previously in opposition. The British case offers the most obvious example of such wholesale alternation, with a single-party Labour government being replaced by a single-party Conservative government, or vice versa. A similar pattern was long evident in New Zealand, with the alternation between Labour and the National party. But while the classic two-party model offers the most obvious examples of wholesale alternation, the pattern can also be seen in more fragmented systems. In Norway, for example, wholesale alternation has regularly ensued on the basis of shifts between a single-party Labour government, on the one hand, and a multiparty bourgeois coalition, on the other, reflecting a pattern of competition similar to that which developed in Costa Rica in the 1960s and 1970s. More unusually, the recent French experience has witnessed wholesale alternation between two competing coalitions, with the Socialists and various left-wing allies, including the Communist party, alternating with a coalition of the Gaullists (RPR) and center–right (UDF). This pattern was also echoed in Germany in 1998, which experienced its first case of wholesale alternation when a coalition of Social Democrats (SPD) and Greens displaced a long-incumbent coalition of Christian Democrats (CDU–CSU) and Liberals (FDP). These latter cases are quite exceptional, however, in that even in systems with four or more relevant political parties, as was the case over extended periods of time in Ireland, Norway, and Sweden, and as was also the case in Japan in 1993, wholesale alternation has usually involved at least one single-party alternative.

The second pattern is *partial alternation,* in which a newly incumbent government in a parliamentary system includes at least one party which also formed part of the previous government. Germany has provided the most obvious example here, in that all of the governments which held office between 1969 and 1998 included the FDP as a junior coalition partner, with the role of senior partner alternating sporadically between the SPD and the CDU–CSU. The Dutch system also approximated this pattern, with the Christian Democrats (CDA) and, prior to 1977, the Catholic People's party (KVP), persisting in office through to 1994, albeit with alternating coalition partners.[6] Indeed, the major contrast between the traditional German and Dutch patterns of alternation was simply that, in the Dutch case, it tended to be the biggest single party that has remained in government, whereas it was usually the smaller partner in the German case. Similar enduring patterns of partial alternation, albeit without involving such pronounced long-term continuity of one particular partner in office, can be seen in Belgium, Finland, and Luxembourg. However, the most striking example of partial alternation was that provided by the Italian case throughout most of the post-war period, with the Christian Democrats (DC) holding office continually from 1946 to 1994, occasionally as a minority single-party government, and more often as the senior partner in a variable multiparty coalition.

The third pattern borders closely on this Italian experience and is marked by a complete absence of alternation, or by *non-alternation,* in which the same party or parties remains in exclusive control of government over an extended period of time, being displaced neither wholly nor partially. Switzerland offers the clearest example of non-alternation over time, in that the same four-party coalition has now held office continually since 1959. A similar pattern of non-alternation characterizes what Sartori has defined as predominant-party systems, as in the case of Japan from 1955 to 1993, with the Liberal Democrats holding office almost consistently alone over this 40-year period, in India, where the Congress party held continuous office until its first defeat in 1977, and in Mexico, where the Revolutionary party (PRI) held the dominant position from the 1920s through to the end of the century.

Innovation and familiarity

Party systems differ not only in their patterns of alternation, but also in the degree to which the alternative governing formulae are either familiar or innovative—that is, whether or not the party or combination of parties has governed before in that particular format (see also Franklin and Mackie 1983). In the British case, for example, familiarity is everything, and no new governing formula has been experimented with since the broad coalition which held office during the Second World War. The formulae were also familiar and hence very predictable over a long period in the Irish case, with governments being made up of either Fianna Fáil on the one hand, or a coalition of all the remaining parties on the other, as well as in Germany, which experimented with no new formula between the advent to office for the first time of an SPD–FDP coalition in 1969 and the eventual incorporation of the Greens for the first time in 1998. Notwithstanding the German case, however, it is in such systems of partial alternation that the greatest scope exists for innovation. In Italy, for example, despite the long-term dominance of the DC, there has been frequent experimentation with new coalition alliances. In the Netherlands, despite the continuity in office of the KVP and, later, the CDA, innovation has also been particularly marked, with differing and novel combinations of parties succeeding one another in office with remarkable frequency. It is important to note here that while innovative formulae are obviously involved when the party or parties concerned have never previously held office, they can also be seen to occur even when the parties have governed before but never in that particular alliance. In the Irish case, for example, the first ever coalition between Fianna Fáil and Labour, which took office in 1993, can be defined as innovative, even though each of the parties involved had already had long experiences of government; similarly, both the People's party (ÖVP) and Social Democrats (SPÖ) single-party governments in Austria (taking office for the first time in 1966 and 1970, respectively) can be treated as innovative, despite the fact that both parties had previously governed together in coalition.

Which parties govern?

The third factor involved here concerns the range of parties which gain access to government. Although not all possible parties can be expected to win a share of office, even with frequent alternation, party systems can nevertheless be distinguished in terms of the degree to which access to office is widely or narrowly dispersed. In other words, party systems can be distinguished in terms of whether all relevant parties eventually cross the threshold of government, as is more or less the case in the Netherlands, for example, or whether governing remains the privilege of just a limited subset of parties, as was the case in post-war Italy. Knowing the range of parties with access to office therefore allows us to distinguish between these latter cases, which otherwise tend to coincide in terms of both of the other criteria indicated above. That is, while both the Netherlands and Italy are similar in the sense of their pattern of partial alternation, in terms of the longevity in office of a core centre party, and in terms of their resort to innovative formulae, they are nevertheless strikingly dissimilar when it comes to the range of parties gaining access to office, with particular parties being persistently excluded in the Italian case prior to the mid-1990s, and with virtually no substantial parties being excluded in the Dutch case.

This distinction may also be related to what Sartori defines as polarized pluralism, which, as noted above, required the presence of anti-system parties at each end of the political spectrum, such parties being defined in part as those which were out of competition for government, thus forcing governments to be formed across the span of the centre. Here, also, the concern is with whether certain parties are persistently excluded as unacceptable partners in office. Where this criterion differs from that used in the definition of polarized pluralism, however, is that the question of whether or not such parties are genuinely and objectively "anti-system", which has always been a point of dispute in the interpretations and criticisms of Sartori's model, becomes irrelevant (see the comprehensive discussion of varieties of anti-systemness in Capoccia 2000). Rather, what matters is whether there are parties which are treated, *in practice*, as "outsiders", and which are regarded by the other parties in the system as unacceptable allies. In this sense, anti-systemness, like beauty, here lies in the eyes of the beholder. It is difficult, for example, to determine whether the right-wing Danish Progress party is genuinely anti-system; on the other hand, it is relatively easy to see that this party has been regarded by its potential allies as an outsider and, up to now, has always languished in opposition (unlike, say, the more ostensibly "anti-system" Communist party in France). Conversely, while the Austrian Freedom party (FPÖ) under the leadership of Jörg Haider has often been regarded as an anti-system party of the extreme right, it has nevertheless been recently incorporated as the junior partner in an innovative coalition government with the ÖVP. In practice, at least, the party is now 'within' the system.

Structures of party competition: closed or open?

The combination of these three criteria yields a fairly broad-brush distinction between two contrasting patterns in the structure of party competition (see Table 4.2). On the one hand, the structure of party competition can be relatively *closed*, and hence highly predictable, with little or no change over time in the range of governing alternatives or in the pattern of alternation, and with new parties and/or "outsider" parties finding it virtually impossible to break through the threshold of government. The British case has afforded perhaps the most obvious example to date of such a closed system, being persistently characterized by wholesale alternation, by a complete absence of innovative formulae, and by the presence of just two governing, and governable, parties. The presidential party system in the United States is similarly closed. On the other hand, the structure of party competition can prove relatively *open*, and hence quite unpredictable, with differing patterns of alternation, with frequent shifts in the make-up of the governing alternatives, and with new parties gaining relatively easy access to office. The post-war Dutch pattern comes quite close to this form, in that new parties have been relatively easily incorporated into government (such as Democratic Socialists 70 in 1971 and both Democrats 66 and the Radicals (PPR) in 1973) and in that innovative formulae have been adopted in almost half of the new governments formed since 1951.

Where the Dutch system deviates from a wholly open pattern, however, is in the long-term presence in government of the KVP and, later, the CDA, and in the fact that alternation has *always* been partial. In this sense, and at least prior to 1994 when the first ever "secular" government was formed, there was always a certain element of predictability involved, and to this extent the structure of competition was at least to some extent closed. Denmark in the post-war period also comes quite close to an open pattern, having experiences of both partial and wholesale alternation, having frequently adopted innovative formulae (in the case of almost one-third of all post-war governments), and having also proved to be relatively open to new parties, such as in 1982, when the Centre Democrats and the Christian People's party were first admitted to government. On the other hand, even Denmark can be seen as partially closed and somewhat predictable as a result of the persistent exclusion from office of the Progress party and the Socialist People's party.

These examples also underline the extent to which the development of a closed structure of competition owes much to the strategies of the established parties, and, in particular, their unwillingness to experiment with innovative formulae and their reluctance to admit new parties into government. In some instances, of course, the parties may feel themselves genuinely constrained in this respect, in that any new governing options might require the bridging of what are believed to be ineluctable divides in policy and/or ideology. The structure of competition may therefore be very predictable, and hence closed, as a result of the distances which separate the

TABLE 4.2   *Closed and Open Structures of Competition*

Closed structure of competition	Open structure of competition
Wholesale alternation in office, or non-alternation in office	Partial alternation, or mix of both partial and wholesale alternation
Familiar governing formulae	Innovative governing formulae
Access to government restricted to a limited number of parties	Access to government open to (almost) all parties
Examples:	*Examples:*
United Kingdom, New Zealand (to mid-1990s), Japan (1955–93), Switzerland, Ireland (1948–89)	Denmark, the Netherlands, post-authoritarian party systems

relevant parties along any one of a variety of different dimensions of competition. Such arguments have been used by DC leaders in Italy, for example, in order to justify the persistent exclusion of the PCI from office, and are equally cited by a number of different party leaderships in Denmark in order to justify the persistent exclusion of the Progress party.

In other instances, however, it is obvious that the maintenance of familiar and closed patterns of competition simply constitutes a strategy of self-preservation on the part of the established parties.[7] In Ireland, for example, the long-term refusal of the dominant Fianna Fáil party to even consider entering a coalition, a refusal which contributed substantially to the long-term closure of competition in Ireland, was clearly designed to maintain its status as the only party capable of offering single-party government, and was thus intended to maintain its electoral credibility. A similar sense of self-preservation can be seen to characterize the long-term reluctance of the two major British parties to consider the possibilities of coalition with the smaller Liberal party, even though Labour did come strikingly close to such a path-breaking option during the Lib–Lab Pact in the late 1970s, and although the Liberals were invited to join certain government committees following New Labour's victory in 1997. To be sure, there are real limits on the capacity, and willingness, of the established parties to maintain a closed structure of competition. New parties might emerge which have to be taken on board; particular party leaders may have their own agendas and priorities; external crises might develop which force the adoption of new strategies, and so on. Nonetheless, any explanation of the degree of closure of any given structure of competition must necessarily focus particular attention on the strategies of the parties themselves.

Closed structures of competition are clearly characteristic of traditional two-party systems, and, of course, of those systems which have experienced a real absence of alternation over time, such as Japan before 1993, the former Stormont regime in Northern Ireland, Mexico before 2000, Singapore, or Switzerland. Conversely, openness, and a lack of predictability, tends to characterize more fragmented systems (that is, systems with a relatively large number of relevant parties), which experience partial alternation and which often lack one large core party of government. Moreover, since closure necessarily requires the development of stable norms and conventions in the patterns of competition and in the processes of government formation, it is also clearly a function of time, and, most crucially, is not something which can be seen to characterize the party "systems" that emerge more or less from scratch following post-authoritarian democratization.

Indeed, what is most striking about such new party systems, including those which have emerged in post-communist Europe, for example, as well as those of Spain and Portugal through to the 1980s, is precisely their lack of closure and hence their lack of *systemness*. Seen from this perspective, the long-term process by which party systems may eventually become consolidated can also be seen as a long-term process by which the structure of competition becomes increasingly closed and predictable. Thus, while a more closed and predictable structure might well develop in a number of the post-communist democracies in the next decade or so, this can prove a relatively lengthy process (but see Toole 2000). The fruits of such a long-term process of structural consolidation can now be seen in the relatively recently democratized Portuguese and Spanish systems (e.g., Morlino 1998), and may also be already beginning in the Czech Republic, not least as a result of the efforts of the two main parties to modify the Czech institutions in a way that is likely to penalize their smaller rivals. Long-term structural consolidation can also be seen in some of the Latin American systems, with one of the most notable examples being the strengthening of two-partyism in Costa Rica. In this latter region, however, as in the United States, the frequent combination of a presidential system of government, on the one hand, and the presence of often undisciplined parties (e.g., Mainwaring and Scully 1995a), on the other, suggests that however closed presidential party politics might be, there remains a significant bias against the development of closed structures of competition in the legislative electoral arena.[8] A similar process can now be identified in Israel (e.g., Medding 2000), where the recent institution of a separate election for the position of the prime minister has effectively undermined the need for parliamentary discipline, and has led to increased fragmentation in the legislative arena and to a wholesale *de-structuring* of the traditional party system. In short, the degree of closure varies, ranging along a continuum from situations in which it is least pronounced, such as in post-authoritarian party systems, to those in which it is most pronounced, such as in those established systems in which there is little or no innovation in the processes of government formation, and in which new parties rarely if ever break through the governing threshold.[9]

A similar pattern of variance is highlighted in Mainwaring and Scully's (1995b) overview of Latin American systems, where they distinguish between "institutionalized"—or what I might call "closed"—party systems, on the one hand, and "inchoate"—or "open"—party systems, on the other. The real question here, however, is whether we can conceive of open or inchoate "systems" as being genuine systems at all. The degree of "systemness" certainly varies from one party system to another. But it is only in cases where this degree of systemness becomes pronounced, and where the party system approaches closure or institutionalization, that we can properly speak of there being a party *system* as such. The idea of a wholly open or wholly inchoate party system may therefore amount to a contradiction in terms. In a similar vein, it can also be argued that the well known Lipset and Rokkan (1967) formulation regarding the "freezing" of party systems can be read as simply another way of referring to the progressive institutionalization or closure of these systems, and hence to speak of the freezing of party systems may simply be another way of saying that collections of parties eventually stabilize their patterns of interactions and thus develop into systems. As systems, they are by definition frozen and institutionalized; de-freezing, in this reading, is system failure (see also Mair 2001).

Party systems and electoral outcomes

The notion of the closure or openness of party systems' structure of competition is also important in that it immediately allows us to move away from the conventional idea that party system change is largely, if not exclusively, a function of, or even a synonym for, electoral change. In other words, it affords a conception of party system change which may owe its origin to factors other than simply the flux in voter preferences. For although party system stability and change, on the one hand, and electoral stability and change, on the other, may certainly be related, they are far from being synonymous. Electoral alignments might shift, for example, even in quite a dramatic way, without necessarily impinging significantly on the structure of competition, and hence without necessarily altering the character of the party system itself. Conversely, the structure of party competition and hence the nature of the party system itself might suddenly be transformed, even without any significant prior electoral flux.

One telling, if now quite dated, example comes from Denmark, where the 1973 election witnessed one of the most substantial electoral shifts to have occurred in post-war Europe up to that time, resulting in an immediate doubling of the number of parties represented in parliament (see Pedersen 1988). Prior to 1973, five parties had been represented in the Danish Folketing, together accounting for some 93% of the total vote. As a result of the 1973 election, five new parties won representation, and the total vote won by the previously represented parties fell to less than 65%. This was a massive shift by any standards, and since the new entrants to the parliament included both the long-established Communist party as well as the newly formed right-wing Progress party, it also resulted in a major increase in the level of polarization. In practice, however, it is certainly possible to question whether this change had any substantial impact on the workings of the Danish party system. To be sure, a new government had to be formed, which, in fact, was a minority, single-party Liberal government, the first such to take office since 1945. On the other hand, this innovative government was then succeeded by a Social Democratic minority government, which was precisely the same formula that had been employed prior to the 1973 earthquake election, and then eventually by a center–right coalition, which was differently composed but otherwise essentially similar to the various other center–right coalitions which had governed Denmark in the early 1950s and late 1960s. The increased fragmentation and the greater degree of polarization after 1973 did of course make governing more difficult: it was not until early 1993 that a government was to enjoy majority status in the parliament (although such a status had also been quite exceptional even prior to 1973); post-1973 governments also tended to collapse more frequently than before; there was a more frequent resort to elections; and finally, as noted above, new parties had eventually to be accommodated into government, although the Progress party has not yet been accorded this particular privilege. But the question still remains as to whether this relatively massive shift in electoral preferences had any real effect whatsoever on the structure of party competition and therefore on the party system itself. Denmark is now, but always has been, quite innovative in terms of governing formulae; it is now, and always has been, reasonably open to new parties coming into government; and now, as before, it experiences both wholesale and partial alternation in government on a regular basis. Moreover, it had once, and still maintains, a relatively open structure of competition and hence a relatively unconstraining party system. In these terms at least, it appears that 1973 has not made any significant difference.

The Italian case in the 1990s also offers a useful example, even though uncertainty still remains as to the direction, if any, in which the party system is being transformed (see especially Bartolini and d'Alimonte 1998). On the face of it, there is no other established Western party system which has undergone such a profound change. At the electoral level, for example, following decades of relative stability, the 1994 election resulted in a level of volatility of more than 37%, which is not only the highest figure recorded in Italian history, but, even more strikingly, is substantially higher than that recorded in almost *any* election held in Western Europe between 1885 and 1989.[10] In terms of format, the system has also became totally transformed, with the emergence of new parties and the reconstitution of established parties leading to a situation in which not one of the parties represented in parliament in the late 1990s had also been represented under the same name or in the same form as recently as the late 1980s. Finally, it can also be argued that there has also been a major change in the level of polarization, as a result of the transformation of the mainstream of the Communist party (PCI) into the Left Democrats (DS), on the one hand, and its eventual leadership of government in 1996, and, on the other, the transformation of the neo-fascist Social Movement (MSI) into the National Alliance (AN) and its incorporation into government in 1994.

These are certainly profound changes. The most relevant question, however, is whether these changes will have any long-term impact on the structure of competition. The structure of competition in the "old" party system was certainly clear. Governments were formed from out of the center, were dominated by the Christian Democrats, and involved shifting alliances with partial alternation across the center–left and center–right while excluding both the PCI and the smaller MSI. Any fundamentally new pattern might therefore seem to require that governments be formed almost exclusively from the left or from the right (creating the potential for whole-sale alternation), that the extremes disappear or be incorporated, and, in this new bipolar world, that the independent position of the center be marginalized. With the formation of the right-wing Berlusconi government in 1994, it certainly seemed possible that this was the pattern that was beginning to emerge, and this seemed to be confirmed when that innovative government was then displaced by an alternative but equally innovative coalition of the center–left, dominated by the DS, which, in turn, was displaced by a recon-stituted Berlusconi coalition in 2001. There remains a question as to what will happen to any new center, however, in that a number of centrist parlia-mentary groups have now been formed which seek to play off left against right, and which appear to be trying to establish an independent pivotal position in the system. As of now, of course, it is too soon to suggest what future patterns or alignments might yet emerge, and in this sense the struc-ture of competition might be regarded as quite open and unpredictable, which, at least in the short term, does represent a fundamental change. Indeed, in this sense the "system" looks increasingly unstructured and hence transformed. Should the center finally split into its own "left" and "right," then this would cement the emerging bipolar pattern, and this would certainly lead to a new structure of competition and hence to a wholly new party system. But should an independent center manage to reconstitute itself, and should it prove capable of taking full advantage of its pivotal position by playing left off against right in a way which would allow it to construct a broad alliance across the center, then, despite the different actors and their different weights in the system, we might well end up by witnessing the recreation of more or less the same structure of competition as had prevailed prior to the 1990s (Bartolini and D'Alimonte 1998).

Question marks also hang over the real extent of change in the Canadian party system, notwithstanding the electoral earthquake of 1993. In this case, as in Italy, the level of volatility rose to an unprecedented and massive high—42%—almost five times that of the average level of volatility recorded in the 1970s and 1980s. The consequences were also very far-reaching, with the once powerful Progressive–Conservative party being reduced to just 16% of the vote in 1993 (its lowest share since 1949), and, even more strikingly, to just two seats (as against 169 in the previous election). In addition, two new parties, the Reform party and Bloc Québécois, won substantial representation in parliament, the first parties outside the mainstream to do so since the effec-tive demise of Social Credit in the mid-1970s. Moreover, precisely because these two new parties were so evidently regional in character, they also signalled a potentially enduring shift in electoral alignments. This was substan-tial change by any standard, and some Canadian scholars have argued that it represents the dawn of a new and distinctively different party system which has yet to fully develop (Carty, Cross, and Young 2000). At the same time, however, there was also one striking continuity, in that the Liberal party returned to government with a powerful majority in 1993, retaining that position with decisive election victories in 1997 and 2000. This suggests the possible return to a "one party dominant" system, similar to that which characterized Canadian party politics in the 1940s and 1950s. At one level, the system has certainly changed: the Liberals now confront an opposition divided across four parties instead of just two, and serious regional divisions have erupted onto the federal stage (Nevitte et al. 1999). An attempt to restructure the Reform party into a new, more broadly based, opposition party (the Canadian Alliance) prior to the 2000 election failed to improve significantly on the electoral gains achieved by Reform when it became the official parliamentary opposition to the Liberals in 1997. While this process of attempting to construct a viable conservative alternative continues, it is as yet impossible to speak of any enduring transformation in the structure of competition in federal politics under the present conditions of uncertainty regarding the future of the Alliance. Meanwhile, the Bloc Québécois continues to provide the only significant opposition at the national level to the Liberals in Quebec, building on the solid base established there in provincial politics by the Parti Québécois since the 1970s.

Finally, we can turn to the Japanese case. Here, in brief, we can also see signs of an Italian-style meltdown, with the traditionally predominant Liberal Democrats (LDP) finally losing office in 1993, following four decades of unbroken rule, in the wake of a highly volatile election in which three new parties suddenly emerged to win some 20% of the seats in the House of Representatives. Three years later, and as the result of further splits, mergers, and formations in what had become a very unstable party environment, two other new groups emerged, the New Frontier party (NFP) and the Democratic party (DPJ), together winning some 40% of the seats. Moreover, and as in Italy, the meltdown of the old order was associated with the formation of innovative coalitions and the arrival in office of parties which had previously either languished in opposition or had just recently been formed for the first time (Mair and Sakano 1998; Watanuki 2001). In effect, then, the old structure of the LDP predominant-party system had dramatically collapsed. In contrast to Italy, however, where no new structure of competition has yet been consolidated, and hence where the party 'system' remains quite inchoate, the Japanese case seems to have adjusted quite quickly to a new form of competition, in which the now diminished but still powerful LDP has taken on the role of a major center party, building a variety of—sometimes short-lived—coalitions to its left and to its right, and thereby returning to office as the power-broker *par excellence*. Thus although the continued survival of the LDP has meant that the changes to the party format have not proved quite so dramatic as in Italy, the new balance of forces has nevertheless led to the emergence of a wholly novel structure of competition.

What we see here, then, is one instance in which substantial electoral change does not appear to have led to significant party system change (Denmark); one instance in which electoral change may be associated with a major shift in the structure of competition (Japan); and two instances in which, despite extraordinary electoral flux, question marks still remain as to whether a new type of party system might yet develop (Canada and Italy). It is precisely the combination of these different experiences which underlines the need to separate out the notion of party system stability/change, on the one hand, and electoral stability/change, on the other.

Not only that, however, for what may be most interesting about the separation of these two processes, and about the recognition that change in party systems may be due to factors other than electoral change, is that it also affords the opportunity to *reverse* the conventional chain of influence, and to probe the extent to which party system stability (or change) *may lead to* electoral stability (or change), rather than simply the other way around. Electoral alignments are, of course, stabilized by a variety of factors, including, most crucially, the cleavage structure (Lipset and Rokkan 1967). Other factors that play a role here include the constraints imposed by institutional structures, such as by the electoral system, as well as those deriving from the organizational efforts of the parties themselves (Bartolini and Mair 1990). In the case of Brazil, for example, as Mainwaring (1998) argues, much of the exceptionally high electoral volatility can be explained not just by social structure, by also the particular character of Brazilian political institutions and by the behavior of the party elites. Even within this broader perspective, however, one additional "freezing" agent that is often neglected is the effect of the structure of party competition itself. As should be evident, a closed structure of competition clearly constrains voter preferences, in that it limits the choice of governing options in a way which is similar to the limits on the choice of parties in non-fragmented systems. A closed structure of competition therefore also clearly enhances party system stability, and, indeed, helps to ensure that party systems generate their own momentum and thus freeze into place. In short, the stabilization of electoral alignments has at least partly to do with the consolidation of a given structure of competition.

What this also implies, of course, and perhaps most interestingly, is that a *change* in that structure may then itself serve to *de*stabilize established electoral alignments. In Italy, for example, the basis for a wholesale change in electoral preferences in 1992 and 1994 was at least partially laid by the "legitimation" of the Democratic Party of the Left, which undermined the terms of reference by which Italian party competition had been structured since the late 1940s. Italian voters, as well as the Italian parties themselves, had long been constrained by the belief that there was no alternative to a Christian Democratic-dominated government. And once such an alternative finally did emerge through the transformation of the unacceptable Communist party into the highly acceptable Democratic Left, this particular anchor was cut loose, and voters began to shift in relatively great numbers, eventually leading to the virtual disappearance of the once dominant Christian Democratic party. In yet another case, in Ireland, and following decades in which there had been no major changes in the electoral balance of the party system, the long-term basis for stability was finally undermined in 1989 when the dominant party, Fianna Fáil decided for the first time ever to enter a coalition with another party. Prior to then, party competition had been structured around the opposition between Fianna Fáil on the one side, and all of the smaller parties on the other, and this had severely constrained and stabilized voter preferences. From 1989 onwards, however, when these constraints were removed, the potential for change was greatly enhanced, and hence while the degree of electoral instability prior to Fianna Fáil's first coalition was relatively muted, the subsequent election witnessed a major upsurge in volatility which resulted in the traditionally marginal Labour party doubling its vote—the result, quite simply, of the removal of what had been up to then the most powerful constraint on electoral mobility.

This is perhaps a roundabout way of saying that the structure of competition, and the structure of competition for government in particular, may impose a major constraint on voter choice, and hence may act to stabilize electoral alignments. In this sense, voters are not simply expressing preferences for individual parties; rather, albeit not always to the same degree in different party systems, and this in itself is an important source of cross-national (and cross-institutional) variance, they are also expressing preferences for potential governments. And in much the same way that a shift in the range of parties on offer can act to undermine established preferences, so too can a shift in the range of governing options, and hence a shift in the structure of competition, act to undermine established preferences and promote electoral instability. In short, it is not only a question of electoral change leading to party system change, as does seem to have been the case in Japan; rather, it can also be the other way around. Party systems do not simply reflect electoral preferences. They also serve to constrain them.

NOTES

1. See, for example, Almond et al. (1993: 117–20), where this traditional distinction is recast as one of "majoritarian" versus multiparty systems; see also the influential study by Lijphart (1999), where one of the key distinctions between majoritarian and consensus democracies is defined as that between a two-party system and a multiparty system, although in contrast to the traditional approach, in Lijphart's case it is the multiparty variant that is associated with consensus politics.
2. For earlier versions of this typology, see Sartori (1966, 1970). An edited version of the Sartori typology, together with those of the other authors discussed here, is reprinted in Mair (1990).
3. Although the predominant-party system constitutes a useful category, it fits rather uneasily into Sartori's framework, since it is defined by wholly different criteria, and can by definition co-exist with every possible category of party

numbers (that is, it can develop within a context of a two-party system, a system of limited pluralism, and a system of extreme pluralism) and, at least theoretically, with every possible spread of ideological opinion.

4. The exception would be those systems which might be categorized as predominant-party systems, and which, as noted above, do not easily fit into the criteria adopted for the typology as a whole.

5. For an application of these criteria to existing party systems in Europe, see Luther and Deschouwer (1999) and Toole (2000).

6. Following the 1994 election, and for the first time since the advent of full democracy, a government was formed in the Netherlands without the inclusion of the Christian Democratic/religious mainstream.

7. It is in this sense that such closure also involves what Schattschneider (1960: 69 and *passim*) has defined as "the mobilization of bias," with the emphasis on particular conflicts and on distinct alternatives acting to preserve the interests of the various protagonists that align themselves in terms of these conflicts.

8. The lack of structuring is also reflected in the persistently high levels of electoral volatility which are strikingly and substantially higher than those occurring in the relatively structured west European systems (see Coppedge 1992; Mainwaring 1998: 535–7).

9. As noted, closure is also probably least pronounced in the legislative electoral arena in presidential systems, notwithstanding any strong structuring which might be evident in the presidential electoral arena in these same systems.

10. The index of volatility measures the net aggregate shift in votes from one election to the next, and is the equivalent of the total aggregate gains of all winning parties or the total aggregate losses of all losing parties (see Pedersen 1979). The average volatility in post-war Europe has been less than 9%, and, apart from the 1994 election in Italy, only four other European elections in the past century have exceeded 35%: Germany in 1919 (47.5%), France in 1945 (36.4%), and Greece in 1950 (47.0%) and 1951 (45.1%)—see Bartolini and D'Alimonte (1995: 443–4); on electoral stability and instability in Europe more generally, see Bartolini and Mair (1990).

5

Candidate Selection

REUVEN Y. HAZAN

This chapter is about the method by which political parties choose their candidates for office, the outcome of this process, and the consequences. Those candidates who are subsequently elected are the ones who will determine much of how the party looks and what it does until the next election. Whether elections are conducted in winner-take-all single-member constituencies, where each party usually selects only one candidate, or according to more proportional systems of representation with party lists, candidate selection is one of the first things that political parties must do prior to an election. The results of this selection process will affect the party and the parliament for a long time after the election itself is over.

Until recently, candidate selection received relatively little attention, and detailed studies of a country's candidate selection methods are rare.[1] This is partially due to the lack of and inaccessibility to data. The dearth of scholarly literature has raised a formidable obstacle for researchers who wish to undertake cross-national analyses of the subject. There have been some attempts to produce a theory or a framework for analysis (Duverger 1959; Czudnowski 1975; Epstein 1980; Ranney 1981; Gallagher and Marsh 1988; Hazan and Pennings 2001), but these remain few and far between. However, the more recent research into this sub-field, particularly in the last decade, eschews earlier assumptions, penetrates new grounds of empirical research, and shows that candidate selection has wide-ranging and significant implications.

In this chapter I elaborate why candidate selection is an essential function of political parties, with significant consequences for representation, party cohesion, legislative behavior, and democratic stability. The analysis works within a new institutionalism perspective and is also in line with the rational choice literature. These two approaches together suggest that the broader institutional context of candidate selection, or reselection, produces institutionally induced incentives and obstacles that shape the attitudes and behavior of both prospective and current legislators. In short, I argue that candidate selection influences a country's politics and that different candidate selection methods have distinct consequences. It is not an exaggeration to state that, in certain spheres, the ramifications of intra-party (candidate) elections can prove to be as important as those of inter-party (general) elections.

What is candidate selection and why is it important?

Candidate selection is not legislative recruitment; the latter is more comprehensive and includes the former. Legislative recruitment involves such aspects of the political system as the legal, electoral, and party frameworks (Norris 1997). Candidate selection, on the other hand, is almost wholly *within* particular parties. That is, there are very few countries in which the legal system specifies the criteria for candidate selection, or in which the electoral system includes regulations for the process of candidate selection. Candidate selection is, according to Ranney (1981: 75), the "predominantly *extralegal* process by which a political party decides which of the persons legally eligible to hold an elective office will be designated on the ballot and in election communications as its recommended and supported candidate or list of candidates."

In the field of candidate selection, the United States is an extreme case in which primaries are controlled by state laws. Candidate selection is thus a public election, similar in many respects to the general election. If American parties wish to change their procedures for nominating candidates, they must change the state law itself. This led Epstein (1986) to liken American political parties to "public utilities" such as water or electric companies. In most other countries, however, the parties themselves are allowed to determine the rules for their selection of candidates.

Candidate selection may be described as "a key stage" (Gallagher 1988a: 2) or even as "the most important stage" (Czudnowski 1975: 219) in the more general recruitment process. This does not mean that parties are autonomous actors in this process. They are embedded in broader institutional contexts to which they respond. In other words, there are many contextual factors that influence the candidate selection processes within parties. These factors include the legal and electoral systems, governmental and party organization, patterns of party competition, legislative turnover, political culture, and so on.[2] For example, when New Zealand changed its electoral system from single-member plurality districts to a mixed-member proportional system, the political parties also had to shift their candidate selection methods to produce a party list alongside their constituency candidates.

Candidate selection determines not only the choices placed before the voters, but also the composition of the parties in parliament—and through them the government and the opposition. It thus influences the interests most likely to be addressed and the resulting policy decisions that will be enacted. Moreover, a party's candidates help to define its characteristics—demographically, geographically, ideologically, etc.—more than its organization, and perhaps even more than its manifesto.

Beyond being a significant stage in the recruitment process, candidate selection is also an important arena for internal party power struggles. Schattschneider's (1942: 64) argument concerning this issue is worth citing in full:

> Unless the party makes authoritative and effective nominations, it cannot stay in business, for dual or multiple party candidacies mean certain defeat. As far as elections are concerned, the united front of the party, the party concentration of numbers, can be brought about only by a binding nomination. The nominating process thus has become the crucial process of the party. The nature of the nominating process determines the nature of the party; he who can make the nominations is the owner of the party. This is therefore one of the best points at which to observe the distribution of power within the party.

Both Gallagher and Ranney endorse this statement, and each takes it a step further. Gallagher (1988a: 3) argues, "the contest over candidate selection is generally even more intense than the struggle over the party manifesto." Ranney (1981: 103) adds, "It is therefore not surprising that the most vital and hotly contested factional disputes in any party are the struggles that take place over the choice of its candidates; for what is at stake in such a struggle ... is nothing less than control of the core of what the party stands for and does." Indeed, after an election, what largely remains as the functioning core of almost any party is its officeholders—its *successful* candidates.

Candidate selection methods: an analytical framework

In any analysis of candidate selection methods, the unit of analysis is a *single* party, in a particular country, at a specific time. Only in those cases where several parties in a particular country use similar methods (usually due to legal requirements), or where a single party uses a similar candidate selection method over time, can one begin to make generalizations about the candidate selection process.

The framework elaborated below offers four dimensions for the classification of candidate selection methods: candidacy; the selectorate; decentralization; and voting versus appointment.[3] All four dimensions are assessed according to a continuum based on the level of inclusiveness or exclusiveness. This continuum will serve as the explanatory factor in subsequent sections of this chapter as well.

Candidacy

Candidacy addresses the question of who can present himself or herself as the candidate of a particular party. At one end, the inclusive pole, every voter might be eligible to stand as a party's candidate. Some states in the United States are close to this pole. At the exclusive pole, we encounter a series of restrictive conditions. Consider Obler's (1974: 180) account of the requirements that applied to potential candidates in the Belgian Socialist party. According to these restrictions, a potential candidate must: (1) have been a member at least five years prior to the primary; (2) have made annual minimum purchases from the Socialist co-op; (3) have been a regular subscriber to the party's newspaper; (4) have sent his children to state rather than Catholic schools; and (5) have his wife and children enrolled in the appropriate women's and youth organizations.

Selectorate

The selectorate is the body that selects the candidates. It can be composed of one person, or several or many people. At one extreme the selectorate consists of the entire (general election) electorate of the nation. At the other extreme, the selectorate—or rather the selector—consists of a single party leader.

Between these two extremes, selectorates are classified according to their amount of inclusiveness. Methods such as the non-partisan primary and the blanket primary used in some US states, in which every registered voter can vote for candidates from both parties, would be located near the inclusive end of the "electorate" zone (Ranney 1981). American closed primaries, which require voter registration by party affiliation, are located toward the more exclusive end of the electorate zone. The exact location of American primaries will, therefore, depend on the restrictions that are defined by the different state laws (Kolodny and Katz 1992).

Still, the electorate zone is not occupied only by American cases. From 1971 on, several parties in Iceland adopted open primaries (Kristjánsson 1998). These were usually conducted in some of the electoral districts, and every citizen in these districts could participate. An additional case, though slightly less inclusive, is that of the Spanish Catalan party, which opened its candidate selection to "registered 'sympathizers'"—non-members who can register as party supporters without paying any membership fee (Hopkin 2001).

European closed primaries (Newman and Cranshaw 1973), as opposed to American closed primaries, usually refer to party primaries (Gallagher 1988b: 239–40) in which the selectors are party members—the second zone of the selectorate continuum. In this "party members" zone, we find different methods of party primaries. Such methods were adopted to select both the party leader and the party candidates in the major Israeli parties in the 1990s (Hazan 1997a).

The selectorates in the party members zone can be distinguished according to the restrictions on party membership, the additional requirements that are placed on members with a conditional right to take part in the party selectorate, and the selector's level of accessibility to the selection procedure. For example, one rule that could restrict membership is the payment of membership dues. Members' participation may also be restricted by the request for a minimal party membership period prior to candidate selection, proof of party activity, etc. Accessibility may also be an important factor in distinguishing between such methods. Levels of accessibility and inclusiveness are higher if a party adopts methods allowing for postal ballots, or spreading polling stations all over the country. A less accessible, yet inclusive, method is an open party convention—while all members can attend such a meeting, it requires more effort on their part than simply voting.

In the "selected party agency" zone we find various party agencies that may be distinguished by different parameters. In a given party, the relative size of each agency is a sign of its inclusiveness: conventions are usually larger than central committees, which in turn are usually larger than executive bodies such as bureaus. The terminology used in each country is rarely equivalent, and one must be cautious when inferring the extent of inclusiveness based solely on what a particular party calls a specific agency.[4] In addition, the more inclusive party agencies often contain delegates selected by party members, while the more exclusive ones tend to include representatives who were selected by such delegates.

In the "non-selected party agencies" zone, the more inclusive selectorates are, for example, special selection committees whose composition is ratified *en bloc* by a selected party agency. The more exclusive selectorates in this zone are represented by a gathering of party founders in new parties, or an informal gathering of faction leaders in older ones. Israel's ultra-orthodox religious parties are an example of a very exclusive selectorate. In one party, a single rabbi was authorized to decide the composition of the party list (Rahat and Sher-Hadar 1999).

Figure 5.1 integrates the two dimensions of candidacy and selectorate, presenting the party candidate selection method according to the level of inclusiveness or exclusiveness with respect to each. A high level of inclusiveness on one dimension combined with a high level of exclusiveness in the other would mean that the party leadership or the party apparatus retains control over the process. For example, the Italian Communist party included non-members as candidates, but this was done under the supervision of an exclusive and centralized selectorate (Wertman 1988).

One final distinction must be made concerning the selectorate, and that is between the one-stage, multi-stage, and mixed candidate selection methods. The one-stage method is a simple, uniform process in which the selection of all candidates is made by the same selectorate. The multi-stage candidate selection method is a process in which the same candidates have

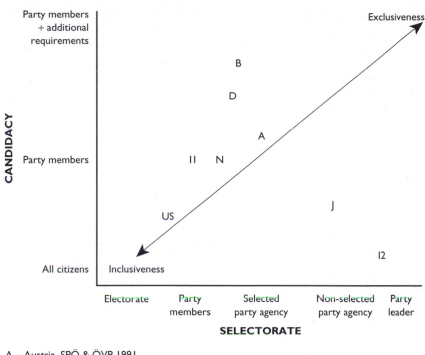

FIGURE 5.1 *Candidacy and Party Selectorates in Candidate Selection*
SOURCES: Austria, Müller (1992); Belgium, Obler (1974); Denmark, Bille (1992); Israel, Rahat and Hazan (2001); Netherlands, Koole and van de Velde (1992); Japan, Shiratori (1988); United States, Kolodny and Katz (1992).

to face more than one selectorate during the selection process. The mixed candidate selection method is one in which different candidates are selected by different selectorates of the same party.

An example of a multi-stage candidate selection method can be found in the British parties, where small executive party agencies screen candidates before they are selected, or have the ability to veto their nomination after they are selected. While it may be the case that those who are screened have no chance of being selected in the first place, and while the veto is activated only on rare occasions, one must still consider the impact of the selected party agency. Thus, a party such as the British Liberals—in which members select candidates but party agencies screen them—would have a multi-stage candidate selection method located on the exclusive end of the party members zone (Denver 1988).

The Belgian parties, from the 1960s until the 1980s, are an example of a mixed system. Inside the larger parties, some candidates were selected by party members, while others were appointed by local and central party agencies (Obler 1974; De Winter 1988). Locating such cases on the continuum requires one to weight the relative impact of each selectorate.

Decentralization

When candidates are selected exclusively by a national party selectorate, with no procedure that allows for territorial and/or functional representation, we have a method that is centralized. Alternatively, in a *decentralized* candidate selection method, the candidates are selected exclusively by party local selectorates or intra-party social groups or sectarian groups. Decentralization can be territorial, that is, when local selectorates nominate party candidates—such as a local leader, a party branch committee, or all party members or voters in an electoral district. In many European cases, the selectorate at the district level plays the crucial role in candidate selection. The Norwegian case is an example. Not only are national party agencies unable to veto a candidacy that is determined at the district level, it is also the case that territorial representation is taken into account *inside* each district (Valen 1988).

Decentralization of the selection method can also be corporate, that is, a method that ensures functional representation for representatives of such groups as trade unions, women, minorities, etc. The Belgian Christian Social party provides examples of corporate decentralization, which was used at the district level. At first, the party decided that in some of the Brussels districts, Flemish and Francophone candidates would alternate on the party list. Subsequently, separate intra-party sub-districts were established when Francophone and Flemish party members in these districts selected their candidates separately (Obler 1974). Establishing quotas for women, such as in the German Social Democratic party, is another example of corporate decentralization.

Voting versus appointment

A voting system, as opposed to an appointment system, is a candidate selection method in which votes determine the party's candidate in the general elections, and (in list systems) his or her position on the list. In an appointment system, candidacy is determined without using such a voting procedure. In a pure voting system, all candidates are selected through a voting procedure, and no other selectorate can change the composition of the list. In a pure appointment system, candidates are appointed with no need for approval by any other party agency beyond the nominating organ itself. When the list is so appointed, its composition is more easily controlled.

From process to outcome

Regardless of the restrictions on candidacy, the inclusiveness of the selectorate, the extent of decentralization or the adoption of a voting system, two clear generalizations can be made concerning the kinds of candidates that are produced as a result of the various candidate selection methods: incumbents have an advantage and women have a disadvantage.

Incumbents have a higher profile than new candidates. They also usually have an organizational base, either of their own or within their party, and they have an easier time collecting funds (Somit et al. 1994). As Gallagher (1988b: 248) stated, "In virtually every country for which we have evidence, incumbents stand a far better chance of being selected than any other group of aspirants." Moreover, incumbents typically have high re-election rates. The extreme case of incumbency success is that of the United States, where well over 90% of the members of the House of Representatives run for reselection and re-election; and of these, over 90% win. Both in 1986 and in 1988, only one member of the House was defeated in the primaries, and only six were defeated in the general election, producing a re-election percentage of 98%.

This phenomenon has resulted in attempts by several parties to curb the advantage of incumbency. For example, the Italian Communist party and the German Greens rotated their parliamentary representatives. Imposing such hurdles can turn the incumbency advantage into a handicap, such as in the case of the Israeli Moretz party in which a two-term incumbent needed the support of 60% of the selectorate in order to be eligible for a third term. Such hurdles can become impenetrable obstacles when they take the form of legal restrictions on the number of terms a person can serve. The US president and many state governors are restricted to two terms in office, and 19 US states have also imposed term limits on state legislators.

If most incumbents will be reselected, then it is safe to say that most reselected incumbents will be male. Despite strong demands for the inclusion of women, the composition of candidates for elected legislatures continues to be overrepresented by males. As Table 5.1 shows, in no country does the percentage of women elected reach 50%. The highest percentages are found in the Scandinavian countries, while women comprise less than 10% in democracies such as India, Japan, and numerous others.

Women may find barriers at the entry level, at the candidate selection level, and at the general election level (Darcy, Welch, and Clark 1994; Norris 1997; Matland 1998). In terms of candidate selection, neither variations in candidacy requirements nor in the inclusiveness of the selectorate, or the existence of a particular voting system, can correct the imbalances that exist. Only decentralization, in its corporate sense, can help here.

TABLE 5.1   *Percentage of Women Legislators in the Lower House*

Country	Election	Number of Seats	Percentage of women
Sweden	1998	349	42.7
Denmark	1998	179	37.4
Finland	1999	200	36.5
Norway	1997	165	36.4
Netherlands	2001	150	35.8
Germany	1998	669	30.9
New Zealand	1999	120	30.8
Mozambique	1999	250	30.0
South Africa	1999	399	29.8
Spain	2000	350	28.3
Austria	1999	183	26.8
Argentina	1999	257	26.5
Bulgaria	2001	240	26.2
Australia	1998	148	23.6
Belgium	1999	150	23.3
Switzerland	1999	200	23.0
Canada	2000	301	20.6
Costa Rica	1998	57	19.3
Portugal	1999	230	18.7
United Kingdom	2001	659	17.9
Dominican Republic	1998	149	16.1
Mexico	2000	500	16.0
Czech Republic	1998	200	15.0
Ecuador	1998	123	14.6
Slovak Republic	1998	150	14.0
United States	2000	435	14.0
Israel	1999	120	13.3
Poland	1997	460	13.0
Mali	1997	147	12.2
Uruguay	1999	99	12.1
Ireland	1997	166	12.0
Bolivia	1997	130	11.5
Philippines	1998	222	11.3
France	1997	577	10.9
Chile	1997	120	10.8
Romania	2000	345	10.7
Lithuania	2000	141	10.6
Italy	2001	630	9.8
Nicaragua	1996	93	9.7
Venezuela	2000	165	9.7
El Salvador	2000	84	9.5
Honduras	1997	128	9.4
Malawi	1999	193	9.3
Thailand	2001	500	9.2
India	1999	543	8.8
Greece	2000	300	8.7
Hungary	1998	386	8.3
Madagascar	1998	150	8.0
Ukraine	1998	450	7.8
Russia	1999	449	7.6
Japan	2000	480	7.3
Benin	1999	83	6.0
Nepal	1999	205	5.9
South Korea	2000	273	5.9
Brazil	1998	513	5.7
Turkey	1999	550	4.2

SOURCE: Inter-Parliamentary Union (www.ipu.org), as of October 2001. Data not available for Taiwan.

That is, only by assuring the functional representation of women—through mechanisms such as quotas—can the number of women candidates and level of women's representation be significantly raised across the board. In those countries where women's representation is low it can be successfully increased, while in countries where it is already high it can be raised even higher (the experience of the Nordic countries is proof of this). Such quotas are rarely found at the systemic level; rather they are the decisions of particular parties. Thus, the level of candidate selection could prove to be the most crucial gatekeeper for getting women into elected office. In light of the prominence this issue has been given in so many countries and parties, it is perplexing that candidate selection has not received more attention in the research on legislative recruitment.

The recent trend in candidate selection: democratization

Democratization of the candidate selection process is expressed as a widening of participation in the process—that is, when the selectorate following a reform of the candidate selection method is *more* inclusive than previously. Adopting more inclusive candidacy requirements (the first dimension in the analytical framework), decentralization (the third dimension), or a voting system (the fourth dimension) may be labeled democratization, but they are not. These are facilitating variables only and do not define nor exhibit democratization. More inclusive candidacy requirements may be adopted, yet the same limited selectorate could still have control over the final results, thereby having no impact on democratization. Decentralization could mean only that control of candidate selection has passed from the national oligarchy to a local oligarchy. Indeed, if the selectorate is decentralized from a national party conference of several thousand participants to a dozen local committees each consisting of a few hundred activists and leaders, the overall selectorate may actually become more exclusive. Voting procedures may replace appointments, but the vote itself could be restricted to a very exclusive body. In other words, it is inclusiveness that is the necessary variable for democratizing candidate selection methods—primarily of the selectorate, but of candidacy as well.[5] Sartori (1973: 19–20) appropriately equated democratization with the "massification" of politics, because the hitherto excluded masses are now allowed to enter.

According to Mair (1997: 148), "many parties are attempting to give their members more say rather than less, and … they are empowering rather than marginalizing them. Many parties now afford their ordinary members a greater voice in candidate selection than was once the case." Indeed, as Table 5.2 shows, parties in a number of democracies have democratized their candidate selection methods in recent years to make them more inclusive (Scarrow, Webb, and Farrell 2000). A study of party rules versus party practice shows that, even where the rules have hardly changed, many political

TABLE 5.2   *Democratizing Candidate Selection in National Legislative Elections*

Country	Statutes give option of member vote on selection	Selection is more inclusive since 1960	Non-members participate in selection	National party leaders can impose or veto selection or change list order
Australia	Lab (in some states)		No	Lab
Austria	Gru, ÖVP, SPÖ	Gru, ÖVP, SPÖ	ÖVP (sometimes)	FPÖ, ÖVP, SPÖ
Belgium	AGA, ECO, PVV		No	AGA, CVP, VU
Canada	All parties		Sometimes	Yes
Denmark	CD, KF, KRF, RV, SD, SF, V	CD, KF, KRF, RV, SD, SF, V	No	CD, KRF, SF, SD
Finland	All parties	All parties	No	All parties
France	PS	PS	No	PS, PC, RPR, UDF
Germany	CDU, Gr, SPD	CDU, Gr, SPD	No	All except FDP and Gr: limited non-binding veto
Ireland	FG, Gr	FG, Gr	No	FF, FG, Gr, Lab
Italy	No		No	All parties
Japan	No		No	All parties
Netherlands	D'66		No	CDA, D'66, PvdA, VVD
New Zealand	Lab	Lab	No	Lab, National
Norway	No		No	No
Sweden	S, C (sometimes)		No	No
Switzerland	No		No	SD
United Kingdom	Con, Lab, LibDem	Lab, LibDem	No	Con, Lab, LibDem
United States	No		All parties	No

NOTE: Party abbreviations follow Katz and Mair (1992).
SOURCE: Adapted from Scarrow, Webb, and Farrell (2000: 139)

parties have shown a trend toward democratizing their candidate selection methods (Bille 2001). And this trend is not limited to candidate selection, but also extends to legislative recruitment in general (Best and Cotta 2000).

The question that remains is: Why are parties moving toward more inclusive selectorates? There are a number of possible explanations, any or all of which may be at work in a specific party at a given point in time. The first is the need to attract new members, particularly in the more elite-based parties that had their origins in parliament. The second is the general decline of social hierarchies, due to developments such as rising educational levels, which has made party members less willing to be blind supporters of the party and more likely to take an interest in party policy and recruitment. The third is the changing nature of the party, such as the move toward less ideology and more inclusion. The fourth is the incentive to mobilize new or underrepresented interests by allowing the voters to take part in the selection of candidates who appeal to them. A fifth answer is to improve the party image and to increase its legitimacy, particularly in the era of the mass media's central role in electoral campaigning where a more open selection process produces candidates more attractive to the electorate. A sixth is electoral crisis, such as a significant defeat that forces the party to adapt in order to maximize its chances for winning. Yet, even collectively these factors do not provide a complete explanation. Thus, for example, democratization of the candidate selection process may be the result of internal factional struggles—such as in Taiwan's Kuomintang party (Wu 2001)—and not necessarily due to any of the explanations outlined above.

The consequences of democratizing candidate selection: two contending approaches

In light of the fact that the democratization of candidate selection methods constitutes a real trend, even if modest, it is important to assess the consequences of this phenomenon for political parties, parliaments, and the stability of government. The analysis of this still quite recent trend is only in its early stages, but there are already two somewhat divergent approaches. The first sees democratization as the internal implosion of political parties, leading to significant consequences for parties, legislatures, and governments. The second perceives democratization as a strategy of the party leaders, in a particular type of party, which does not necessarily lead to such consequences.

According to the first approach, if party lists are assembled not by the party organs, but instead by more inclusive selectorates such as party members, the party's ability to aggregate policies and present a cohesive ideological image is weakened (Hazan 1997b, 1999). As Gallagher (1988a: 15) has argued, "Where nominations are controlled centrally, we might expect to find that deputies follow the party line faithfully in parliament, as disloyalty will mean deselection. ... If they do not depend on any organ of the party for reselection, one might expect to find low levels of party discipline in parliament. ... Party cohesion may be threatened unless control of selection procedures is maintained." The ability of prospective politicians to appeal directly to the party membership thus changes the locus of responsibility in the now more inclusively selected party representatives. If the party does not function as a filtering mechanism, then the key actors in the process may become the candidates themselves, who will mobilize supporters directly. The whole selection process could then be driven by the candidates and not by the parties. The results, as Figure 5.2 suggests, could be a weakening of partisan discipline and cohesiveness, leading to a decline in the ability of the parties to operate effectively in the parliamentary arena.

Candidates who are chosen by an inclusive selectorate owe their loyalty to their voters in the candidate selection process, and not only to their party. Such candidates are no longer assured of a future in politics by being loyal team players; instead they must stand out and be recognized—not by the party leaders but by their now more inclusive selectorates. Democratizing candidate selection thus produces *dual sources of legitimacy* for candidates—party legitimacy and selectorate legitimacy. The former is

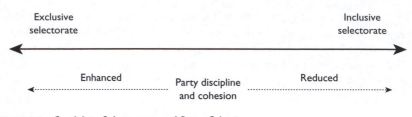

FIGURE 5.2 *Candidate Selectorates and Party Cohesion*
SOURCE: Rahat and Hazan (2001: 314)

exclusive and organizational in nature, while the latter is inclusive and popular. The immediate results are:

1. a shortening of the political time-frame based on an almost constant fixation with both inter- and intra-party elections;
2. a behavioral dependence on an amorphous group of party members or voters (that is, the selectorate);
3. a tendency to disregard the group(s) with which the candidate/legislator is associated (that is, the party, coalition, opposition, etc.);
4. a dramatic increase of the trend towards individualist and populist politics;
5. a significant growth in the influence of the mass media on politics in general, and on the candidate selection process in particular;
6. a need to enhance financial resources in order to reach a wide voter base.

Transferring the functional responsibility of choosing party candidates to a more inclusive selectorate could also expand the influence of well organized groups, thus producing lists that include both independent and special interest candidates.

In short, the narrow personal and special interests of candidates selected by more inclusive selectorates could overwhelm the more general party interests that legislators must take into account. As Epstein (1964: 55) claimed, "it appears illogical to combine primaries, intended to make legislators independent of party, with a parliamentary system that requires cohesive legislative parties in order to provide stable government."

Democratizing candidate selection can lead to additional, and related, consequences, such as (1) increasing even further the power of incumbents; (2) decreasing the representativeness of the selected lists; or (3) exacerbating intra-party conflict (Hazan and Rahat 2000).

How can parties, after democratizing, still exert an important impact on the candidate selection process in order to avoid such consequences? If parties maintain, or reassert, their control over certain phases in the candidate selection process, the phenomenon of democratization will not necessarily lead to a loss of control for the party organization, nor to a decline in its functional capacities. For example, if the party can filter prospective candidates prior to allowing a more inclusive selectorate to rank them, or if its agencies can produce a final list after the more inclusive selectorate has voted for prospective candidates, the party might still remain the master of its own internal fate.

Parties can also reassert their control by reversing the process of democratization. The Australian Labor and Liberal parties began shifting away from party primaries as early as the 1950s. From the 1970s onward, several Belgian parties phased out or abolished the use of membership balloting as part of the candidate selection process, and most Dutch parties eliminated the option of balloting local party members in the 1980s and 1990s. The Austrian ÖVP and SPÖ ceased to use party primaries as a candidate selection method in the two most recent elections, after changing their statutes to recognize this method and implementing it in 1994. In Israel there was a wholesale reversal in 1999, with all but one party abandoning party primaries after experimenting with this method of candidate selection for only a single election. In sum, parties have been able to undemocratize their candidate selection methods and reassert both party discipline and cohesion.[6]

The second approach to the consequences of democratizing candidate selection is based on the developing model of the cartel party (Mair 1994, 1997; Katz and Mair 1995; Katz 2001). It is still in its early stages with respect to research questions regarding its consequences. According to this approach, there must be a considerable degree of elite autonomy for the parties to participate effectively in the cross-party cartel. The cartel model suggests that one possible strategy used by the party leaders in order to achieve this necessary autonomy is to empower the party members. In other words, an increase in the nominal power of the base of the party will come at the expense of the middle-level activists, as they are the ones who might be able to coordinate an effective challenge to the autonomy of the party leaders. Moreover, this strategy will maintain, or even increase, the power of the party leaders, rather than diminish it and bring about the associated consequences outlined in the first approach. According to this approach, power has not shifted in a single direction, but rather it has simultaneously moved both up and down, at the expense of the middle.

In order to understand why party leaders might wish to empower their party members, it is important to make two distinctions: first, between party activists and party members, and second, between leaders in a cartel party and those in other types of parties. Party activists, as opposed to rank-and-file party members, are more likely to be motivated by ideology and ideological solidarity. Because of their activism, these more ideologically motivated members are usually influential within the party and may impose constraints on the ability of the party leaders who hold public office—the successful candidates—to pursue a strategy of compromise with other parties.

The cartel party model describes a type of party whose leaders are professional politicians. They are professional because leadership in the age of the cartel party requires specialized skills and expertise that can be achieved only through experience in office. Moreover, the leaders and parliamentary members of the cartel party are professionals for whom politics is not only a passion, but also a job. The willingness of this group to trade such concerns as ideology or policy for such needs as office and income is higher than it was for the leaders of other party types (Katz 2001). And, since cartel party leaders see the problems of government in managerial rather than in ideological terms, they desire autonomy— particularly from those who are motivated by ideology or interest.

In short, the cartel model requires that the party leadership be able to compromise across party lines. This, in turn, necessitates a leadership that is not limited by constraints imposed on them by party activists. Logically, then, the leaders of the cartel party have two options, or two strategies, to limit the impact of the ideological activists. The first is to disempower the party on the ground. In the arena of candidate selection, for example, this would take the form of centralizing control. Such a strategy might be costly in electoral terms, it may be illegal in certain countries, and it could alienate not only the ideologically motivated activists, but other members as well. A second option is to decapitate the party on the ground. This strategy is aimed at denying the ideologically motivated activists the opportunity to organize and speak for the party members. A most prominent example of this strategy is to have party decisions, such as candidate selection, opened up to the full membership. The rationale behind this option is that the less intensely involved rank-and-file party members are more likely to take cues from the highly visible party leadership. Mair (1997: 148–50) explains this strategy:

> The somewhat curious pattern that is developing therefore seems to be one in which the party in public office is afforded more power or autonomy ... and in which, at the same time, through enhanced democratization, the ordinary members themselves, albeit sometimes fewer in number, are being afforded a greater role. ... The process of intra-party democratization is being extended to the members as individuals rather than to what might be called the organized party on the ground. In other words, it is not the party congress, or the middle-level elite, or the activists who are being empowered, but rather the "ordinary" members, who are at once more docile and more likely to endorse the policies (and candidates) proposed by the party leadership and by the party in public office. This is, in fact, one of the most commonly distinct trends we see today. ... It may well be the case that a fully democratized party is more susceptible to control by the party in public office.

The most significant aspect of this strategy is that despite its leading to a more inclusive selectorate, this democratization of the candidate selection process is only an elusive empowerment of the party's base. If successful, this strategy might avoid the consequences elaborated in the first approach— no weakening of partisan discipline and cohesiveness, and no decline in the ability of the parties to function as a stable base for the political process or to operate effectively in the parliamentary arena. One apparently successful example of this strategy is New Labour in Britain.

Leadership selection

As politics becomes increasingly focused on individual candidates, the party becomes identified more and more with its leader. As a result, leaders have assumed greater electoral importance, even in parliamentary systems – such as Britain or Canada – where the electorate cannot vote for them directly. When it comes to selecting the party leader, as opposed to the parliamentary candidates, it would be reasonable to expect candidacy for the leadership to be more exclusive for several reasons (except where candidate selection is controlled by law rather than by party regulations). First, parties would prefer to be led by someone who has already proven his or her loyalty along with his or her abilities in party politics. Second, those who have an impact on party regulations – aspirants for leadership and their supporters – would tend to limit competition. Third, parties would prefer to refrain from having to deal with an inflation of irrelevant or unqualified candidates.

Despite this rationale, the process of leadership selection has shown similar trends to those of candidate selection (Blake and Carty 1999; LeDuc 2001). Marsh (1993: 230), in his introduction to a series of articles focusing on selecting party leaders argued that "an opening up of the selection process has been part of the wave of 'democratisation' that has affected political institutions." In other words, greater democratization is evident here as well, not only in the arena of candidacy requirements, but also in the makeup of the selectorate. Several party systems have demonstrated clear trends toward membership selection of leaders in the 1990s, including Belgium, Canada, France, and the UK, where even the Conservative party chose its leader by a postal ballot of the party membership in 2001. As Table 5.3 shows, membership selection is still a minority of the cases, but it is the fastest growing of the leadership selection methods, is the second-most favored method, and already encompasses the second largest number of countries.

A possible reason for this democratizing trend is that the choice of the method for the selection of its leader sometimes reflects a party's view of its competitive position more generally (LeDuc 2001). That is, because the choice of a candidate for the country's highest office is so important, parties may devise more inclusive processes of leadership selection in order to attain electoral goals. For example, a party that has suffered a serious electoral defeat may attempt a process of renewal, an important component of which may be to democratize the process through which it selects its leader. However, such a democratization will induce changes and produce significant consequences not only for the parties themselves, but for the party system as a whole.

TABLE 5.3   *Democratizing Party Leadership Selection*

Country	Parliamentary party	National committee	Party congress	Party members/ voter primary
Australia	2			1
Austria		1	4	
Belgium		1	1	5
Canada			2	2
Denmark	6		3	
Finland			6	
France		2	2	5
Germany		1	3	
Ireland	3			1
Italy		3	1	
Netherlands	5		1	1
New Zealand	1			
Norway			5	
Sweden			6	
United Kingdom			1	2
United States (presidential)			2	2
United States (congressional)	2			
Total	19	8	37	19

NOTE: Table entries denote the number of parties that employ a particular method for selecting their leaders.

SOURCE: Adapted from Scarrow, Webb, and Farrell (2000: 143)

In short, different selectorates, particularly more inclusive ones, will choose different types of leaders. The movement toward increased democratization in the US Democratic party, the British Labour party, the Spanish Socialist party, the Canadian Progressive Conservative party and the two main Israeli parties, Labor and Likud, has produced challengers from both inside and outside the party or brought a shift in the kind of individuals that contested and won the leadership contest. In the United States, for example, a shift from national office holders to state governors, such as Carter, Reagan, Clinton, and Bush.

Moreover, leadership selection and candidate selection are intrinsically related. The process of candidate selection at one level influences the pool of candidates available at a higher level, particularly in a country such as Britain which selects its party leaders only from within parliament. As the selection of parliamentary candidates changes, in both process and outcome, so too will the pool of eligible candidates for leadership positions.

By opening up the contest for party leadership to a more inclusive selectorate, a party may become more permeable to outside forces. As pressure for, and movement toward, greater democratization of leadership selection builds momentum, parties run the risk of losing control over the selection of their own leaders. This is already the case in the United States. While it is unlikely that many other countries will adopt the American presidential primary as a model for leadership selection, the shift towards more inclusive mechanisms is already under way. Such a trend will, inadvertently or not, import at least some of the consequences of American-style party permeability.

Conclusion

In most modern representative democracies, the relationship between the party and the voter is weakening (Schmitt and Holmberg 1995; Poguntke 1996; see also Dalton, Chapter 9 below). The consequences of these trends for political parties are well known. Most parties are confronted with declining membership rates, which creates financial problems and hampers the recruitment of candidates (Daalder 1992; Scarrow 1996; Dalton and Wattenberg 2000). Another consequence is that the number of floating voters is growing. This increase in electoral volatility causes potentially greater fluctuations in the vote shares of the parties, increasing the vulnerability of party elites whose positions increasingly depend on factors they cannot control.

If parties no longer possess a stable electoral base, they will feel the need to seek new methods of increasing their popularity and of gaining votes in elections. Shifts in party strategy are becoming more and more important for parties in order to secure and enlarge their vote shares (Wattenberg 1991; Kaase 1994; Scarrow 1999). Examples of this include the intensification of campaigning prior to elections and the focus on individual candidates rather than on the party.

Yet, there is another strategy that parties are adopting in order to increase their popularity—the reform of candidate selection methods in general, and the democratization of candidate selection in particular. By enlarging the number of those who can select candidates, parties can try to strengthen the sense of involvement of either members or voters. This can be done through varying degrees of membership participation.

The importance of candidate selection is not only associated with the elections to parliament but is also directly related to the parliament itself. That is, the "demise of parliaments" thesis may be partially explained by the nature of the parliamentarians (Longley and Hazan 2000). A candidate selection process that produces autonomous legislators at the cost of party discipline and cohesiveness may yield a weak parliament.

Whether the result is the demise of parties or the erosion of parliaments, candidate selection is a key variable in this process. Institutional arrangements such as candidate selection can be altered more easily than behavioral regularities, and a modification in institutional arrangements, in turn, can alter behavioral patterns. Yet the consequences of institutional reforms are sometimes just as unpredictable as those resulting from attempts to alter behavioral patterns. Institutions and the rules of the game affect power distributions, the distribution of preferences, and the management of control.

As such, different candidate selection methods influence actors who are affected by this institution, the most prominent among them being political parties and their associated legislatures, candidates, and selectorates.

Interests and preferences can develop within the context of institutions or change as a result of institutional reform. Institutions are, indeed, driven by the individuals who inhabit them; but institutions can also drive their inhabitants, alter their cohort structures, influence their turnover rate, affect their professional standards, and modify their collective behavior. The organization of political life does make a difference, and within this context, institutions such as candidate selection do matter. Researchers of comparative democracies who focus strictly on inter-party electoral systems and ignore the intra-party selectoral system do so at their own risk.

NOTES

I am indebted to Larry LeDuc, Pippa Norris, and Gideon Rahat for their comments and suggestions on an earlier draft of this chapter. I would like to thank Richard Katz for his assistance regarding democratizing candidate selection in the cartel party.

1. A notable exception is Ware (1996), who includes a comparative chapter on the selection of candidates and leaders.
2. Gallagher suggests five influences on the selection process: legal provisions; structure of government; electoral system; political culture; and the nature of the party. Yet, he concludes that even collectively they do not provide a complete explanation of the selection process in any party: "To some extent, each party must be looked on as being *sui generis*. Parties do have some autonomy; their behaviour is not determined absolutely by their environment" (1988b: 265).
3. This section is largely based on Rahat and Hazan (2001).
4. Gallagher (1988b: 237–45) outlined seven party agencies, or actors, in his attempt to assess the locus of greatest influence over candidate selection: party voters, party primaries, subset of constituency party members, national executive, interest groups, national factional leaders, and party leader. Yet he, too, acknowledges the terminological obstacles involved.
5. If the selectorate is made more inclusive, but candidacy is not—that is, the party leadership selects an approved list of candidates that is similar in size to the number of "safe" seats—the expanded selectorate will only be able to rank the candidates, not select them.
6. This process of reasserting party control is all the more difficult if there are legal regulations concerning the method of candidate selection, such as in the United States.

6

Campaign Communications

PIPPA NORRIS

Political communication is an interactive process concerning the transmission of information among politicians, the news media, and the public. The process operates downwards from governing institutions towards citizens, horizontally in linkages among political actors, and upwards from public opinion towards authorities. This chapter begins by providing a schematic model of campaign communications and proceeds to outline a conceptual framework for understanding how campaign communications have evolved over time. It then examines evidence about the impact of campaign communications, and concludes by considering the broader systemic consequences of this process for representative democracy.

The study of campaign communications

At the most general level, campaigns can best be understood as organized efforts to *inform, persuade, and mobilize*. Campaigns can be directed towards multiple goals such as pursuing elected office or lobbying government, persuading the public about the health risks of smoking, breast cancer, or AIDS (Siegel and Biener 1997), or pressuring multinational companies over the price of drugs or the use of sweatshop labor (Sage 1999). Campaigns include four distinct elements, as illustrated in Figure 6.1: the *contextual environment* based on the legal regulations and structure of the mass media within each country, the *campaign organizations* with strategic objectives that they are seeking to communicate, the direct and mediated *channels of communication* employed by these organizations to convey their messages, and the *effects* of these campaign messages on their targeted audience. Effective campaigns also include a dynamic feedback loop as organizations learn about the response of their targeted audience and adjust their goals and strategies accordingly. The literature on *electoral* campaign communications

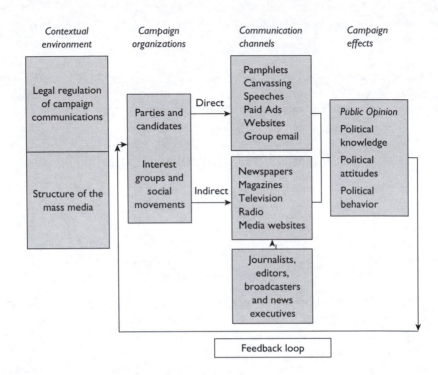

FIGURE 6.1   *Model of Campaign Communications*

during the last decade can be subdivided into these schematic categories, focusing on understanding the contextual environment, the strategic objectives of campaign organizations, the direct and mediated channels of communications, and impact of the messages upon the public.

Contextual environment

At the broadest level in election and referendum campaigns, the legal rules of the game—such as the regulation of campaign finance and advertising or the formal directives governing political broadcasting and freedom of the press—determine the overall campaign context. The most striking development since the early 1980s has been the dramatic transformation of public broadcasting in Western Europe and in new democracies in Central and Eastern Europe, following the growth of commercial competition from alternative terrestrial, cable and satellite, and now broadband, channels (Siune and Truetzschler 1992; McQuail and Siune 1998; Smith 1998). This trend has generated considerable concern about the possible consequences for traditional standards of journalism evident on public television and the most appropriate regulation of political coverage for broadcasters in a multichannel environment (Weymouth and Lamizet 1996; Østergaard 1997; Tracey 1998).

The context of election campaigning is also determined by the structure of the mass media within each country. As shown in Table 6.1, the diffusion of newspapers and television sets per 1,000 population varies considerably among nations. Among post-industrial societies, there is widespread access to these mass media, although some countries, like the United States and Canada, are more television-centric while others, like Norway and Japan, are more newspaper-centric. There are similar variations in media access among nations with slightly lower levels of development, such as Israel and Portugal, or Romania and Lithuania. Among poorer societies, however, there is far less access to either mass media. Similar patterns are evident in terms of the diffusion of radios, telephones, and the Internet population (Norris 2000b, 2001).

Research has also examined the changing ownership of newspapers and magazines following the growth of multinational corporations like Bertelsmann and News Corporation, as well as mega-mergers between organizations like Time–Warner and AOL (Bogart 1995; Bagdikian 1997; McChesney 1999). Comparative studies have also commonly analyzed the news culture, especially the values that journalists, broadcasters, and editors employ as gatekeepers in deciding what's news, as well as the organizational structure of newsrooms (Blumler and Gurevitch 1995; Weaver 1998). The rise of digital communication and information technologies has generated much new research, particularly on the use of websites by parties, social movements, transnational policy networks, and the traditional news media (Davis and Owen 1998; Davis 1999; Margolis and Resnick 2000; Norris 2001).

Campaign organizations

Research has long focussed on understanding the role of campaign organizations like parties, traditional interest groups, and new social movements. In recent decades the most striking development has been the increased professionalization of political marketing campaigns, evident in many countries, including the rise of political consultants, pollsters, advertising executives, and their coterie, and the consequence of this process for strategic communications by political parties and interest groups (Swanson and Mancini 1996; Newman 1999; Thurber and Nelson 2000, Thurber, Nelson, and Dulio 2000). Some researchers have highlighted changes in the symbiotic relationship between parties and the press, with the rise of a more autonomous news industry, often concerned primarily with generating a mass audience to maximize newspaper sales and TV advertising revenue (Mazzoleni 1987; Panebianco 1988). The mass media are widely regarded as playing a more autonomous role than in the past, not merely passively reflecting but also shaping the process of electioneering, the salient issues on the policy agenda, and the legislative and policy-making process in government. In the post-war era, mainstream political science has commonly

TABLE 6.1   *Access to the Mass Media in Democratic Nations*

Country	Newspapers per 1,000 1996	Radios per 1,000 1997	TV sets per 1,000 1997	% population with telephones 1998	% population with PCs 1998	% population online 2000
Argentina	123	681	289	19.7	4.4	1.0
Australia	293	1376	639	51.2	41.2	37.4
Austria	296	753	516	49.1	23.3	5.5
Barbados	—	—	—	42.2	7.5	1.9
Belgium	160	793	510	50.0	28.6	19.8
Belize	—	—	—	13.8	13.0	4.3
Benin	2	108	10	0.7	0.1	0.1
Bolivia	55	675	116	6.9	0.8	0.1
Botswana	27	156	20	6.5	2.6	0.2
Bulgaria	257	543	398	32.9	—	1.8
Canada	159	1077	715	63.4	33.0	41.9
Chile	98	354	232	20.6	4.8	1.0
Costa Rica	94	271	387	17.2	3.9	0.8
Cyprus	—	—	—	58.5	—	4.3
Czech Republic	254	803	447	36.4	9.7	2.8
Denmark	309	1141	585	66.0	37.7	20.8
Dominica	—	—	—	25.2	—	0.3
Dominican Republic	52	178	95	9.3	—	0.2
Ecuador	70	419	293	7.8	1.9	0.0
El Salvador	48	464	375	8.0	—	0.5
Estonia	174	693	480	34.3	3.4	10.9
Finland	455	1496	640	55.4	34.9	28.0
France	218	937	601	57.0	20.8	10.6
Germany	311	948	580	56.7	30.5	15.0
Greece	153	477	466	52.2	5.2	1.0
Grenada	—	—	—	26.3	9.6	2.0
Hungary	186	689	437	33.6	5.9	5.0
Iceland	—	—	—	64.7	32.6	40.4
India	—	121	69	2.2	0.8	0.1
Ireland	150	699	403	43.5	27.2	12.0
Israel	290	520	318	47.1	21.7	10.2
Italy	104	878	486	45.1	17.3	15.7
Jamaica	62	480	182	16.6	3.9	2.0
Japan	578	955	707	50.3	23.7	15.5
Kiribati	—	—	—	3.5	0.7	0.4
Korea, Republic of	393	1033	346	43.3	15.7	21.9
Latvia	247	710	492	30.2	—	4.1
Lithuania	93	513	459	30.0	5.4	2.2
Luxembourg	—	—	—	69.2	73.2	11.9
Malta	—	—	—	49.9	26.0	5.3
Mauritius	75	368	226	21.4	8.7	3.5
Micronesia, Fed Stat	—	—	—	8.0	—	0.9
Mongolia	27	151	63	3.7	0.5	0.0
Namibia	19	144	37	6.9	1.9	0.6
Netherlands	306	978	543	59.3	31.8	24.4
New Zealand	216	990	508	47.9	28.2	14.8
Norway	588	915	579	66.0	37.3	41.6
Panama	62	299	187	15.1	2.7	1.1
Papua New Guinea	15	97	24	1.1	—	0.0
Philippines	79	159	108	3.7	1.5	0.4

(Continued)

TABLE 6.1   *Continued*

Country	Newspapers per 1,000 1996	Radios per 1,000 1997	TV sets per 1,000 1997	% population with telephones 1998	% population with PCs 1998	% population online 2000
Poland	113	523	413	22.8	4.4	5.2
Portugal	75	304	542	41.4	8.1	2.0
Romania	300	319	233	16.2	1.0	0.7
Slovakia	185	580	402	28.6	6.5	9.4
Slovenia	199	406	356	37.5	25.1	23.0
South Africa	32	317	125	11.5	4.7	4.2
Spain	100	333	506	41.4	14.5	7.8
St. Lucia	—	—	—	26.8	13.6	1.3
St. Vincent & Grenadine	—	—	—	18.8	8.9	1.8
Sweden	445	932	531	67.4	36.1	44.4
Switzerland	337	1000	535	67.5	42.2	16.4
Taiwan	—	—	—	52.4	15.9	21.8
Thailand	63	232	236	8.4	2.2	0.2
Trinidad & Tobago	123	534	334	15.2	4.7	1.6
Tuvalu	—	—	—	—	—	—
United Kingdom	329	1436	645	55.7	26.3	23.9
United States	215	2146	847	66.1	45.9	39.1
Uruguay	293	607	241	25.0	9.1	2.7
Western Samoa	—	—	—	4.9	0.5	0.2

SOURCES: Newspapers, *UNESCO Statistical Yearbook, 2000;* radios and TV sets, *World Development Indicators,* World Bank 2000; telephones and PCs, International Telecommunications Union, *Basic Indicators* 2000; online, www.NUA.ie. Shown are all "free" states as defined by Freedom House 2001, www.freedomhouse.org

regarded political parties and interest groups as the primary channels linking citizens and the state. Yet in many political systems today, the role of the mass media has come to be regarded as equally important, not just for campaigns and elections, but also for governance.

Communication channels

Another related mainstream research tradition has examined the contents of campaign messages in different channels of communication, such as the amount of campaign reporting presented in television news, the partisan balance in the press, or the positive or negative tone of political advertisements. Most comparisons are among different media within a particular country—for example, contrasts in the campaign messages conveyed by parties and candidates through political advertisements or press releases, and what journalists cover in newspaper columns and TV news stories during an election campaign (Kaid and Holtz-Bacha 1995; Just et al. 1996; Norris et al. 1999). Other comparisons examine trends in the content of campaign coverage over time, such as changes in news coverage of presidential elections (Patterson 1993), stories about political scandals (Lull and

Hinerman 1997), or the treatment of social minorities (Entman and Rojecki 2000). Less often, collaborative teams have attempted cross-national comparisons of media messages—for example, how selected major national newspapers covered a specific event (Jensen 1998) or European Union politics (Norris 2000b). And there have been only a few attempts to compare the contents of election communications in different societies (Blumler 1983; Dalton et al. 1998). To move beyond description, the content of the campaign messages needs to be related to either the prior structural context (to examine their possible causes), or to their potential impact (to understand their effects). Content analysis can document a certain pattern of coverage but, by itself, it cannot assess whether these messages have any impact, given variations in the response of the audience.

Campaign effects

Perhaps the largest body of research, certainly in American political science, has focussed on understanding the potential effects at the individual or micro-level of attention and exposure to different types of campaign communication. The literature is too extensive to cite in any systematic fashion here, but an excellent summary can be found in Bryant and Zillmann (1994). It is conventional to identify three distinct periods of effects research on the study of elections and voting behavior.

The early *"direct effects"* school of social psychology attempted to identify the impact of government propaganda via the new mass media of movies and radio, often using innovative experimental techniques (Hovland 1959). This approach was succeeded by survey methodology, and the results of those studies helped to fuel the *"minimal effects"* model (Lazarsfeld, Berelson, and Gaudet 1944). The conventional wisdom by the early 1960s, exemplified by Klapper (1960), was that the earlier propaganda school had adopted a naïve "stimulus-response" model which assumed that media messages had the direct power to change the attitudes and opinions of the mass public. Instead, it was argued, although use of the partisan press reinforced the attentive public, the power of the mass media to *alter* deep-rooted political attitudes and values was strictly limited, not least because the undecided voter paid less attention to campaign messages.

In the past two decades, however, the minimal effects model has come under increased challenge. It has become more common to study media effects using dynamic rolling cross-section or panel surveys and also experimental methods, ideally combined with content analysis data. More sophisticated research techniques, including experimental methods, are capable of capturing even modest campaign effects (Iyengar and Simon 2000), and the shift in the central focus of the campaign first from newspapers to television studios, and more recently to the Internet (Davis 1999) has altered the research agenda. Recent research has focussed on analyzing the potential impact of exposure and/or attention to different types of mediated messages (such as watching a campaign debate, TV ad, or news story) upon three dimensions of public opinion—*political knowledge*, such as awareness or opinions about an issue, information about "civics," and recognition of political candidates (Bartels 1993; Delli Carpini and Keeter 1996); *political attitudes and values*, such as party identification, political trust, or issue salience (Dearing and Rogers 1996; Norris et al. 1999; Norris 2000b); and *political behavior*, such as voting turnout (Ansolabehere and Iyengar 1995; Lau et al. 1999).

The study of political communications is inherently interdisciplinary, bringing together legal theorists, cultural historians, sociologists, economists, professional journalism schools, and social psychologists, as well as students of media studies and political scientists. But there is an important distinction in the focus of different approaches. Communication studies often treat the contents of political messages as the core *dependent* variable, and then seek to explain these phenomena in terms of the broader social, economic, and political context, as well as specific features of the production process, such as the predominant journalistic values in the news culture, or patterns of rhetoric in presidential speeches. This tradition typically asks such questions as: How far is the news shaped by the predominant values of broadcasters and journalists (Weaver 1998)? How far do gender stereotypes influence the depiction of female candidates in the media (Kahn 1996)? How do newspapers report news about campaign opinion polls (Andersen 2000)? Are there significant differences in the ways that the local, regional, and national press cover a campaign (Wasserman 1999)?

In contrast, political scientists tend to regard the contents of political communications mainly as *independent* variables, in seeking to explain patterns of mass attitudes and behavior, such as the impact of leadership speeches on presidential popularity (Brace and Hinckley 1992), or the influence of partisan balance in the press on levels of voting support (Dalton et al. 1998). Common questions within this approach are whether negative party political broadcasts or political advertisements have a significant impact on turnout (Lau et al. 1999); whether television coverage of crime, the economy, or the environment heightens viewers' concern about these issues on the campaign agenda (Dearing and Rogers 1996; Iyengar and Kinder 1987; Semetko et al. 1991); how far the results of opinion polls affect voting (Schmitt-Beck 1996); and, at the more diffuse level, how changes in the nature of election communications may have altered the context for voters' choices.

Developments in campaign communications

While methodological innovations and changing intellectual frameworks have revived interest in understanding political communications and the role of the news media as a more autonomous actor in the electoral process, interest has also been generated by key political developments. We can identify three distinct stages in the evolution of election communications, namely, the shift from premodern to modern to postmodern campaigns, which simultaneously transformed campaign organizations, the news media, and the electorate (Table 6.2).

Many accounts have noted the decline of traditional forms of party campaigning, like local rallies and door-to-door canvassing, and developments like the growth of spin-doctors and political consultants. A growing series of case studies has documented these trends in established and newer democracies (Gunther and Mughan 2000). These changes have been alternatively interpreted as representing the "rise of political marketing," or the "Americanization of campaigning." The interpretation offered in this chapter is that changes in campaign communications can best be understood as an evolutionary process of *modernization* that simultaneously transforms campaign organizations, the news media, *and* the electorate.

In this theoretical framework, *premodern* campaigns are understood to display three characteristics: the campaign organization is based upon direct forms of interpersonal communications between candidates and citizens at the local level, with short-term, ad-hoc planning by the party leadership. In the news media the partisan press acts as core intermediary between parties and the public. And the electorate is anchored by strong party loyalties. Typically in these types of campaigns local parties selected the candidates, rang the doorbells, posted the pamphlets, targeted the wards, planned the resources, and provided all the machinery linking voters and candidates. For citizens, the model is one that is essentially *local-active*, meaning that most campaigning is concentrated within local communities, conducted through more demanding political activities like rallies, doorstep canvassing, and party meetings.

Modern campaigns are defined as those with a party organization coordinated more closely at a central level by political leaders, advised by external professional consultants like opinion pollsters. In the news media, national television becomes the principal forum of campaign events, supplementing other media. And the electorate becomes increasingly decoupled from party and group loyalties. Politicians and professional advisors conduct polls, design advertisements, schedule the *thème du jour*, leadership tours, news conferences, and photo opportunities, handle the press, and battle to dominate the nightly television news. For citizens, the typical experience of the election becomes more passive, in the sense that the main focus of the campaign is located within national television studios, so that most voters become more distant and disengaged spectators in the process.

Lastly, *postmodern campaigns* are understood as those in which the coterie of professional consultants on advertising, public opinion, marketing, and strategic news management become more co-equal actors with politicians, assuming a more influential role within government in a "permanent" campaign, as well as coordinating local activity more tightly at the grassroots. The news media fragments into a more complex and incoherent environment of multiple channels, outlets, and levels. And the electorate

TABLE 6.2 *Typology of the Evolution of Campaign Communications*

	Premodern (Mid-19thC to 1950s)[a]	Modern (Early 1960s to late 1980s)[a]	Post-modern (1990s+)[a]
Campaign organization	Local and decentralized party volunteers	Nationally coordinated with greater professionalization	Nationally coordinated but decentralized operations
Preparations	Short-term, ad hoc	Long campaign	Permanent campaign
Central coordination	Party leaders	Central party headquarters, more specialist advisors	Special party campaign units and more professional consultants
Feedback	Local canvassing and party meetings	Occasional opinion polls	Regular opinion polls plus focus groups and interactive websites
Media	Partisan press, local posters and pamphlets, radio broadcasts	Television broadcasts through main evening news, targeted direct mail	TV narrowcasting, direct and mediated websites, email, online discussion groups intranets
Campaign events	Local public meetings, whistle-stop leadership tours	News management, daily press conferences, controlled photo-ops	Extension of news management to routine politics and government
Costs	Low budget	Moderate	Higher costs for professional consultants
Electorate	Stable social and partisan alignments	Social and partisan dealignment	Social and partisan dealignment

[a]Dates of predominant era are given.

becomes more dealigned in their voting choices. For some citizens, the election may represent a return to some of the forms of engagement found in the premodern stage, as the new channels of communication potentially allow greater interactivity between voters and politicians.

The essential features of this model can be expected to vary from one context to another. Rather than claiming that all campaigns are inevitably moving into the postmodern category, this view emphasizes that contests can continue to be arrayed from the premodern to the postmodern, due to the influence of a range of intermediary conditions such as the electoral system, campaign regulations, and organizational resources. And instead of a specifically American development, with practices like negative advertising, personalized politics, or high campaign expenditures which are subsequently exported to other countries, it seems more accurate to understand changes in campaigning as part of the modernization process rooted in technological and political developments common to many post-industrial societies.

The premodern campaign

Premodern campaigning originated in 19th century democracies with the expansion of the franchise and continued in recognizable form in most post-industrial societies until at least the 1950s. In general elections the premodern era was characterized by a campaign organization with the party leader at the apex, surrounded by a few close political advisers, running a relatively short, ad hoc national campaign. The base was a loose organizational network of party volunteers dispersed in local areas. The party organization was predominately locally oriented, involving politicians, party workers, and citizens in direct, face-to-face contact through activities like town-hall hustings, canvassing, and branch party meetings. Party members provided the unpaid labor, advised by the constituency party agent. Premodern campaigns relied heavily upon the partisan press as the main source of mediated information, either directly owned and subsidized by party organs, or independently owned and managed but providing sympathetic partisan-spin through editorial columns and political commentary. Newspapers were indirectly supplemented in the 1920s by radio and movies, important sources of news in the inter-war period, and these media started to nationalize campaigns even prior to the age of television. Classic theories of voting behavior stressed the stability of the electorate during this era, anchored by social and party loyalties. Lipset and Rokkan (1967) emphasized that European parties were based on stable sectoral cleavages in the electorate, with the divisions of class, religion, and region providing the solid bedrocks of electoral support. Accounts of American electoral behavior argued that voters were guided by enduring partisan loyalties or "standing decisions" influencing voting decisions over successive contests (Campbell et al. 1960). If voters were largely stable, the main function of party organization was to energize and mobilize their traditional bases of electoral support.

Today direct forms of campaigning have often been supplemented, rather than replaced. The traditional campaign, built on personal networks of volunteers and face-to-face candidate–voter communications, continues to be common when mobilizing voters in no-frills contests for local, municipal, and state-level elected office, for minor parties without generous financial resources, and in countries like Britain and Canada where mass-branch party organizations maintain networks of active party members (Bell and Fletcher 1991; Denver and Hands 1997; Carty and Eagles 1999). Electoral systems with multimember seats where politicians compete with others within the same party often emphasize the importance of local campaigning to maintain support. This pattern is evident in Ireland under STV, as well as in Japan, where politicians traditionally relied upon local associations, or *koenkai*, in competing with others from within their own party under the multimember single nontransferable vote system used until 1994 (Flanagan et al. 1991). Direct campaigning also remains characteristic of elections in developing societies, such as India and South Africa, with relatively low levels of literacy and little access to television.

Even in the United States, "retail" politics survives in the New Hampshire primaries, in district and state caucuses, and in general elections, with candidates meeting activists in local living rooms and diners, and displays of yard signs and bumper stickers (Aldrich 1995). Huckfeldt and Sprague (1995) emphasize the political importance in presidential elections of local mobilization efforts, party canvassing, and discussion networks within American communities. Analyses of long-term trends in the proportion of Americans engaged in campaign activism show no consistent and substantial decline across most dimensions of activity other than the display of buttons and bumper stickers (Norris 2000b). There has been no fall in the proportion contacted by the major US parties, either face-to-face or, more commonly today, by telephone. Pew post-election surveys suggest that about 38% of Americans were contacted over the phone during the 2000 campaign by candidates, parties, or other groups urging them to vote in a particular way, including 53% of all voters in the key battleground states (Pew 2000). Nevertheless, technological changes, notably the rise of television and of opinion polls, mean that in post-industrial societies direct forms of campaigning often become ancillary to mediated channels of party-voter communication.

The modern campaign

The evolution of the modern campaign from the early 1950s to the mid-1980s was marked by several related developments in established democracies—the move from dispersed state and local party organizations to a nationally coordinated strategic campaign; from party officials and volunteers contributing time and labor to paid professional consultants specializing in communications, marketing, polling, and campaign management; the shift from more partisan newspapers towards national television news; and the development of a more detached and instrumental electorate, less strongly anchored to party loyalties and social cleavages. The "long campaign" in the year or so before polling day gradually became as important strategically as the shorter formal campaign.

In most post-industrial democracies, the critical shift towards the modern campaign developed during the 1950s with the rise of television and the introduction of regular public opinion polling. This process gradually shifted the primary location of political communications from the print media towards broadcasting, particularly the mainstream national evening news on the major television channels. The printed press remained politically important, particularly in newspaper-centric systems, since the per capita circulation levels of newspapers in OECD countries has remained stable (Norris 2000b: 65). Nevertheless, many countries have experienced weakening press–party linkages, as newspapers have become increasingly politically independent.

In the Netherlands, for example, at least until the 1960s there were strong sectoral cleavages, producing "polarization" as people within a community attended the same schools and churches, joined the same social clubs, sports clubs, and community associations, tended to vote for the same party, and read the party newspaper. The *"zuillen"* or pillars were formed around Protestant, Catholic, and labor mass movements, which mobilized politically in the early 20th century, at the same time that mass circulation newspapers developed in the Netherlands, creating stable cleavage sub-cultures reflecting the Protestant, Catholic, and Socialist pillars (van der Eijk 2000). The de-pillarization process leading to the decline of the partisan press in the Netherlands started in the mid-1960s. Other countries seem to have followed a similar process, yielding greater internal diversity within newspapers but reducing the degree of external diversity among different print media.

Newspapers did not necessarily decline in importance as sources of political communications, but they became supplemented by television. The main effort of party campaign organizations, from the morning press conferences through the day's events, visits and photo opportunities to the evening rallies and speeches, became increasingly focused on achieving favorable coverage through the main evening news, current affairs programs, and leadership debates on television. Such efforts were exacerbated by the mainstream audience for these programs, given that until the early 1980s there were only two or three television stations broadcasting in most OECD countries. Major news programs occurred at regular prime-time slots in the evening rather than on a 24-hour cyclical basis, and most countries offered no opportunities for paid political advertising on television. To a large extent, therefore, what was reported on the flagship news programs on Britain's BBC and ITN, on Sweden's SVT, or on Japan's NHK, to a largely captive electorate, *was* the heart of the modern election campaign, setting the agenda for the following morning's newspapers. The role of television news heightened the party leadership's control over the campaign, which became increasingly nationalized.

Swanson and Mancini (1996) suggest that the focus on television campaigns has strengthened the spotlight on the party leadership, moving from cleavage-based and issue-based conflict towards a greater "personalization" of politics. Case studies suggest that this trend is particularly marked for presidential elections, but it is apparent in parliamentary elections as well. The shift in emphasis from newspapers to television probably heightened the visibility of leaders, especially those like Tony Blair and Bill Clinton who seem most comfortable in this medium, although systematic evidence is unavailable to confirm whether this is a general trend in many democracies. Moreover, it is not clear whether the focus on leaders in campaign coverage has necessarily led to an increasing importance of party leaders in determining votes in parliamentary systems (Mughan 1995; see also Hazan, Chapter 5 above).

In the modern campaign, parties developed coordinated national and regional strategies with communications designed by specialists skilled in advertising, marketing, and polling. One study of European political marketing terms this process a "shopping model," as parties grafted particular practical techniques which seemed useful or successful in other campaigns onto the existing machinery on a more ad hoc basis (Plassner Scheucher, and Senft 1999). The move from amateur to professional campaigns was marked by more frequent use of specialist experts, PR consultants, and professional fund-raisers influencing decisions formerly made by candidates or party officials (Thurber and Nelson 2000). The new professionals were frequently "hired guns" external to the party organization, sometimes working on campaigns in different countries. Increased use of paid consultants, public opinion polls, direct mail, and professional television broadcasts during the long campaign led to rising costs and the shift from labor-intensive towards more capital-intensive campaigns.

The professionalization of the political consultancy industry has developed furthest in the United States, fuelled by the traditional weakness of American party organizations, the rise of candidate-centered and advertising-driven campaigns, and the number and frequency of American primary and general elections. Outside of the US, the rise of independent political consultants has been slower, mainly because parties have more often incorporated professionals within their own ranks (Panebianco 1988).

The rise of the modern campaign was also related to major changes in the electorate, discussed fully in Chapters 8 and 9. Many studies have highlighted how dealignment has eroded traditional social cleavages and partisan loyalties, producing a more instrumental electorate supporting parties on a more contingent basis based on their policies and performance. The familiar cleavages of class and religion, which had long anchored the European electorate, proved weaker predictors of voting behavior in many countries as party competition over issues, images, and leadership became increasingly important from the 1970s onwards. Earlier theories suggested that dealignment was largely a product of long-term socioeconomic secular trends gradually transforming the mass public, stressing rising levels of education, class mobility, and crosscutting cleavages like race and gender. Some more recent accounts have emphasized that parties have both contributed to, and sought to benefit from, these changes in the electorate by developing more "catch all" strategies, designed to attract voters from outside their core constituency (Evans and Norris 1999). The modern campaign evolved into a familiar pattern from the early 1950s until the mid-1980s, with similar, although not identical, changes becoming evident across many post-industrial societies.

The postmodern campaign

Accounts commonly identify only two steps in this historical sequence, regarding the age of television as the culmination of the modernization process. But during the past decade there is evidence of the rise of the "postmodern" campaign marked by several related developments. Among these are the fragmentation of television outlets, with the shift from national broadcasting towards more diverse news sources including satellite and cable stations, talk radio, and 24-hour rolling news bulletins. Opportunities for newer forms of party–voter interaction have been facilitated by the rise of the Internet, and parties have attempted to reassert control in a more complex, fragmented, and rapidly changing news environment through strategic communications and media management during the permanent campaign, with continuous feedback provided by polls, focus groups, and electronic town meetings. This last stage of the modernization process remains under development, and it is more clearly evident in some societies than in others, but it seems likely to represent the future direction of political campaigning in post-industrial societies. The concept of "postmodernism" is usually understood to include the characteristics of greater cultural pluralism, social diversity, and fragmentation of sources; increased challenges to traditional forms of hierarchical authority and external standards of rational knowledge; and a more inchoate and confused sense of identity. While the term is subject to multiple interpretations, it does seem to capture many of the developments that are currently transforming the process of campaigning, at least in post-industrial societies.

Two qualifications need to be made. As Swanson and Mancini (1996) argue, many other factors may well be transforming society in general, like a greater differentiation of roles, rising educational levels and cognitive skills, and more complex social identities. However, the focus here is restricted only to the developments within the area of campaign communication. Many have characterized recent changes as the rise of political marketing, placing primary emphasis on the strategic activities of parties, politicians, and campaign advisers in their attempt to maintain or expand their share of the electorate. This approach does provide useful insights but in contrast the conceptualization of the postmodern campaign in this interpretation places greater emphasis on the way that technological and socioeconomic developments have altered the context of campaign communications. Even in recent campaigns, the use of systematic marketing to inform party policies has often proved limited. The postmodern conceptualization sees politicians as essentially lagging behind technological and economic changes, while running hard to stay in place by adopting new techniques.

Instead of a linear development, the postmodern campaign may symbolize a return to some of the more localized and interactive forms of communication that were present in the premodern period. Digital technologies allow forms of political communication that can be located schematically somewhere between the local-activism of the premodern campaign and the national-passive forms of communications characteristic of the modern television campaign. The development of political discussion user-groups on the net, party intranets, interactive websites by government agencies, community associations, or transnational policy networks, and the use of email or listserves to mobilize and organize, as well as the use of the web by "traditional" news media, represents a mid-way point in the model. These formats continue to evolve, along with the political uses of the web, but parties, governments, and social movements have been rapidly adapting to the digital world.

To document just how far the Internet has penetrated, within the space of less than a decade, in June 2000 a worldwide comparison of 1,244 electoral parties (defined as those that contested seats for the lower house in the most recent election) in 179 nations found that 39% had developed their own website; the proportion online was particularly high among Green parties (71% online), as well as Christian Democrats (62%), Liberals (57%), Social Democrats (52%), and Conservatives (51%) (Norris 2001). The distribution varied by size, but there was only a modest gap between fringe parties (31% online), minor parties (47%), and major parties (52%). Similar patterns were found in the function and content of party websites, measured by their levels of information transparency and interactive communications. Comparisons of the world of online newspapers in 179 nations found that about 2,500 newspapers were online in mid-2000, representing about 40% of all daily papers. Access to the Internet varies substantially even among postindustrial societies, as well as among major world regions, and differences in levels of technological diffusion are strongly related to the development of online political institutions (Norris 2001). Nevertheless as political use of the Internet expands, the postmodern campaign adds yet another distinctive layer of communications to the process, supplementing existing channels.

To illustrate the potential impact of these developments, we can compare recent trends in the United States, one of the countries at the leading edge of the information society. A Pew Center survey in 2000 reveals a dramatic erosion in the size of the audience for early evening network TV news, which plummeted from a main source of election news for over half of all voters to only one-fifth in just eight years. American newspapers are also in decline, along with local TV and magazines. In contrast, use of radio news, cable TV, and especially the Internet surged during this period. While many of those using the Internet were turning to traditional news media outlets, like CNN, MSNBC, or the *New York Times* online, rather than more specialized news outlets or candidate websites, this process has none the less altered the form and speed of transmission, accelerating the 24/7 news cycle, and motivating parties and candidates to use direct rather than mediated channels to contact supporters, encourage fundraising, or foster voluntary activities like emailing friends with support messages on behalf of one of the candidates. Among those Americans who went online for news in campaign 2000, fully 43% said that this information affected their vote. Most of this group (69%) used online sources to get information about the candidate, although one-fifth (22%) also sent email about the candidates, 16% got civic information about when and where to vote, 8% participated in campaign chat rooms, and 5% donated money online. The United States has moved online more rapidly than most other post-industrial societies; nevertheless, these figures point the way towards the radical potential for new technology to alter and supplement the traditional channels of campaign communications.

Mediating conditions

The way that campaign communications have evolved over time in different countries, and the pace of change, remain heavily dependent upon mediating conditions. Postmodern campaigns are exemplified most clearly by contests, like US presidential and congressional elections, characterized by two major catch-all parties with minimal ideological baggage in winner-take-all elections, with an army of technical consultants for hire, widespread use of capital-intensive TV ads in a fragmented multichannel environment, the rapid expansion of political uses of the Internet, and an electorate with weakened party loyalties. Such an open environment is ideal for an entrepreneurial approach designed to maximize electoral support. In contrast, premodern campaigning continues to characterize many other types of contest, such as British local elections which are second-order, low-salience contests where the major parties rely primarily upon volunteer grassroots members, activists, and candidates in each community to canvass voters and mobilize partisan support. In some countries, since financial resources are restricted, there is minimal national coverage on television or in newspapers and the chief means of publicity remains in the form of hand-bill displays and printed pamphlets.

Four major factors can be identified as important mediating conditions affecting the modernization process:

- The **regulatory environment,** including the *electoral system* (whether single-member majoritarian or proportional party list); the *type of election* (including the frequency of elections, the type of office, such as presidential or parliamentary, and whether sub-national, national or supra-national levels); and the *laws* governing campaigning (such as rules on party funding and state subsidies, campaign expenditures, the publication of opinion polls, and access to political broadcasts or ads).
- The **media system,** including the level of development of the *political consultancy industry* (including the availability of professional market researchers, opinion pollsters, advertisers, and campaign managers); and the *structure and culture of the news media* (such as the contrasts already discussed between newspaper-centric or television-centric systems, between the partisan-leaning or "objective" models of journalism, and whether broadcasting reflects a public service or commercial ethos).
- The **party system,** including the structure, organization, membership, and funding of parties (such as whether elite-led, mass-branch, "catch-all," or cartel); and the system of *party competition* (such as one-party predominant, two-party, moderate or polarized pluralism).
- The **electorate,** including the pattern of *voting behavior* (such as whether electors display strong or weak party loyalties, and whether there is limited or extensive electoral volatility).

Other parts of this book have discussed changes in the electorate (Chapters 8–9) and party systems (Chapter 4) so here we can focus on comparing the regulatory framework and party campaign organizations.

The regulatory framework

Regulations governing television coverage during elections concern three main areas: the purchase of paid commercial advertisements, the allocation and contents of free party political broadcasts, and rules governing political balance in campaign debates, news coverage, and current affairs. During the era when public service channels predominated in most countries, there were severe restrictions on the ability of political parties to purchase any airtime on television. A comparative survey of Western societies in the late 1970s found that only five of the 21 countries surveyed had commercial channels, and paid political advertising on television was allowed only in Australia, Canada, Japan, and the United States (Smith 1981). By the mid-1990s, following deregulation and the explosion of commercial channels, about half the OECD countries allowed paid political advertising on television (see Table 6.3). In practice the use of this facility varied substantially between countries, as well as between public service and commercial channels. In the Netherlands, for example, although political commercials are now allowed, in practice few have been aired because of the limited financial resources of Dutch parties (van der Eijk 2000). In contrast, in the United States campaign ads are employed for every level of office, producing highly capital-intensive campaigns; for example, about 60% of expenditures in recent presidential campaigns were devoted to paying for, producing, and airing TV and radio commercials (West 1997).

Following the long tradition of public service broadcasting, all OECD countries other than the United States allocate some free airtime to parties, either on a legal basis or by virtue of a long-standing agreement with broadcasters. The length of these slots varies substantially, from the 30 or 60 second ads common in Italy, to 2.5 minutes in Germany, 4 minutes in France, and an allocation of up to 10 minutes (usually only partially used) for British party political broadcasts. Three formulas are commonly used for allocating time between contestants. Strict equality between all parties is used in countries like the Czech Republic and Mexico; in the latter the Federal Electoral Institute buys 15 minutes per month of advertising on television and radio for each party. Other countries provide allocations based upon the results of the previous general election—for example, Greek parties are given airtime based on the size of their membership in the previous parliament, with a modest allocation for parties with no elected representatives. Lastly, countries like Australia and Britain divide the time according to an agreement between parties and the broadcasting authorities.

In addition, all OECD countries have some fair balance rules, either formally or informally regulating the amount of party political coverage on

TABLE 6.3   *Campaign Communication Regulation in OECD Nations, mid-1990s*

Country	Paid political ads on TV	Free TV airtime to parties	Fair balance rules	Leader debate last election	Ban on publication of opinion polls prior to election	US consultants involved in recent campaign	Direct funding subsidy to parties or candidates	Contribution limit
Australia	✓	✓	✓	✓			✓	✗
Austria	✓	✓	✓		✗		✓	
Belgium	✗	✓	✓	✓	✗	✗	✗	✗
Canada	✓	✓	✓	✓		✓	✓	
Denmark	✗	✓		✓	✗	✓	✓	
Finland	✗	✓	✓	✓	✗	✓	✓	✓
France	✓	✓	✓	✓	✓	✓	✓	✗
Germany	✓	✓	✓	✗	✗	✓	✓	
Greece					✗	✗		✓
Ireland	✗	✓	✓	✓	✗	✓	✓	✓
Italy	✓	✓	✓	✓	✗	✓	✓	✓
Japan	✓	✓	✓	✓	✓	✓	✓	✓
Mexico	✓	✓						✗
Netherlands	✓	✓	✓	✓	✗	✗	✗	
New Zealand	✓	✓		✓		✗		
Norway	✗	✓	✓	✓	✗	✗	✓	
Poland		✓		✓			✗	
Portugal			✓	✓	✓	✗		✓
Spain	✗	✓	✓	✓	✓	✗		✗
Sweden	✓	✓	✓	✓	✗	✓		✓
Switzerland	✗	✓	✓	✗		✓	✗	✓
Turkey	✗	✓	✓		✗		✓	✓
United Kingdom	✓	✓	✓	✗	✗	✓	✓	✓
United States	✗	✗	✓	✓		✓	✓	✓
OECD Total	11/21	21/22	18/18	16/18	5/16	13/18	15/20	8/13

television news, current affairs programs, and leadership debates during election periods. In Britain, for example, the ratio used to allocate party political broadcasts is also used to distribute the time balance of news coverage of the parties, following the "stop-watch" principle. In the 1997 election the allocation was a 5:5:4 ratio whereby the major parties each received five 10-minute party election broadcasts during the campaign, the Liberal Democrats got four slots, and other minor parties with at least 50 candidates got one each, with additional arrangements for the regions. In the United States, presidential debates have followed different formats and schedules—for example, the questions have been asked either by selected journalists or by members of the public in an invited audience, or by a mix of both. But all debates follow a strict allocation of time designed to be impartial to all candidates (Coleman 1999).

Party campaign organizations and funding

An extensive literature has documented changes in the structure, membership, and finances of party organizations. The role of parties has evolved or adapted since the 1960s in Western democracies, rather than simply weakened (Katz and Mair 1992, 1995; Mair 2001). Documenting trends in twenty European countries from the early 1980s to 2000, Mair recorded a decline in total party membership whether measured in absolute numbers or as a percentage of the electorate. Studies based on survey evidence in 15 West European countries reached similar conclusions—showing a modest long-term erosion of party membership in many established democracies (Widfeldt 1995).

   Katz and Mair (1995) also found that, since the 1960s, many countries experienced a substantial increase in the proportion of staff employed by parties, most notably parliamentary party staff paid by state funds, as well as a considerable rise in central party income. Where these personnel and resources are derived from state subventions, they suggest a shift from "mass-branch" parties based primarily upon volunteers towards a "cartel" party organization, more dependent upon public resources. This pattern is clearer in some countries than others; state subsidies towards parties are far more generous in Germany, Sweden, and Norway, for example, than in Ireland, Britain, and the Netherlands, where party income remains more dependent on membership dues. Table 6.3 shows that by the mid-1990s direct funding for parties or candidates was common; 15 out of 20 countries provided public funds, although at different levels of subsidy. In some countries, like Canada, France, and Australia, public subsidies are designed to reimburse some election expenditures, while in others, like the Netherlands, Ireland, and Denmark, such funds are designed for purposes such as general administration, policy research, political education, or to promote participation by young people or women. Public funding is often justified to lessen the risk of parties and candidates becoming dependent upon large donations or falling under the influence of lobby groups.

The question of whether the "cartel" party represents the emergence of a new and distinctive type of party organization that is evident in many countries remains controversial. There are also important questions concerning how we interpret the consequences of the decline of party membership, and in particular whether the fall has been concentrated mostly among less active older members, or whether it involves an across-the-board contraction (Scarrow 2000). Nevertheless, what does seem well established by these studies is that many European countries experienced a gradual shrinkage in grassroots party membership from the 1960s to the late 1990s, reducing the overall pool of voluntary labor available for traditional local campaigning. In counterbalance, parties have growing numbers of professional staff as well as more generous financial resources from public funds. These developments, accompanied by the technological and economic changes in the news system, have contributed towards the shift from direct to mediated forms of campaigning.

Conclusions: understanding campaign communications

Many commentators have noted the transformation of traditional forms of political campaigning, and a growing literature has started to distinguish the key features of these developments. Much of this has been conceptualized as involving an "Americanization" of campaigning. Swanson and Mancini (1996) provide one of the most ambitious theoretical accounts along these lines, suggesting that the "Americanization" of campaigning has produced similar developments across post-industrial societies. They stress four major developments: the "personalization" of politics as leaders and candidates rise in importance; the "scientificization" of campaigning as technical experts like opinion pollsters come to take decisions formerly exercised by party officials; the detachment of parties from citizens as politicians come to be increasingly reliant upon opinion polls rather than direct contact with grassroots activists and voters; and the development of more autonomous structures of communications, as the modern news media are more determined to pursue their own interests rather than to serve the needs of politicians.

Yet the impact of these practices varies substantially between nations depending upon the institutional context of election campaigns, such as the legal rules governing campaigning, the strength of traditional mass-branch party organizations, and the structure of the electorate. There are sharp contrasts between newspaper-centric and television-centric news environments, as well as major differences between broadcasting systems that are predominantly commercial, mixed or public service oriented (Norris 2000b). The predominance of almost purely commercial television in America is atypical of most democracies. The regulation of campaign ads or party political broadcasts, and systems of campaign finance, also vary substantially across nations. Rather than following the American model, election campaigns in different post-industrial societies continue to display striking differences. The rise of television-dominated, personality-driven, and money-driven campaigns, often seen as characteristic features of the "Americanization" of campaigning, has probably gone further in Italy, Venezuela, and Israel, for example, than in Britain, Germany, and Sweden. National case studies suggest complex and varied patterns of campaigning worldwide, rather than a simple and uniform process of "Americanization."

Instead this chapter has proposed that the major developments can be understood as a process of *modernization* with campaigns evolving through the premodern, modern, and postmodern stages. These changes did not displace local constituency activity, as the ritual of canvassing and leafleting continues in many countries characterized by mass-branch party organizations. Dedicated party volunteers and candidates continue to engage in the day-to-day activity of organizing, canvassing, leafleting, telephone polling, and mobilizing support. Nevertheless, due to new technology, central campaign headquarters can now tightly coordinate even such local activities. Many of the features of premodern campaigns also continue in the United States; retail face-to-face politics remains important for presidential candidates in the Iowa caucus and the New Hampshire primary, as well as in local and state races. In the same way, the printed press remains a vital channel of political communications, particularly in newspaper-centric societies characterized by high readership. Nevertheless, the primary focus of campaign activities shifted during the 1950s towards national television news and then subsequently into a wide range of venues like talk shows, Internet websites, and cable stations in a more fragmented electronic environment. The shift towards the "postmodern" campaign has moved towards the permanent campaign, in which the techniques of electioneering become intertwined with those of governing.

7

The Dynamics of Electoral Participation

MARK N. FRANKLIN

Participation is the lifeblood of democracy, involving different numbers of people in different activities at different times. Maintaining viable party organizations requires the commitment of a few people over a considerable period. Campaigning, lobbying, or protesting require a greater commitment by more people, but over a shorter period. Voting requires a minimum commitment for a brief period, but involves by far the greatest number of people. In a book primarily about elections it seems natural to focus on voting. Indeed, the health of a democracy is often seen in terms of its level of turnout.

This chapter starts by examining variations in voting turnout by country, variations over time, and variations by social characteristics. In seeking to explain these variations we consider three theories that have dominated research in this area since the start of behavioral political studies—one based on individual resources, one based on political mobilization, and one based on instrumental motivation. The central argument in this chapter is that *instrumental motivation*, largely determined by the context in which elections are held, has been unduly neglected yet plays a critical role in driving variations in electoral turnout. The salience of elections, the use of compulsory voting and postal voting, and the presence of a highly competitive party system provide the most plausible explanations of cross-national differences in voting turnout because these influence the costs and benefits of casting a ballot.

However, it is not enough to be able to explain the differences between countries in average turnout. Any such explanation is incomplete if it cannot also explain changes in turnout within countries from one election to the next. This is a chapter about the dynamics of electoral participation. It demonstrates that the same variables accounting for country differences also account for a large part of the differences in turnout that occur with the passage of time. In over-time perspective we focus on aspects of the competitiveness of the electoral situation—the closeness of the race and the likelihood that one party will win control of the legislature—as prime candidates for explaining turnout variations.

We measure turnout, except in the United States, in terms of the number of those voting as a percentage of registered voters. In the United States the denominator in the calculation is derived from the voting age population.[1] In studying turnout, we will use three different data sets: one containing survey responses from individuals living in 23 countries in the early 1990s, another containing cross-sectional data relating to average turnout between 1960 and 1985 in an overlapping set of 31 countries, and a third containing time-series data relating to turnout in the successive elections conducted in each of these 31 countries between 1945 and 1999.

Turnout in democracies

We can begin by comparing turnout in 40 democracies. Table 7.1 shows average turnout in these countries (ordered by turnout) at free elections for the lower house conducted between 1960 and 1999, along with the number of elections upon which each average is based.[2] Countries marked with † in Table 7.1 are countries for which we have obtained survey data from the early 1990s. These countries are used in the individual-level analyses reported later in this chapter. Countries marked with # in Table 7.1 are countries for which systemic characteristics have been compiled by Katz (1997). These countries are used in the country-level analyses reported later in this chapter. Since the systemic characteristics are reported by Katz for the period 1960–85, turnout in the country-level analyses is also restricted to that period. The period is one of stability in electoral arrangements impacting significantly on turnout, which makes it a convenient window in which to look at the country-level effects of independent variables.[3] Later in the chapter we will analyze data for free elections conducted between 1945 and 1999 in these countries. Because those data are presented in the context of an over-time analysis, changes in the characteristics of particular countries can be accommodated. The overlapping data sets provide a picture of electoral participation across a wide variety of political systems, including those with emerging and established democratic institutions, parliamentary and presidential systems, and very different electoral and party systems.

Turnout has varied somewhat over the 50 years since the end of the Second World War. Figure 7.1 plots average turnout for elections grouped into five-year intervals for 23 of the countries marked with # in Table 7.1 (all except Argentina, Brazil, Chile, Costa Rica, India, Portugal, Spain, and Venezuela, for which the series does not extend back to the 1940s). The solid line on that graph shows what appears to be a precipitous decline in turnout, starting in the late 1960s; however, too much should not be made of this. In the first place, turnout during the late 1960s was at a historically high point, as Topf (1995) has pointed out. In the second place,

TABLE 7.1 *Average Turnout (%) in Free Elections to the Lower House in 40 Countries, 1961–1999*

Australia (16)#	95	Greece (11)#[†]	82	Spain (7)#[†]	74
Malta (9)#	94	Netherlands (9)#[†]	82	Bulgaria (3)[†]	73
Belgium (13)#[†]	92	Brazil (9)#	81	Ireland (12)#[†]	73
Italy (10)#[†]	90	Venezuela (8)#	81	Japan (12)#	69
Austria (11)#	90	Norway (10)#	81	Estonia (4)[†]	68
Iceland (11)#[†]	89	Costa Rica (10)#	80	India (10)#	59
Luxembourg (8)#	89	Israel (11)#	80	Russia (3)[†]	58
Sweden (12)#	88	Latvia (4)[†]	79	Hungary (6)[†]	57
New Zealand (12)#	87	Portugal (10)#[†]	77	Switzerland (9)#	52
Denmark (15)#[†]	86	Romania (2)[†]	76	United States (9)#[†]	52
Germany (11)#[†]	86	Finland (11)#	76	Poland (4)[†]	51
Argentina (13)#	83	Canada (12)#	75	Lithuania (2)[†]	50
Czech Republic (4)[†]	83	United Kingdom (10)#[†]	75		
Chile (7)#	83	France (10)#[†]	75		

NOTES: US presidential election years only, Dutch elections only from 1968, elsewhere from 1945 or the earliest democratic elections. The number of elections included in each average is in parentheses.

\# Included in country-level data set (31 countries).

[†] Included in individual-level data set (23 countries).

SOURCES: Mackie and Rose (1991); Katz (1997); *Electoral Studies* (vols 5–19)

the amount of change is greatly exaggerated by the scale used to plot the solid line (on the right-hand side of the graph). The broken line at the top of the graph gives a more balanced perspective by presenting the decline on a scale that has zero as its minimum (on the left-hand side of the graph). In fact, the net change in turnout between 1945 and 1999 is only 4.4 percentage points—a very small amount compared to the differences between countries shown in Table 7.1. Nevertheless, we will give consideration to the apparent decline in turnout when we later investigate the reasons for turnout change.

Who participates?

Tables 7.1 and 7.2 show turnout variations between countries and across the social characteristics of individuals. The most striking message is that turnout varies much more from country to country than it does between different types of individuals. It matters whether one is rich or poor, educated or uneducated, interested in politics or not; but none of these things matters nearly as much as whether one is an Australian or an American. Five countries show turnout averaging 90% or more, while six show turnout averaging 50–60%—an average difference across these 11 countries of nearly 40%. No difference in turnout levels across categories of individuals averages more than two-thirds as much. The strongest

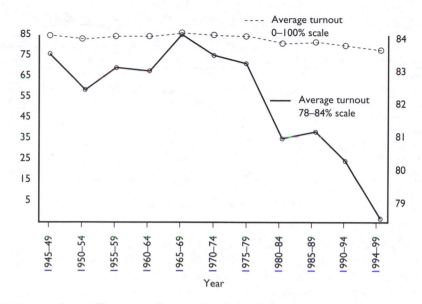

FIGURE 7.1   *Average Turnout over Five-year Periods for 23 Countries since 1945*

individual-level effect that might be subject to manipulation—political discussion—averages only 13% (83.1 less 69.7 in Table 7.2). Individual-level differences are very similar across Eastern and Western Europe, though greater in the United States where education accounts for a 41% difference in turnout levels, while age, income, and political discussion have effects that exceed 30%. Only the first of these differences even comes close to matching the difference between the United States and the high-turnout countries (but see note 4).

To make it clear that within-country effects never approach between-country effects, the final columns of Table 7.2 compare the variance explained by particular variables with that explained by country differences in a two-way analysis of variance. Only three variables have more than a tenth of the explanatory power of country differences and only one has more than a fifth (that one being age, a variable hardly subject to manipulation).

This comparison suggests that if one wants to increase electoral participation in a low-turnout country, the answer lies not in increasing levels of education or prevalence of political discussion of the citizens of that country—the only individual-level characteristics that appear amenable to manipulation. Even if everyone in the United States were college educated, for example, this would not bring turnout there even to levels found in medium-turnout countries such as Britain.[4] Of course the effect of education might be additive with effects of political interest, party identification, and other variables so as to cumulatively raise turnout considerably; or the

TABLE 7.2   *Average Turnout (%) for Different Groups of Individuals in 23 Countries*

Variable (no of categories)	Average turnout in group with		Variance explained by	
	Lowest turnout	Highest turnout	Individual effects	Country effects
Age (5)	58.8	88.9	6.3	9.9
Political discussion (2)	69.7	83.1	2.1	9.9
Party identification (4)	70.1	89.2	1.6	9.9
Religious participation (3)	76.3	83.0	0.7	9.9
Education (2)	73.8	86.1	0.6	9.9
Union membership (2)	76.8	81.6	0.3	9.9
Income (5)	75.4	89.2	0.3	9.9
N	21,601	21,601	21,601	21,601

NOTE: Countries included in this table are marked [†] in Table 7.1.

SOURCE: Eurobarometer 41a; US National Election Study 1988; East European Barometer 2

effects of those other variables might be largely subsumed by education. This question can only be evaluated by means of multivariate analysis (see below). In the meantime, our preliminary findings clearly imply that to increase the level of turnout in the United States, India, or Switzerland, we need to establish what factors make people more likely to participate in some countries than in others, and then see whether these factors can be imported by the low turnout countries (cf. Powell 1986).

Why participate?

Although a great many theories have been proposed to explain variations in political participation, these essentially boil down to explanations involving three different features that distinguish people from one-another: *resources, mobilization,* and the desire to affect the course of public policy (what we shall call *instrumental motivation*). Resources are what people individually bring to the democratic process: knowledge, wealth, and time. Mobilization is the heightened awareness of their role that can be inculcated in people through the operations of the media, parties, and groups. Instrumental motivation is the sense that individuals may have that their actions (at least taken in concert with the actions of other individuals who share the same concerns) might affect an election outcome.

Of these, the resource theory of political participation has been most widely studied. According to this theory, people participate who have the skills, time, and money to do so (Verba and Nie 1972). The trouble with this approach is that it cannot explain the large differences in turnout that exist between countries. We have already seen that differences in turnout by levels of education and income are less than differences in turnout by country. Moreover, high turnout countries do not have richer or more educated people than low turnout countries. Indeed two of the richest and most highly educated countries (Switzerland and the United States) are among the lowest in terms of turnout.

Taking account of the activities of groups and organizations (especially unions and political parties) has recently gained prominence in studies of political participation (Rosenstone and Hansen 1993; Verba, Schlozman, and Brady 1995; Gray and Caul 2000). However, variations in mobilizing activities do not go far towards remedying the problems of the resource approach. According to Rosenstone and Hansen (1993), citizens (even those with most resources) are more likely to participate if encouraged to do so, and one source of encouragement comes from efforts made to "get out the vote." Yet in European countries, at least in the context of the European elections of 1989, country differences in mobilizing activities are smaller even than country differences in education or political interest.[5]

Both the resource and the mobilization theories indirectly address the instrumental motivations of citizens to affect the course of public policy. Those whose education and experience lead them to feel politically efficacious will vote because they are motivated to do so; and those who are mobilized to vote are evidently motivated by this mobilization (Verba, Schlozman, and Brady 1995). The role of the election *contest* as a source of instrumental motivation, however, has often been neglected by scholars who focus on the behavior of individuals. Among scholars who study differences between countries, on the other hand, the importance of institutional and contextual differences in affecting turnout has been a major theme in the literature of political participation since the earliest studies (Tingsten 1937; Powell 1980, 1986; Crewe 1981; Jackman 1987; Jackman and Miller 1995); and a link can be made between institutions and motivations if we consider differences between elections in how much is at stake (van der Eijk, Franklin, et al. 1996: ch. 19). An election that does not decide the disposition of executive power (an election for the European Parliament or a US midterm election, for example) can be expected to prove less important (and therefore less likely to motivate voter turnout) than a national election in Europe, or an American presidential election. If executive power is at stake, then we would expect that more people will turn out—especially if the election is a close one, the outcome seems likely to determine the course of public policy, and there are large perceived differences between policy alternatives. For example, the unprecedentedly high turnout in the 1992 Louisiana gubernatorial primary contested by the former Klu Klux Klan member David Duke shows the possible consequences in terms of turnout of an election whose outcome is expected to be close and whose protagonists arouse strong feelings. This also means that an electoral system that ensures no votes are wasted will presumably motivate more people to vote; and that a country like Switzerland, where the outcome of parliamentary elections has no discernible policy implications (because the same coalition will take office whatever the outcome and all important policy decisions are in any case subject to referendum) will see lower turnout than a country like Malta, where the fact that there is a unicameral legislature with no other level of government (no mayors, no local government) means that every important political decision hangs on the outcome of a single electoral contest (Hirczy 1995). Of course, the mobilization approach can also to some extent take account of differing electoral contexts since important elections will stimulate more electoral activity by parties and candidates; but the instrumental approach subsumes such activities. A contest that stimulates voters to turn out in large numbers will evidently also stimulate parties and candidates to redouble their efforts to obtain the participation of those who might still stay at home.

In brief, the instrumental approach to understanding electoral participation is superior to the other two common approaches because it largely subsumes them both, while explaining additional aspects that neither of the other approaches can address. Indeed, this approach is the only one that makes sense when we focus on the importance of the electoral context in conditioning people's motivations; and only differences in context show promise of explaining country differences in turnout.

Nevertheless, the fact that instrumental motivation has mainly to do with the benefits of voting should not blind us to the fact that voting also involves costs. Countries may differ not only in terms of how important elections seem to voters but also in terms of how difficult it is to vote. Later we will describe some relevant ways in which countries differ from each other in these respects, but first we need to validate what so far has merely been suggested: that what matters in explaining turnout are differences between countries not differences between individuals.

Effects on individual-level electoral participation

We saw earlier that differences between types of individual in terms of turnout were generally much less than differences between countries. The implication of that finding was that individual-level differences have less effect than country-level differences. This implication can be more formally confirmed if we conduct a multivariate analysis that attempts to explain individual-level electoral participation on the basis of demographic and other characteristics of individuals, and contrast the effects with those that can be seen when the country contexts in which individuals find themselves are taken into account. Such an analysis can assess the cumulative effects of many attributes at once, in contrast to our earlier descriptive approach.

A great many variables have been suggested as determining the resources that individuals bring to the participatory context and the success of parties in mobilizing these voters to turn out. In the data available to us for 23 countries (those of Western and Eastern Europe, together with the United States), relatively few variables are included that are relevant to electoral mobilization—only strength of party identification and extent of

TABLE 7.3 *Effects on Individual-level Electoral Participation in 23 Countries*

Variable (no. of categories)	Individual level only		With national effects considered		With missing data indicators	
	b	SE	b	SE	b	SE
Constant	0.636	(0.017)*	0.065	(0.022)	0.069	(0.022)
Age (5)	0.064	(0.002)*	0.063	(0.002)*	0.062	(0.002)*
Political discussion (2)	0.097	(0.006)*	0.091	(0.006)*	0.093	(0.006)*
Strength of party identification (4)	0.010	(0.004)	0.040	(0.004)*	0.039	(0.004)*
Religious participation (3)	0.008	(0.004)	0.024	(0.005)*	0.030	(0.004)*
Education (2)	0.005	(0.003)	0.025	(0.003)*	0.025	(0.003)*
Union member (2)	−0.081	(0.006)*	-0.023	(0.006)*	−0.024	(0.006)*
Income (standardized)	0.001	(0.001)	0.004	(0.009)*	0.004	(0.001)*
Average country effect (proportion)			0.478	(0.017)*	0.489	(0.017)*
Missing religious participation (2)					−0.041	(0.009)*
Adjusted R^2	0.055		0.195		0.195	
N	21,601		21,601		21,601	

NOTE: Countries included in this table are marked [†] in Table 7.1.
*$p<0.001$.

SOURCE: See Table 7.2

political discussion might be construed as variables that would make voters responsive to mobilizing efforts. However, other analysis of specifically West European data (van der Eijk, Franklin, et al. 1996) has shown that campaign mobilization contributed less than one-eighth of total individual-level effects on electoral participation; and the resource variables at our disposal do include most of those suggested in past research (cf. Oppenhuis 1995; van der Eijk, Franklin, et al. 1996).

Table 7.3 shows the effects of variables found to have statistically significant (at the 0.001 level) influences on individual-level electoral participation in three separate models: the first where only individual-level influences are considered,[6] the second where these effects are considered within their national contexts,[7] and the third where missing data indicators are taken into account.[8] As can be seen, individual-level characteristics explain only 5.5% of variance in electoral participation. Taking account of national context (in the central column of the table) multiplies this variance explained virtually fourfold. Taking account of missing data adds trivially (but significantly) to variance explained.[9] Effects (b) of the variables included in the table are readily interpretable. The important finding is the extent to which national context (indicated in the table by average country effects) exceeds in importance the effects of individual-level variables. This is shown not only in terms of variance explained but also in the size of the average country effect. Explicating these country differences is the purpose of the next section.

Country differences in the costs
and benefits of voting

We have already suggested that the extent to which policy outputs are expected to depend on an election outcome will be important in determining both the costs of failing to vote and the benefits of voting. Our example was Switzerland—a country where election results for the lower house are hardly linked to the political complexion of the executive. Another country with tenuous linkage between legislative election outcomes and government complexion is the United States, where the separation of powers ensures that even if a party wins control of the legislature it will not necessarily be able to put its preferred policies into force. In these two countries public policy outputs evidently rest on many imponderables—for example, interest group lobbying in the United States and referenda in Switzerland—that have nothing to do with the outcome of legislative elections (cf. Hirczy 1992), reducing the stakes of such elections (and hence the benefits of voting) compared to what they would be in systems where the linkage was tighter.[10] A second feature of the electoral context that we have suggested will differentiate low-turnout countries from others is the number of electoral contests that are held. A country with federal as well as state elections, and frequent referenda (or propositions) is likely to see lower turnout than other countries. This feature will be hard for us to separate in practice from poor legislative/executive linkage, because the two countries in our data with least evident linkage between legislative electoral outcomes and government complexion are the same two countries (the United States and Switzerland) that have the largest number by far of electoral contests.[11] Because of the coincidence that these two countries are the only ones with both these reasons for low turnout, we cannot readily disentangle the two influences, and in the analyses conducted in this chapter we thus take both effects together, indicating their presence by means of a dummy variable (which we refer to as "electoral salience" in the tables that follow) that picks out these two countries in contradistinction to all others. A third factor of the electoral context is the total size of the electorate, with votes perhaps counting for more in small countries like Malta than in large countries like the United States and especially India (Radcliff 1992).

Another variable already proposed as contributing to the benefits of voting is the proportionality of the electoral system (Blais and Dobrzynska 1990; Franklin, van der Eijk, and Oppenhuis 1996). A country with single-member districts and a winner-takes-all electoral system will be one in which a large number of electoral contests have foregone conclusions because one candidate is known to be virtually certain of winning. People are less likely to vote in such contests, so overall turnout will be lower than in countries where a proportional electoral system ensures that fewer votes are wasted. In this research we measure disproportionality rather than proportionality, and do so according to the average votes/seats ratio, calculated over all parties in each country (data from Mackie and Rose 1991).[12]

A series of important variables have to do with the competitiveness of the electoral situation at the time of an election. As already mentioned, turnout is likely to be higher when a close race makes people feel that every vote counts (Jackman 1987; Blais and Dobrzynska 1990; Jackman and Miller 1995) and turnout is likely to be higher if the most recent previous election is some time in the past (Boyd 1981; LeDuc, Chapter 3 above).[13] Although not previously suggested, one aspect of competition at election time is how close the leading party is to obtaining an absolute majority. Evidently, if the largest party will be able to govern alone there is more reason to expect it to be able to put its policies into effect. A party that needs the support of other parties in order to govern is likely to have to compromise its policies, making the stakes of even a close election lower.[14] Rather different reasoning leads us to suppose that a party that has much more than majority support will fail to draw people to the polls to the extent of a party whose expected support is close to 50%. If a party is a clear winner then the stakes of the election are lower and fewer people can be expected to vote. These three variables—margin of victory, time since the previous election, and majority status (the absolute difference between a party's vote share and 50%)—are more likely to be powerful predictors in over-time perspective. However, to the extent that countries differ in the average values of these variables we may also find them playing a role in the explanation of cross-country turnout variations; and, in fact, countries do vary from 3% to 26% in terms of the average deviation of the largest party from 50%, and between 2% and 23% in terms of the average margin of victory, quite enough to yield significant effects of these variables even averaged over time. Average time since the last election, however, varies only between 2 and 5 years. The fact that really short periods between elections are so rare that they are "averaged out" in cross-country perspective means that this variable is likely to show its power only in over-time perspective.

Several potentially important variables have not yet been mentioned. Whether voter registration is automatic (as in most countries) or voluntary (as in the United States, France, and some Latin American countries) will make a difference to the number of people registered to vote and hence able to respond to a late awareness of an election's importance to them. Voluntary voter registration is the reason customarily given for low turnout in US elections (Piven and Cloward 1977; Wolfinger and Rosenstone 1980; Crewe 1981).[15] Whether the election occurs on a weekend or working day should evidently affect the ease with which working people can vote (Crewe 1981). In many countries compulsory voting provides an incentive to vote (even if the penalties for non-voting are nominal) and most previous studies have included this variable, while in some countries advance voting or postal voting will make it easier to obtain the participation of those away from their homes due to employment and other reasons (though this variable has only been tested across countries in the previous edition of this chapter).

Effects of country differences on turnout

Across the countries for which we have adequate data, the country characteristics we have posited as being important prove somewhat sensitive to precisely which countries are included. This can be seen in Table 7.4, which displays the findings from three different analyses. The first focuses on the 25 countries included in Mackie and Rose's *International Almanac of Electoral History* (1991)—the only countries for which we have complete data on all the variables. The second adds another six countries for which we have most but not all of the relevant data.[16] The third repeats this analysis with Switzerland and the United States omitted.

The first two models explain a highly respectable 95 and 93% of variance in turnout, but time since the last election and the size of the electorate did not prove significant in the first of them. Eight other variables are significant in both models. Of these, by far the most potent is electoral salience. Salient elections give rise to some 30% greater turnout than non-salient elections. Because of the nature of this variable our findings are driven by the low turnout in Switzerland and the United States together with a plausible but unproven supposition about the reason for the anomalous turnout in these countries. These countries are omitted from the third model, with the consequence that salience plays no role in explaining turnout, but the remaining coefficients are little changed and variance explained remains high at 90%. In the next section we will report the results of an independent test of the importance of electoral salience in determining turnout, but first we should list the other variables that help to distinguish one country from another.

Compulsory voting, postal voting, weekend voting, and the proportionality of the electoral system between them can have an impact approaching that of electoral salience. Compulsory voting apparently increases turnout by about 6–7% in countries that make voting obligatory. Postal voting is worth another 5–6%. (Dis)proportionality is worth about half a percentage point in turnout for every per cent by which the distribution of seats in the legislature approaches proportionality with the distribution of votes. Countries vary in terms of the proportionality of their electoral systems from a low of 79 in Britain to a high of 99 in Germany; that is a twenty point difference which (multiplied by 0.5) translates into a difference of about 10% in turnout. Sunday voting is worth 6–7%. Finally, from among the independent variables that will have remained relatively constant over the 25-year period investigated in this table, size of the electorate proves to have a slight effect of 0.03 to 0.04 per million voters (though this effect is significant only when the universe of countries is extended beyond those included in the Mackie–Rose *Almanac*). When considering the difference in size of electorates between Malta and India, this effect could translate into differences of as much as 8% in turnout, but most countries would not be much affected.

Turning to the three variables whose values are not generally fixed, two of these (majority status and margin of victory) show quite strong

TABLE 7.4   *Three Models Explaining Turnout in 25–31 Countries, 1960–1985*

Variable (range of values)	Mackie–Rose		31 countries		No Switzerland or United States	
	b	SE	b	SE	b	SE
Constant	61.07	(5.57)**	62.80	(4.54)**	88.11	(5.18)**
Majority status (3–26%)	−0.21	(0.09)*	−0.23	(0.10)*	−0.16	(0.10)*
Margin of victory (2–23%)	−0.26	(0.13)*	−0.33	(0.12)**	−0.22	(0.13)*
Time since last election (2–5yr)	−1.41	(1.11)	−1.85	(0.95)*	−0.98	(1.08)
Disproportionality (0–20%)	−0.57	(0.13)**	−0.51	(0.13)**	−0.50	(0.13)**
Compulsory voting (0,1)	7.36	(1.93)**	5.56	(1.51)**	7.15	(1.82)**
Postal voting (0,1)	6.08	(1.41)**	5.29	(1.45)**	5.81	(1.34)**
Weekend voting (0,1)	5.60	(1.75)**	6.81	(1.47)**	6.06	(1.67)**
Size of electorate (million)	−0.03	(0.03)	−0.04	(0.01)**	−0.08	(0.04)*
Electoral salience (0,1)	29.56	(3.18)**	29.54	(2.98)**		
Adjusted R^2	0.949		0.929		0.897	
N	25		31		29	

NOTE: Countries included in this analysis are marked # in Table 7.1.
*$p<0.05$, one-tailed; **$p<0.01$, one-tailed.
SOURCE: Analysis of data from Mackie and Rose (1991); Katz (1997); *Electoral Studies* (vols 5–19)

effects of 0.2 to 0.4, giving rise to turnout differences of 4–8% given average differences between countries in these two characteristics reported earlier. Time since the last election proves (barely) significant only when all 31 countries are included in the analysis, presumably because (as already mentioned) countries do not in practice differ very much from each other on average in terms of this variable. Evidently, when we come to deal with specific elections, rather than averages over a series of elections, the effects of this variable could prove much stronger.

On the basis of these findings we can assert (as we have elsewhere, see van der Eijk, Franklin, et al. 1996) that there are many routes to high turnout. Electoral salience is most important, but cross-sectional findings suggest that even a country with low salience elections might raise turnout to 80% or more by means of compulsory voting, a highly proportional electoral system, postal voting, and weekend polling—especially if it was a country that also tended to have close elections between parties that stand a real chance of gaining a majority of the votes. However, we will see in a later section that, when these variables are indeed allowed to vary over time, not all of them have the effects that cross-sectional analysis would lead us to expect.

One proposed variable did not yield significant effects in any of the analyses. Voluntary voter registration does not seem to reduce turnout.[17] This finding may come as a surprise to those who have assumed that low turnout in the United States can be largely attributed to this factor. Yet it is not possible that the factor has simply been included within the effects of low salience. Not only does Switzerland not have voluntary voter registration, but several other countries do have this attribute. So our research design should have succeeded in detecting any general effect of voluntary voter registration. It failed to do so, reinforcing suggestions made elsewhere that the effects of this variable, even in the United States, may be less than had been supposed (see note 15).

Later we will return to the analysis reported above in order to elaborate it in over-time perspective, employing free elections conducted since 1945. But first we need to validate our assumptions about the importance of electoral salience.

Effects of the nature of the electoral contest on turnout

We have pointed out that the most powerful influence reported in Table 7.4 has not been unambiguously identified. Switzerland and the United States may indeed be low turnout countries because of low electoral salience, but not unless we can show that electoral salience does affect turnout. One way to validate our assumption about the centrality of electoral salience is to establish its operation in a different context. While there might be some question as to whether elections in Switzerland and the United States are of lower salience than elsewhere, there is little dispute among scholars that elections to the European Parliament are of lower salience than national elections in European countries. The difference between the two types of elections is supposedly due to the fact that national executive power is not at stake in elections to the European Parliament (Reif and Schmitt 1980; Reif 1985; van der Eijk, Franklin, et al. 1996) any more than it is in Swiss or US legislative elections. But European Parliament elections have an additional feature that makes them particularly suited to investigating the importance of electoral salience: they occur at different times in relation to elections in which national political power is at stake.[18]

Analysis of votes cast in European elections held at different points in the national election cycle has validated the assumption that time until the next national election can be employed as a surrogate for electoral salience (van der Eijk, Franklin, et al. 1996: 301–2). The validation did not involve a study of turnout variations. Instead it looked at the parties voters chose to support. The theory was that in elections of lowest salience—those occurring immediately after national elections—voters would have no reason to vote other than for their most favored party. Such elections have no role even as barometers of opinion, because better indicators of the standing of political parties already exist in the results of the recent national elections. However, as those most recent elections fade into the past, commentators and politicians become interested in the outcome even of elections that do not decide the allocation of political power—simply as markers of what might happen in national elections. The resulting media attention gives them more salience for voters too. The additional salience of these elections in such circumstances is attested to by the increasing tendency of voters to vote other than for their preferred party: indeed, to vote tactically in such a way as to signal their displeasure (if any) with the performance of the party they really prefer, or to signal their approval of parties they would never support in real elections (van der Eijk, Franklin et al. 1996, 302).

In other words, even European elections become useful as vehicles for transmitting information from voters to leaders as they occur later in the electoral cycle. At such times turnout should be higher because the elections have greater salience; and it has been shown (van der Eijk, Franklin, et al. 1996: 317–18) that in European elections held at the start of the electoral cycle (as much as 5 years before the next national election in some countries) turnout will be 18% lower than turnout in European elections held on the same day as national elections. This finding does not prove that electoral salience is the variable that chiefly accounts for low turnout in the United States and Switzerland, but it does confirm the importance of electoral salience—a necessary condition for our assumption to hold. So it adds plausibility to our assumption about the distinctiveness of Switzerland and the United States without definitively ruling out other possible explanations.

Effects on turnout variations over time

Turnout not only varies between countries but also over time (which is to say within each country from one election to the next). If the theoretical approach we have adopted in this chapter is correct, these variations should be largely explicable on the basis of changes in the importance of successive elections to voters. Of course, the most important variable that changes from election to election in one country—the policy stakes of what is at issue—is a variable not readily measured in comparative perspective (but see below). However, to the extent that countries alter their electoral arrangements (adopting or discarding compulsory voting, or changing the day of the week on which elections are held, for example), these changes should give rise to turnout variations. Moreover, three variables whose average levels were already employed for differentiating between countries (majority status, the closeness of the race, and time since the most recent election) do vary considerably in practice from one election to the next. When races are tight, and when one party has a good chance of winning a majority in its own right (especially if it is a long time since the most recent previous election), we can expect turnout to be higher than when the most recent election was very recent, when the race is a foregone conclusion, or when the largest party will need to share power in a coalition government (if, indeed, it holds power at all).[19]

Determining the importance of different variables in conditioning turnout variations over time is complicated by the fact that successive elections in one country are not really independent events. A high turnout

TABLE 7.5   *Two Models Explaining Turnout Variations in 31 Countries, 1945–1999*

Variable	Within country		Panel corrected	
	b	SE	b	SE
Constant	25.06	(3.93)**	52.63	(2.14)**
Majority status (0–50%)	−0.13	(0.04)**	−0.16	(0.04)**
Margin of victory (0–70%)	−0.06	(0.04)*	−0.08	(0.03)**
Time since last election (0.6–5)	0.52	(0.18)**	0.37	(0.14)**
Disproportionality (1–20)	−0.01	(0.04)	−0.06	(0.04)
Compulsory voting (0,1)	5.99	(1.99)**	10.92	(0.76)**
Postal voting (0,1)	4.07	(1.96)**	6.79	(0.84)**
Weekend voting (0,1)	−1.57	(0.89)	−0.26	(0.54)
Size of electorate (million)	−0.01	(0.01)	−0.04	(0.01)**
Electoral salience (0,1)			25.46	(2.06)**
Turnout_{t-1}	0.66	(0.04)**		
Missing margin (0,1)	−5.59	(1.66)**	−5.89	(1.58)**
Adjusted R^2	0.506		0.709	
N	403		436	

NOTE: Countries included in this table are marked # in Table 7.1.

*$p < 0.05$, one-tailed **$p < 0.01$, one-tailed.

SOURCE: Mackie and Rose (1991); *Electoral Studies* (vols 5–19); Katz (1997, Table 13.3)

country will tend to have high turnout at all elections, and vice versa for low turnout countries. Treating each election as an independent event when it is not can greatly bias the estimates we make of the effects of independent variables and grossly overestimate their importance. On the other hand, taking explicit account of over-time dependencies by using a lagged version of the dependent variable as an additional independent variable (as we do in the first of the models we present below) can attenuate the effects of independent variables, attributing to consistency some of what actually is the result of independent variables having the same effects again and again. Alternatively, we can deal with the lack of independence of successive elections by treating each country as a panel and correcting the analysis for within-panel homogeneity. By presenting both these models we hope to demonstrate that our findings are in fact very robust: we reach much the same conclusions whichever way we deal with the problem of lack of independence between successive elections.

Table 7.5 shows the effects of the same independent variables as were employed in Table 7.4, but this time uses them to explain turnout variations in over-time perspective at free elections conducted in 31 countries between 1945 and 1999.[20] The first model does a quite respectable job of explaining turnout variations by incorporating turnout at the previous election as one of the predictors (thereby focusing on change in turnout from one election to the next). This model explains over half the variance in turnout change on average across countries. The second model does rather better by making the adjustments needed for treating each successive election as an independent replication of the test for significant effects on turnout in each country, obviating the need to include a lagged version of the dependent variable.[21]

Evidently, taking account of turnout variations over time somewhat changes the picture that we got when we considered only differences between countries. In particular, weekend voting and the proportionality of the electoral system have effects that are much reduced in over-time perspective (to the point where these effects are not significant in either model). Evidently countries that move to or from Sunday voting do not thereby clearly increase or reduce their turnout, as might have been expected from the cross-sectional findings. Equally, countries that increase or reduce pro-portionality in the conversion of votes into legislative seats do not see turnout clearly responding to this change. These two findings are somewhat surprising. They suggest that the cross-sectional effects of these variables are perhaps spurious, capitalizing on chance differences between countries rather than being indicative of a real effect of proportionality or of opening the polls on weekends. Alternatively, at least when considering Sunday voting, perhaps the changes in this norm mainly took place quite recently, at a time when the meaning of the Sabbath (and its implications for turnout in Sunday elections) has fundamentally changed. Other variables appear to have very much the same effects in over-time perspective as they have cross-sectionally, even size of the electorate, whose effects remain slight and inconclusive in over-time perspective.[22]

Most interestingly, the effects of variables that do change over time are confirmed in this analysis. Time since the last election reduces turnout by close to half of a per cent for each year that a government cuts short its term of office. Margin of victory reduces turnout by about one-tenth of a percentage point for each 1% that the leading party runs ahead of its major competitor. The majority status of the leading party (how close it comes to gaining 50% of the votes) is also important, taking about one-sixth of a percentage point from turnout for each 1% that the largest party deviates from 50%. So a country whose leading party loses support to the extent of dropping from 50 to 32% of votes will show a decrease in turnout of about 3%, while a 10% lead over its nearest competitor will reduce turnout by a further 1%. Quite normal changes in these three variables from election to election will easily cause turnout fluctuations of 5% or more.

Turnout decline?

Much has been made in recent years of the supposed decline of turnout, and books and articles with titles like *The Disappearing American Voter* (Teixeira 1992) or "Exploring Declining Turnout in Western European Elections" (Flickinger and Studler 1992) are almost commonplace. In 2000, Harvard University's Kennedy School of Government was home to the "Vanishing Voter Project." We saw in Figure 7.1 that there does seem to have been a decline in turnout since the late 1950s of some 5.4 percentage points, on average, over the 23 countries for which we have over-time data going back that far. But this decline was from a high point in electoral turnout that may well have coincided with a series of important elections (see below). If we measure the recent decline from a base consisting of the 1950–89 average, it is much more modest—only 3.5%, which is considerably less than the accuracy with which we can confidently predict turnout levels.

Elsewhere I have argued (Franklin, Lyons, and Marsh 2000) that the rise and decline of turnout seen in Figure 7.1 can perhaps be understood in terms of the changing salience of elections in established democracies. What we have found in this chapter is that voters respond to differences in the electoral context that make their votes appear more or less important; but we have not been able to measure all such differences. Above all, we have not been able to measure the importance of the issues at stake. However, we do know something about these issues. We know that in established democracies a number of critical elections were held in the late 1950s which largely resolved the long-standing conflict between labor and capital by establishing welfare states in country after country (Franklin, et al. 1992). It seems plausible that the general pattern seen in Figure 7.1 of first a rise and then a fall in turnout reflects the coming and the passing of a peak of interest generated by electoral decisions relating to this conflict. So elections in recent years may see lower turnout for the simple reason that these elections decide issues of lesser importance than elections did in the late 1950s; but until we have some way to measure the substantive importance of electoral contests in terms that are comparable cross-nationally it will not be possible to be definite about this.[23]

Conclusions

In this chapter we have shown that going to the polls is an activity motivated primarily by the desire to affect the course of public policy. It is true that the stick of compulsory voting and the carrot of postal votes do lead more people to vote than otherwise would do so, but the major factors determining turnout—the importance of the electoral contest (what we have called electoral salience) and the likelihood that one's vote will be influential (indicated by the closeness of the race and size of the largest party)—could only operate if people were motivated to use their votes to achieve a political goal.

A country with low salience elections and a party system that was not very competitive can easily show turnout levels 45% below a country with high salience elections and a highly competitive party system. Such differences arise purely from differences in the institutional and political context within which elections are conducted—differences affecting the extent to which a political system will be responsive to the electoral choices made by voters. Voters are not fools, and an unresponsive system will motivate many fewer of them to vote.

It seems likely that voters also respond to the importance of the issues at stake, and on this basis the lower turnout seen in many countries in recent years may well be a symptom of the fact that few great issues are currently being decided at elections in most countries. But the contemporary decline in turnout, if it is even real (see note 1), is much smaller than commentators would often have us believe.

The fact that voters are not fools is also suggested by the extent to which they bypass electoral routes where those routes prove unresponsive. The United States suffers much in terms of turnout from the unresponsive nature of its institutional character;[24] but other research has shown (Verba, Nie, and Kim 1978; Barnes, Kaase, et al. 1979) that the United States is the country (among those for which we have relevant data) in which citizens most frequently turn to non-electoral modes of political participation. This concomitant of low turnout is only speculative, but the conjecture is highly consonant with the instrumental basis of political action that seems so clear in our findings.

NOTES

1. In recent years it has become increasingly common to analyze turnout figures that are based on voting age population for all countries. This procedure has a number of disadvantages. First, these figures are not officially validated and are thus subject to greater error. More importantly, voting age population everywhere includes an unknown but variable number of individuals not eligible to vote. It has been estimated that, in the United States, changes in the denominator used in the conventional calculation of turnout have alone been responsible for all of the apparent turnout decline in that country since 1972 (Mcdonald and Popkin 2000). The denominator used in the calculation of US turnout for this chapter has been corrected for estimated changes in the ineligible portion of the US voting age population (cf. Mackie and Rose 1991: 458).

2. US midterm elections do not respond to the same forces as elections elsewhere, since executive power is not at stake, and so they have been excluded. For the Netherlands, the series starts in 1968, after the abolition of compulsory voting.

3. See Katz 1997, Table 13.3. After 1985 several countries held elections under new electoral systems, adopted weekend voting, or made other changes that would have required us to truncate the series for those countries or include complex interaction terms in our models. Before 1960 there was also a certain lack of stability in regard to these arrangements. The only major changes that occurred during the 1960–85 period was a lowering of the voting age in many countries; but this (contrary to expectations) did not significantly impact turnout (see below).

4. The 41% increment mentioned above would only apply to those who would not otherwise have completed high school (11% of the sample). For 37% of the sample there would be no gain, because they already have a college-level education. The remaining half of the population might find its turnout increased by about 30% if everyone were college educated—an overall gain in turnout of 16%. Add the 4% (one-tenth of 40) from those who now do not even have a high school education, and turnout in the United States might be raised 20% by this stratagem, bringing it to 72%—still 3% below Britain's, and 20% below the level found in high turnout countries.

5. Powell (1986) found significant effects from a variable he termed "group–party linkages" but his data are from the 1960s. By the 1970s such linkages had

declined in many countries (Franklin, et al. 1992) and analysis of turnout in the late 1980s found no remaining trace of this effect (van der Eijk, Franklin, et al. 1996: ch. 19).

6. Because the dependent variable in this analysis is a dichotomy (voted or not), many scholars consider regression analysis to be an inappropriate statistical method. Other work with similar variables (but whose case base was restricted to West European countries) did not indicate any way in which researchers would have been misled by relying on OLS regression (van der Eijk, Franklin, et al. 1996: ch. 19) which, because of the interpretability of its results, is the method employed here.

7. To measure the maximum possible effect of national context, 22 dummy variables were included in the analysis whose results are reported in the second and third columns of Table 7.3—one for each country less one for the base country (the United States in this instance). These variables will encapsulate differences between countries that go beyond anything that can specifically be measured at the national level, but we will see that in practice we can account for some 95% of the variance explained by these variables.

8. In the analyses reported in this chapter, data missing on any variable were replaced by mean values of that variable. Dummy variables were then defined that indicated the presence or absence of missing data for the corresponding substantive variable and included in each analysis as recommended by Cohen and Cohen (1983: 275–300). However, only here and in the analysis reported in Table 7.5 did any such missing data indicators prove significant.

9. Respondents who fail to disclose their extent of religious participation are 4% less likely to vote than those who are willing to disclose this information.

10. The United States has so many unique features as a democracy that it is difficult to attribute low turnout to one of these features in particular. However, if separated powers are bad for turnout then anything that causes powers to become more separated should result in turnout decline. This is found to be the case when divided government is treated as a phenomenon that accentuates the separation of powers (Franklin and Hirczy de Mino 1998).

11. The Swiss are called to the polls on average seven times a year, mainly to render referendum verdicts (see this volume, Chapter 3). Americans face federal, state, or local elections more than twice a year on average (Boyd 1981: 145), less often than the Swiss, but many times more often than anyone else.

12. For countries not included in the Mackie and Rose compendium, this value is estimated from the votes/seats ratio for the largest party in the legislature. In the over-time analyses this variable is measured separately at each election.

13. If frequent elections are bad for turnout then the length of time since the most recent legislative election may well have the same sort of effect. It is well known that when countries have not held free elections for some time (and especially when they have never previously held a free election) turnout is particularly high. Where an election is preceded by a period without regular elections, the variable is coded as one more than the maximum period of time allowed by law between elections in that country.

14. A similar line of reasoning led Jackman (1987) and others (Blais and Dobrzynska 1990; Jackman and Miller 1995) to suppose that the number of parties in a legislature would affect turnout. However, findings from these studies were mixed, and the variable is evidently closely related to the size of the largest party which in our work overrides any effect of the number of parties. Several other variables have been proposed by various authors as likely causes of turnout changes over time, and especially of turnout decline (Powell 1986; Radcliff 1992; Jackman and Miller 1995; Franklin and Hirczy de Mino 1998; van Egmond, de Graaf, and van der Eijk 1998; Blais and Dobrzynska

1990; Wattenberg 2000). However, these are either variables that would only be appropriate for analyzing turnout variations within one country or they have not proved successful in explaining turnout variations in a model as fully specified as the one we employ here (cf. Franklin, Lyons, and Marsh 2000).

15. But see Ayres (1995) and Mitchell and Wlezien (1995) for suggestions that the effects of this variable might have been overstated even in the United States. A study of the effects of "motor voter" and other reforms on turnout in the 1996 US presidential election (Knack 1999) concludes that registration effects are too small (at about 4%) to prove significant in a study such as this one, and in a comparative study similar to ours, Jackman and Miller (1995) failed to find any effect of this variable.

16. Spain and Portugal (which are also included in the first model) did not hold free elections until the late 1970s, and it proved impossible to obtain the necessary statistics for elections held prior to 1958 in Venezuela, 1966 in Brazil, 1967 in India, 1969 in Chile, 1973 in Argentina, or 1974 in Costa Rica.

17. Countries without automatic voter registration that did have compulsory voting were coded as though registration was automatic.

18. This is because elections to the European Parliament occur on a fixed cycle, every five years, whereas elections to national parliaments in most European countries occur when they are called, though with a legal limit on the maximum length of time allowed between elections. This means that European elections occur at different times within the national electoral cycles of different countries, and even at different times within successive electoral cycles in the same country.

19. Note that we do not expect to explain as much variance in an analysis of turnout variations over time as we do in an analysis of turnout variations between countries. In the latter analysis (conducted earlier in this chapter) we average the turnout at successive elections, removing a lot of the variation which, in over-time perspective, does have to be explained.

20. The number of elections for each country varies from 5 to 22. See note 16 for details of countries for which we do not have election data over the full span of years included in this table. In certain Latin American countries we are missing some specific variables for particular elections. Missing data was treated as described in note 8.

21. This analysis employs Prais–Winston regression with panel corrected standard errors to provide significance tests that take account of the structure of the data (Beck and Katz 1995). It also takes account of the (autoregressive) AR(1) process underlying the data (which in the first model is accounted for by the lagged dependent variable).

22. These models all find significant effects of the missing data indicator for the margin of victory variable, which (as it happens) invariably signals missing information about the size of the second largest party (see note 8 for an explanation of this test). This is probably because one reason for failure to report the size of the second largest party would be that it received very few votes— very many fewer than the average for second parties (which is the value assumed when data are missing).

23. The spectacularly low turnout in the 2001 British General Election (which took place after the period covered by analyses in this chapter) appears to have been due to expectations of a foregone conclusion, especially in safe Labour constituencies (Norris 2001). By contrast, the higher than expected turrnout in the US presidential election of November 2000 occurred in a breathtakingly close race. It may be that voters in many countries are responding in greater numbers than in earlier years to variations in the salience of elections. Adding two variables to Model B of Table 7.5—to measure the interaction of margin of

victory and majority status with a measure of time elapsed since 1945—increases variance explained in that model by 1.5%. On this interpretation, the decline of turnout observed in some countries in recent years might be the result of greater responsiveness to the unimportance of certain elections, as well as to the fact that "unimportant" elections are nowadays more frequent.

24. To say it "suffers" from its institutions is to look at things purely from the perspective of electoral turnout. The founding fathers, of course, designed a system that would be unresponsive to the popular will, and their system works pretty much as intended. Our findings suggest that low turnout is an inevitable concomitant.

8

Voting: Choice, Conditioning, and Constraint

WILLIAM L. MILLER and
RICHARD G. NIEMI

The vast empirical literature on electoral behavior has contributed greatly to our understanding of the knowledge, values, and motivations of individual voters. It has increasingly become comparative, at least in the sense of examining elections in multiple countries through a common set of variables or a single theoretical perspective. But insightful as this work has been, it has conveyed a highly individualistic view of voting that overstates the very real but also rather limited significance of voters' choices in democratic politics. More realistic is a model of "constrained and conditioned voters" in which voters' choices are *constrained* by the electoral system and the limited range of voting options available and *conditioned* by the social and geographic context in which voters live and by the way in which politics is presented to them. That does not eliminate voters' freedom of choice, but it restricts it severely— and usually far more severely than voters themselves consciously recognize.

Much of the time, conditioning and constraint are invisible to the voter and almost as invisible to the analyst. The power of electoral systems to aggregate voters' choices in different ways to produce distinct outcomes is a well recognized fact of arithmetic. But the power of electoral and party systems to influence the choices made by the voters themselves only becomes fully obvious when the electoral system is changed or when several electoral systems operate simultaneously. Similarly, that issues are influenced by voters' social contexts and interpreted by the media is well known, but the dependence of voters' choices on what options are presented to them and how they are interpreted becomes fully obvious only when voters are offered new choices or are offered different ranges of choice at different levels of government. As long as the electoral system and the range of voting options remain unchanged, the potential for voter volatility will be underestimated and the individual component of voter decision-making will be overestimated. Conversely, changes in patterns of voting behavior may not reflect changing voters so much as changing constraints (Crewe 1992).

In this chapter, we begin by reviewing the literature that falls conventionally under the heading of voting behaviour—that is, research that uses an individualistic approach. Our primary goal, however, is to call attention to the way in which voters' choices are conditioned by their surroundings and by the media and constrained by electoral and party systems. By bringing together these different strains of research (in the last two sections), we hope to present a fuller, more realistic picture of how voters operate and to begin the integration of "individual-level postulates" with the "institutional environment underpinning mobilization [and choice]" that Scarbrough (2000) and others have called for.

Predispositions

Ignoring for the moment the impact of conditioning and constraint, what factors explain individual voting preferences? Conventionally, they have been divided into two categories: *long-term predispositions* and *short-term factors*. In the metaphor of an electoral battleground, long-term dispositions define the terrain and the balance of forces while short-term factors influence the action. Short-term factors such as (new) issues, (new) candidates, and (variations in) media coverage or the day-to-day performance of parties and politicians can explain voting change. Long-term predispositions reflect voters' more enduring interests, values, and identifications, and these explain the large element of stability in voting preferences.

Interests

Elections, and the resulting distribution of governmental power, help determine the balance of interests between different sectors of society—the center and the periphery, urban and rural residents, rich and poor, men and women, public and private sector workers, and those with different religious, linguistic, racial, or ethnic backgrounds. Consequently, rational if narrowly self-interested voters might vote for policies and parties that further their group's interests. Thus arises social cleavage voting—voting that reflects economic, religious, linguistic, ethnic, and other interests.

Social cleavages in democratic politics have long been a focus of attention and debate. In part, this is because the divisions themselves can be very persistent. Indeed, noting the similarity between social cleavages in the 1920s and 1960s, Lipset and Rokkan (1967) raised the possibility that they might become "frozen," persisting long after the conflicts of interest that originally created them had faded.

But research suggests the ice has now broken. Nieuwbeerta and Ultee (1999) used surveys from 20 Western countries over the half-century

1945–90 to investigate trends in class cleavages (see also Dalton, Chapter 9 below). They found the lowest levels of class voting in the United States and Canada, and the highest in Scandinavia and the UK. But levels of class voting had declined, and declined most where class cleavages had originally been greatest. So by the 1990s, the 20 countries had "slowly converged into a situation where class was relatively unimportant to voting behaviour" (1999: 147). Rising living standards within a country correlated with the decline in class voting. Paradoxically, so did increasing trade union membership, as union membership spread through the ranks of non-manual and professional workers.

Evans (1999) does not dispute the decline in class voting but he does dispute such sociological explanations. In his view, there is too much cross-national variation in the shape and timing of trends in class voting for it to be explained in terms of social change. Detailed case studies argue against the "thesis of declining class distinctiveness derived from processes of social change generic to advanced industrial societies" (1999: 328). Nor, in his view, do different trends in class voting simply reflect varying paths toward modernity or "postmodernity." Instead, Evans emphasizes that voting options are defined by political elites, not just in terms of the available parties but also in terms of the available policies and programs put forward by those parties. His reasoning is echoed by Hout, Manza, and Brooks (1999), who see class dealignment in the United States as driven by changes in the policy appeals of the Democratic and Republican parties, and by Dalton, who notes that parties respond to initial declines in cleavage voting in ways that reinforce the process.

Dalton (1996b) compared not just class cleavages, but also sectarian, religious/secular, urban/rural, and regional cleavages in 18 Western democracies (including Japan), using data from the 1990–91 World Values Survey (see also Chapter 9 below). On average, the religious/secular cleavage was strongest, while class, sectarian, urban/rural, and regional cleavages were significantly weaker but roughly equal to each other in strength. His primary conclusion, however, was that cleavage voting was significantly weaker than in the past. Perhaps as significant as the strength of any particular cleavage was the fact that some countries seemed riven by social cleavages while others were relatively unaffected by them. On average, social cleavage voting was notably strong in Belgium, the Netherlands, and Austria, and notably weak in the United States and Japan. Elsewhere, the balance of the cleavages varied, but their average strength generally remained close to the cross-country average.

Yet we need to think in terms of elites and parties here, too. World Bank data indicate that the Gini Index of inequality stands at 25 in Belgium (as in famously egalitarian Norway, Denmark, and Sweden) but rises to over 40 in the United States—a figure only exceeded in the former Soviet Union and the developing world (World Bank 2000: 238–9). So what is weak in the United States is not social cleavages as such, but only the *expression* of these social cleavages in voting patterns. And that, as Hout,

Manza, and Brooks (1999) remind us, reflects the character of the parties as much as the character of the voters.

Cleavage voting is not in universal and inexorable decline, however. Changing circumstances can stimulate new voting cleavages or reinvigorate old ones. In Britain, Canada, and Spain, constitutional changes have stimulated rather than reduced voting for nationalist or even secessionist parties, at least in regional elections (Hamann 1999; Jones 1999; Miller 1999; Nevitte et al. 1999). In India, the BJP (Bharatiya Janata Party), which was a sectarian fringe party with around 10% of the vote until the 1980s, suddenly advanced to around 30% by 1998 (Mitra and Singh 1999).

The significance of social cleavages can also ebb and flow because of changes in the size of social groups as well as changes in their relevance to political issues. Heath, Jowell, and Curtice (1985) argued that the apparent decline in class voting in Britain reflected changing class sizes rather than changing class behavior—though they now admit (Evans, Heath, and Payne 1999: 100) that there has also been a real decline in class cleavages in Britain. Similarly, Gluchowski and von Wilamowitz-Moellendorff (1998) stress the declining number of union working class members in Germany (see also Boy and Mayer 2000 on France). Conversely, the growth of Hispanics in the United States has increased the significance of that ethnic cleavage (Stanley and Niemi 1999). And immigration into Western Europe has not only prompted the growth of anti-immigrant parties but increased the significance of the immigrant vote (van der Brug, Fennema, and Tillie 2000).

Values

Ideology or values provide an alternative basis for long-term predispositions. Voters may split along enduring ideological or value-dimensions—with or without any expectation of advantage for themselves or for any associated social group. Since voters' value orientations are relatively stable, and parties themselves are historically associated with particular values, such orientations provide a basis for long-term voting predispositions.

In its simplest form ideology can be expressed in terms of a voter's position on a single *left/right* value-dimension. But that often ignores a *nationalist/cosmopolitan values* dimension that contrasts nationalist or parochial versus universalist or cosmopolitan values. And it compounds (and sometimes confuses) two other dimensions: first, an *egalitarian/free-market values* dimension that contrasts egalitarian or socialist versus laissez-faire or free-market values; and second, a *liberal/authoritarian values* dimension that contrasts liberal or libertarian versus traditional or authoritarian values.

Voters who take opposite sides on the egalitarian/free-market dimension are likely to differ on such issues as progressive income tax, universal health-care, public enterprise, and perhaps gender and racial equality as well as class equality, even (reflecting its notoriously biased application) capital punishment. Those who take opposite sides on the liberal/authoritarian dimension are likely to take different sides on issues of policing, censorship, human rights, lifestyles, and personal freedoms.

A single-dimensional analysis in terms of self-assigned labels "left" and "right" often works tolerably well since it combines both the egalitarian and the liberal/authoritarian dimensions. In Britain, and probably most European countries, both egalitarian and liberal voters describe themselves as "on the left" while both anti-egalitarians and authoritarians describe themselves as being "on the right." And at the level of political elites, though not so much among the general public, these two dimensions are correlated: liberal elites tend to be relatively egalitarian and vice versa (Miller, Timpson, and Lessnoff 1996: 100–1, 304). But the two dimensions are conceptually and empirically quite distinct.

These value-dimensions are recognizably similar in different places and at different times although terminologies, definitions, and measurements vary across authors and countries. In the early 1950s, Eysenck (1954) analyzed political attitudes in terms of cross-cutting "radical/conservative" and "tough/tender" values dimensions—roughly equivalent, respectively, to our "egalitarian/free-market" and "liberal/authoritarian" values dimensions. Inglehart (1977) has popularized the term "post-materialism"—essentially a new way of measuring liberal/authoritarian values. Inglehart argued that the peace and prosperity of post-war Western democracies was rapidly satisfying brutish needs for security and allowing new generations to focus on their higher needs—that is, to become more liberal and less authoritarian than their parents and also to put more weight on the liberal/authoritarian dimension when making voting choices. Across eight countries, Dalton (1996a: 96) found a modest drift towards more "post-materialist" values between 1973 and 1990, though the ranking of countries did not correspond to levels of prosperity.

Election surveys have tended to focus on more immediate issues to the relative neglect of value-orientations. Nonetheless, Heath et al. (1991: 175, 198) have constructed scales of "left/right" (egalitarian/free-market) and liberal/authoritarian values and shown that both had statistically significant impacts on voting choice. Palmer's (1995) analysis of Eurobarometer data from 1979 to 1987 indicates that libertarian/authoritarian values were a more powerful determinant of Conservative and Labour support than income throughout that period, and as powerful as occupational class after 1983. A later and much more extensive study of British political values in the 1990s found that voting preferences were strongly affected by both liberal and egalitarian values, though more strongly by the latter. More importantly, once both these value dimensions were taken into account, social cleavages had little or no additional impact on voting preferences (Miller et al. 1996: 438).

Values may provide a particularly significant foundation for voting choice in the absence of strong social cleavages or long-established partisan identities. Toka (1998: 607) argues that "value preferences" provide a "more solid, stable basis [than social cleavages] for enduring partisan attachments, at least in the relatively new democracies" of eastern Europe. Even when elite maneuvering creates different parties at successive elections and therefore prevents values from fostering stable party choices, values can still provide a coherent and continuing basis for voting choice—albeit from a changing menu of parties (Miller and White 1998). In France, as well, it is thought that value preferences, in the form of left–right self-placements, play an especially important role, perhaps even more important than partisan identities (Lewis-Beck 2000: 8–9).

Identifications

Psychological identifications provide yet another basis for long-term predispositions. Here, "psychological identification" means some deeply held and enduring emotional attachment, sometimes without any community of interest or values—or, indeed, any other rational basis. That is, identification can be pure emotion.

In fact, what appears on the surface to be interest-based cleavages is often more identity-based than interest-based. This is most obvious in terms of *religious and ethnic* divisions—divisions that, in the modern world, increasingly reflect little more than identity. Religious divisions, in particular, have often declined from differences of faith to differences of group-interest and in some cases to mere differences of identity. USIA surveys, for example, show that many ex-Soviet Muslims were intensely conscious of their Muslim identity without being able to name the five obligations that define a good Muslim (the "Five Pillars of Islam"). They started with a strong Muslim identity and only gradually learned what it meant to be a Muslim—though very few, even of those who knew their obligations, claimed to practice them (USIA 2000: 14). Many Christians have an equally tenuous grasp of their own professed faith and few could claim to practice it. Observers who visited Polish churches during the late communist period noted that many Poles were willing to assert their Catholic—and Polish—identity by attending Mass, but were "prepared to do no more than attend" (Beeson 1974: 164). Among Western countries, the United States is an exception in this respect, in that church attendance is relatively high and doctrinal awareness and the willingness to apply it with respect to issues such as school prayer and abortion are relatively strong, especially for the Christian Right (Wilcox 2000).

Even class cleavages in voting increasingly reflect mere *class identity*. Indeed, the connection between occupations and self-assigned class is so weak and variable that self-identification with a class can take on a trend in the opposite direction to trends in occupationally defined class. Voters may identify with the occupational class of their parents or neighborhood. Retired voters identify with the occupational class of their middle-age.

Students who do not yet have an occupation, or who temporarily work in bars and burger-outlets, most certainly do not see their current occupation (or lack of it) as defining their class. Thus even class and other "social" cleavages may be primarily psychological.

The more directly political concept of *party identification* was viewed by its proponents as "similar to the concept of religious identification. ... Confessional loyalties and political loyalties often begin with the socializing influence of the family and of others, but they come to be incorporated in the self. The maintenance of rituals becomes important to the person's sense of identity. Over time, the definition of self is extended to include belong-ingness within the group" (Miller 1976: 22).

Voters may also identify with familiar and charismatic politicians or with long-established governments. In mature democracies, parties may last so much longer than personalities that they constitute the natural focus for politi-cal identification. But there are times and places where politicians, particularly incumbents, last much longer than their parties or their policies—Russia under Boris Yeltsin for example. In such circumstances voters may evaluate new policies and new candidates not according to which party endorses them, but according to which familiar leader endorses them, or according to whether the government or the opposition recommends them. Vojislav Kostunica gained support so rapidly in Serbia because he was endorsed by the ill-defined and badly organized but well understood "democratic opposition" rather than by his relatively insignificant political party—and because he enjoyed the negative endorsement of a regime with which he had no connections.

None the less, in mature democracies, *party* identification is the most significant aspect of political identity and as such it holds a special place in voting studies.

Party identification: a special predisposition

The concept of party identification has prompted much debate, focused on such overlapping questions as:

- What is *meant by* party identification—is it purely a matter of emotion and feeling as originally defined by the Michigan team (Campbell et al. 1960), or is it a more rationally based "running tally" of past evaluations (Fiorina 1981)?
- How should it be *measured*? (Jowell, Witherspoon, and Brook 1987; Flanagan et al. 1991; Miller and Klobucar 2000)
- Should it include *negative* as well as positive feelings towards parties (Rose and Mishler 1998: 162–6), *dual* or even *multiparty* identification (van der Eijk and Niemöller 1983; Uslaner 1989) or, when parties themselves are unstable at the top, *political families* or *tendencies* (Shabad and Slomczynski 1999: 692)?

There has been an equally vigorous debate about the application and usefulness of the concept for understanding and predicting voting behavior, centered on such questions as:

- *How many* party identifiers are there in the electorate?
- Is party identification *declining* around the world (Schmitt and Holmberg 1995; Dalton 2001)?
- How *stable* is party identification? (Niemi and Weisberg 2001: ch. 17; Schickler and Green 1997)
- What *can it do* that other indicators of predispositions cannot?
- Does the concept *travel*?

Some of these questions of application and usefulness are inseparable from questions of definition. The extent of partisanship, for example, depends upon the definition we adopt. There is no "correct measure," and consequently no uniquely "correct level" of identification; the more extreme the commitment to party required by a survey question, the fewer respondents will agree to it. But whatever scale is used, provided only that it distinguishes the more committed from the less committed, it can be used to study the variation in partisan predispositions across individuals, groups, countries, and times—and to predict the likely incidence of voting change among individuals or electorates with higher or lower levels of party identification.

Paradoxically, the concept of party identification is most analytically useful when it fails to predict voting choices. It was precisely in those circumstances that the Michigan team originally focused upon it in the 1950s. It was banal to discover that a Democratic identifier voted for a Democratic candidate. What was fascinating was to discover that a quarter of Democratic identifiers voted for the Republican presidential candidate (Eisenhower) without abandoning their identification with the Democratic Party.

In the United States, such "defection" rates increased in the 1970s but have recently decreased as partisanship has taken on some of its earlier strength (Bartels 2000). In Britain, defection rates have generally been lower than in the United States, but among Labour identifiers they peaked at over 18% in 1983. Within both countries, however, the rate of voter defections at any election has always been much higher among weak identifiers than among strong identifiers. Party identification can thus predict which individuals are most likely to defect at any one time, as well as whether that defection is likely to be permanent or not. Within a campaign, party identification can be used to distinguish "hard" from "soft" support and predict likely trends in support for different parties (Miller, White, and Heywood 1996). Party identification can also predict which individuals are more or less likely to participate in politics; weak identifiers are more likely to abstain from voting altogether, especially in "second-order" elections such as those for the European Union (van der Eijk and Franklin 1996:

ch. 19) or for local governments (Butler and Stokes 1974: 41; Rosenstone and Hansen 1993: ch. 5).

By any measure, there is widespread evidence of slowly declining levels of party identification in mature democracies. Schmitt and Holmberg's review of regular Eurobarometer surveys across the nine "old-EC" members between 1978 and 1992 showed that the numbers of party identi-fiers declined at a rate of almost 1% per annum from an initial high of 71% (1995: 107). Dalton's (1999: 66; 2001) analysis of national election study data for 19 mature democracies over a longer period suggests that the level of party identification declined in all these countries, by an average of one-half a per cent per annum from an initial high of 75%.

In new democracies, however, levels of party identification appear to be increasing from a low base. Schmitt and Holmberg (1995: 107) showed that party identification in the EU's new democracies (Portugal, Greece, and Spain) increased at an annual rate of one-half a per cent per annum from an initial low of 53%. And among post-communist countries there is some, though mixed, evidence of party identification increasing from a low base in east-central Europe and an even lower base in the former Soviet Union. In the early 1990s, only about one-tenth in Ukraine, a quarter in Russia, and a third in Hungary, Slovakia, and the Czech Republic thought of themselves as party "supporters" compared with more than half in Britain (Miller, White, and Heywood 1998: 170, 411). On this measure, party "supporters" had reached only 23% in Ukraine, 14% in Moldova, and 11% in Belarus by the first half of 2000 (White, private communica-tion). Using a less strict measure, whether one party "best represents your views," there is evidence that partisanship "skyrocketed" in Russia and Lithuania between 1992 and 1997—though there was only a modest increase in Ukraine (Miller et al. 2000: 462, 486–87).[1]

There is also disagreement about whether the cause of the decline in party identification in mature democracies is sociological or political. The *sociological explanation* stresses the "autonomous process of socio-structural change." Post-industrial society is producing "newly independent and resourceful post-materialist citizens" who can act as individuals or through ad hoc issue organizations (Schmitt and Holmberg 1995: 122–3). They need parties less than the citizens of traditional mass societies. Such an explanation is supported in the United States by the fact that partisanship declined little among older voters but sharply among younger generations (Miller and Shanks 1996). Related to this is the post-1960s personalization of politics in the United States, along with some evidence of personalization in the UK (Wattenberg 1991, 1998; Foley 1993; Pryce 1997).

The *political explanation* argues that "general macro-sociological expla-nations cannot do justice to ... the variety of country-specific findings" (Schmitt and Holmberg 1995: 121). The upward trend in party identification in new democracies reinforces this interpretation. In addition, Schmitt and Holmberg point to evidence that the level of party identification in mature democracies depends on the degree of political polarization and ideological conflict between the parties. That view is echoed in Bartels' (2000) analysis. Declining partisanship in the United States reached its nadir in the mid-1970s, and its strength and impact have risen since then. Bartels attributes that not to social or psychological change but to public perceptions of important ideological differences between the parties. Thus the level of party identification—like so much else—depends upon the parties as much as the voters.

There is also disagreement about whether declining overall levels of party identification are a harbinger of political instability, as originally suggested by Converse (1969). Certainly, very low levels of party identification in post-communist Russia coincided with high levels of voter instability (White 2000: 60–1) but that reflected much more than lack of psychological commitment among voters. Russian parties are created and dissolved with such rapidity that over half the party identifiers voted in 1999 for a party created since the preceding election and for the new election (Rose, Munro, and White 2001: 429). Studies focusing on identification with political families or tendencies indicate more structure and stability (Shabad and Slomczynski 1999).

Over the long period from 1918 to 1985, Bartolini and Mair (1990) found that electoral volatility in 13 European countries was influenced about equally by four factors. Volatility was higher when and where the number of parties was higher or there were changes to the franchise or the electoral system. Conversely, volatility was lower where party (or trade union) membership was high and where society was riven by deep socio-cultural cleavages. But overall they were impressed by the trend towards more rather than less stability.

How can this increase in stability be reconciled with a decline in social cleavages and party identification? First, value cleavages might substitute for social cleavages as the basis for political cleavages. Second, as Schmitt and Holmberg and Bartels pointed out, the alleged decline in partisanship may have been exaggerated. But it may simply be that partisanship and stability are not that closely connected. Even in Britain, where Dalton (1999: 66) found that the decline in the number of strong identifiers from 1964 to 1992 was greater than in any of the other 18 countries he studied, panel surveys show there was no increase in gross volatility (the percentage of individuals changing their votes) during those years. In six inter-election panels that together covered the years 1959–87, there was evidence of nothing more than "trendless fluctuation" in levels of voter volatility (Heath et al. 1991: 20). Even such modest and temporary fluctuations that were apparent could be explained by "changing political circumstances" (for example, changing numbers of Liberal Party candidates) rather than by "changing social psychology" (that is, declining party identification). Volatility increased sharply when Blair won in 1997 (Heath and Taylor 1999a: 170)—yet there was no dramatic drop in party identification at that time.

Similarly in Italy, Eurobarometer data show only a slow long-term decline in party identification between 1978 and 1992. And in every year, the percentage of "closely attached" party-identifiers was higher in Italy than the EU average (Schmitt and Holmberg 1995: 126). So neither time-trends nor cross-national analysis of these figures could plausibly have predicted the remarkable stability in the old Italian party system until the late 1980s followed by its sudden collapse in the early 1990s. Psychological changes among Italian voters contribute almost nothing to the explanation of trends in party support. The end of the Soviet Union in 1991 and the eruption of the *tangentopoli* ("bribesville") scandal in Italy in 1992 changed the choices open to voters and supply a far more plausible explanation for voter volatility than sociologically driven trends in party identification.

Thus, while the strength of an individual's partisanship remains a good predictor of whether that individual is more or less likely than others to switch votes, the British and Italian experiences imply that the strength of party identification in the electorate as a whole is not the main determinant of voting stability or volatility throughout the country.

Short-term factors

Since the introduction of party identification into the vocabulary of political scientists, no one has doubted that long-term factors play an important role in voting decisions and election campaigns. Yet the thrust of much recent work has been that pre-determined factors have been overrated and that more immediate factors—issues, candidates, and election campaigns—have been underrated.

When British Prime Minister Harold Macmillan was asked what he found the most difficult aspect of government he famously replied: "Events, dear boy, events!" Predictable events hardly count. What politicians mean by events are those that are unpredictable: a sudden international oil crisis, an unexpected outbreak of armed conflict, or a high-level corruption scandal. A potent example was the widespread industrial unrest during the 1979 "Winter of Discontent" that led to a sudden and massive swing against the Labour government and the election of Mrs Thatcher.

Changes of leaders can have an equally dramatic effect—and not just in presidential systems. Much of the time it is difficult to separate the impact of leader and party images on voters. In party-dominated Scandinavia, "evaluations of parties are more important for voters than evaluations of political leaders" insofar as they can be distinguished at all (Aardal and Oscarsson 2000; see also Gidengil et al. 2000). But leaders can have a significant role in defining what a party means: Tony Blair even rebranded his party as "New Labour" and formally changed its historic mission statement ("Clause 4")—with visible effects on Labour support. Still more clearly, when Thatcher, who also defined her party, resigned after outstaying her welcome, her resignation turned a 16% Labour lead into a 20% Conservative lead between the second and fourth week of November 1990.

Truly "candidate effects" also exist and should be distinguished from "leader effects." Collectively, a party's many candidates in a parliamentary or congressional election contribute to the definition of the party itself, but individually they differ one from another. It is at this level, of truly "individual candidate" effects, that the United States differs most clearly from Western Europe—and has much in common with post-communist Russia. Russian and American candidates differentiate themselves from their parties even if they have a nominal affiliation, fight candidate-centered campaigns, and score personal victories or suffer personal defeat to a degree that is without parallel in Western Europe (Wattenberg 1991; White, Rose, and McAllister 1997: 120–9).

New research in the United States has also found direct support for the importance of campaign events (Holbrook 1996; Campbell 2000). Past research has typically assumed that events influenced respondents only if they were able to recall them. But most individuals can recall only a few such events, and when they do, remember them only vaguely. That led to the "minimal effects model" of political campaigns. A strikingly new model was proposed by Lodge, McGraw, and Stroh (1989) and tested experimentally by Lodge, Steenbergen, and Brau (1995). In their "impression-driven model" of candidate evaluation, voters integrate information about candidates into a "running tally" or "on-line" evaluation (like the running tally sometimes used to describe party identification). The specific ingredients (campaign events, candidate information) are most often quickly forgotten, but voter evaluations none the less reflect their impact.

Issues, especially new or newly salient issues, are also thought to be significant short-term factors. Because they are so variable, however, it has been surprisingly difficult to generalize about their influence on voter behavior. Yet one such factor—the state of the economy—has been found widely influential on candidate and leader evaluations and on voting decisions. Since the early studies some 30 years ago, assessments of economic influence have been increasingly extended to one country after another, including new and reinvigorated democracies (Wilkin, Haller, and Norpoth 1997). The literature is voluminous (Lewis-Beck and Paldam 2000). The analytical questions have also expanded to include the role of "pocketbook" versus national-economy effects (Markus 1992; Palmer 1999), the relative influence of retrospective versus prospective assessments (MacKuen, Erikson, and Stimson 1992; Norpoth 1996), and the mechanisms of influence, including the role of experts and the media (MacKuen et al. 1992; Nadeau, Niemi, and Amato 2000).

Most interesting perhaps from a comparative perspective has been evidence that institutional factors affect the relationship between economic factors and voting decisions. Powell and Whitten (1993: 398) noted that assignment of responsibility for economic performance to the government "strongly reflect[s] the nature of policymaking in the society and the coherence and control the government can exert over that policy." Anderson (2000),

Nadeau, Niemi, and Yoshinaka (2001), and others have extended this argument in various ways.

Research in Poland, Peru, and Mexico on new democracies introducing promarket reforms suggests that although voters' patience is eroded if reforming governments "persist indefinitely" in their promise of a better future (Stokes 1996: 516), voters agree that they "must suffer hard times in the near future if they are to enjoy prosperity later" (p. 505). Thus, the ordinary rules of electorates in mature democracies punishing incumbents for economic hardship may not apply. Other studies in Poland, Hungary, Lithuania, the Czech Republic, Slovakia, and Bulgaria have found that although former Communist parties won back office from anti-communist reformers in the harsh economic conditions of the mid-1990s, personal experience of economic hardship was of surprisingly "little importance" (Powers and Cox 1997: 617) or had only "a modest effect" (Harper 2000: 1191) on party choice. During a period of transition, economics appears to be primarily a "position" issue rather than a "valence" issue—that is, an issue that polarizes winners against losers and affects patterns of support for challengers as well as incumbents, rather than an issue that focuses primarily on consensual goals and the merely technical competence of the incumbents (Fidrmuc 2000: 199).

Conditioning

Even though they may have the freedom to choose between parties or candidates, voters' choices are unconsciously conditioned by barely visible influences of various kinds. Apart from the family, the most important are two very different but equally invisible influences: first, the media—outside the confines of its explicit advertising and editorializing which are, of course, easily visible. Second, the sociogeographic context in which the voter lives.

Early media studies, including the classic election studies by Lazarsfeld, Berelson, and Gaudet (1948) and Berelson, Lazarsfeld, and McPhee (1954), replaced intuitive notions of an all-powerful mind-conditioning media with a "minimal effects" model in which the media did little other than possibly reinforce existing public opinion. This model, which extended to television as well as newspapers (Blumler and McQuail 1968; Patterson and McClure 1976), was so dominant that few media studies of elections were even conducted.

In the 1970s, however, a new role was found for media-conditioning when the notion of "agenda-setting" took hold — that is, the notion that the media play a major role in determining what people talk about (Norris, Chapter 6 above). When combined with the theory of "issue-ownership" (Petrocik 1996)—that particular parties are widely accepted as the best able to handle particular issues—this notion of "agenda-setting" points to potentially powerful media effects. It has been used in this way to explain electoral outcomes in Germany and the Netherlands (Kleinnijenhuis and de Ridder 1998). Later, this notion was enlarged to include "priming"—the idea that the media not only determine what people think about, but how they think about it (for example, the standards by which they evaluate political leaders) (Iyengar and Kinder 1987). Even when expanded in these ways, however, media were still given a limited role in that they were thought not to change people's opinions and choices.

Recently, however, an increasing number of both experimental and survey studies have suggested that the media in fact persuade voters (Miller 1991; Bartels 1993; Zaller 1992, 1996). Moreover—and this gets closest to the notion of *media-conditioning*—even apparently objective phenomena are not free of media influence. For example, while the media are to some extent neutral reporters of uninterpreted economic statistics or simply the mechanism for transmitting experts' opinions (MacKuen et al. 1992; Zaller 1992: ch. 12), they also inject an independent element into the news (Sanders, Marsh, and Ward 1993; Nadeau and Niemi 1999; Nadeau et al. 2000).

Media influence is likely to be most insidiously effective where the media develop a consensus about how the facts should be interpreted. Dunleavy and Husbands complain that "we should be less concerned about trying to gauge the political impact achieved by any one media source—such as a single newspaper—and focus attention instead upon the overall climate of media influence to which people have been exposed" (1985: 110). While that presents a severe methodological challenge and goes well beyond the narrower concerns found in most of the literature on voting, it none the less highlights the role of the media as a conditioning factor on voters' choices. From this larger perspective, Page and Shapiro (1992: ch. 9) present considerable evidence of opinion manipulation, much of it attributable to media coverage, if not media invention.

The evidence for *context-conditioning* is less ambiguous and its effects are large. An initial effect of context is the socialization of young people by their parents. Despite possibly weaker intergenerational ties than in the 1950s, young people still very often share partisan tendencies with their parents. In later life, the impact of this early socialization experience may fade, but only to be replaced by the ongoing influence of friends, neighbors, colleagues in the workplace, leisure-associates, and partners. At no stage in the life cycle is it realistic to view voters as insulated from their social environment.

The local environment has a particularly significant impact on voting patterns because it tends to intensify partisan choice whenever people of the same type live and work in close proximity. It intensifies left-wing partisan-ship in working-class areas that would already be inclined towards the left, and intensifies right-wing partisanship in more affluent areas that would already be inclined towards the right. And the effect is large—enough to double the natural class-polarization of constituency voting patterns (Butler and Stokes 1974: 130–7; Miller 1978).

The existence of such contextual effects has long been obvious. It was highlighted by Berelson Lazarsfeld, and McPhee (1954) in the early 1950s and later by many others.[2] But whether these effects were caused by inter-personal communications or by some statistical artifact was less obvious. Recent questions about "conversational partners" now provide direct evidence about the impact of "discussion networks", "party networks" (interactions with party members), "social class networks," and residential or "neighbor-hood networks" (Zuckerman, Kotler-Berkowitz, and Swaine 1998; see also Lalljee and Evans 1998; Pattie and Johnston 2001). These new studies confirm the powerful impact of context. Statistically, "discussion networks rival party identification as predictors of vote choice" (Zuckerman et al. 1998: 291). Moreover, discussion networks affect the consistency of attitudes and the stability of voting choices: "in the absence of reinforcing discussion networks and encounters with party activists, people are almost as likely to change their vote between two adjacent elections as to repeat it" (p. 307).

Constraints

Conditioning is largely invisible to the voter, and its effects are internalized. Constraints are different. They are visible, they remain external, and they encourage voters to make a conscious distinction between party preferences and voting choices.

Some constraints on voter choice are imposed by the electoral system, others by the parties. Different electoral systems offer voters different numbers of votes, and count them in different ways—which may either widen or narrow the range of effective choices. But choice is never infinite. Voter choice is also constrained by the number and nature of the available options (parties, candidates) standing for election—and by coalition deals made by parties.

The number and nature of available options

Where voters dislike all existing voting options there is an opportunity for new political entrepreneurs to widen the range of options by standing as independent candidates or by inventing new political parties. Yet the "start-up" costs are high. To become a realistically available option a new party needs large-scale funding, wide access to the media, a favorable electoral system, and—presidential systems excepted—hundreds if not thousands of personally credible candidates. So for much of the time the main source of innovation in the political market-place consists of new or revised models from old entrepreneurs—new parties that emerge from elite-level party splits, or just revised policy programs from old parties. Consequently, the available options determine the voter's choice, not the other way round.

Parties can have a dramatic effect upon voting choice simply by changing the number of seats they contest. The British Liberal party took roughly the same share of the vote in seats that it contested at elections in 1951 and 1997. But it contested 639 seats in 1997 compared to only 109 in 1951—which allowed many more Liberal sympathizers to vote Liberal in 1997. Parties can also have a dramatic, though less mechanical, effect upon voters' choices when they shift sharply to the left or right or when they enter or leave formal or informal coalitions with other parties. Similarly, party elites can affect voting behavior by emphasizing certain differences thereby intensifying some voting cleavages, or by de-emphasizing other differences thereby reducing or suppressing other potential voting cleavages.

More generally, parties may move closer together or further apart, with implications for both the structure and the intensity of voters' partisanship and voting choices. A recurrent theme of Heath, Jowell, and Curtice's series of voting studies is that voting change has been produced more by party-change and by system-change than by changes in the psychology of the voters (e.g., Heath et al. 1991). If parties differ sharply on issues, so will their voters. If parties use explicitly ideological language, so will their voters. If parties focus their appeals on candidates' personalities, voting cleavages will reflect candidate appeal. Crewe (1992) sums up this conclusion in his phrase "changing votes and unchanging voters."

The impact of electoral systems on voters' choices

Voters' influence over electoral systems is even less than their influence over the range of available party options. Occasionally public unrest can produce a change in the electoral system.[3] More often electoral systems remain unchanged for long periods, or are changed to satisfy the ambitions of the governing elite. So, it is usually the electoral system (or elite-imposed changes in it) that determines voters' choices, not the other way round.

Tactical voting and demobilization under majoritarian electoral systems

The Anglo-American first-past-the-post system (FPTP) has well-understood implications for voter turnout and choice. Supporters of parties that are likely to come in third (or worse) in a local constituency are thought to be "wasting" their votes if they "vote their preference." They would do better to vote tactically, casting their vote for whichever of the top two parties they find more acceptable or less distasteful (cf. Blais and Massicotte, Chapter 2 above).

The argument has implications for parties as well as voters. Parties that are likely to come in third (or worse) in a constituency are wasting their efforts if they attempt to maximize their voter turnout. It might improve their vote share but is unlikely to gain them the seat. They may withdraw their candidates in such places, discretely hint that their supporters abandon them in favor of a coalition partner or informal ally, or simply avoid over-exerting themselves. Conversely, a party should not waste campaign effort in a seat where it expects to win a big majority. Extra effort would only increase an already adequate victory margin. The party would do better to neglect its "core" areas and shift resources to marginal seats where the outcome is less certain.

Less obviously, parties and voters face similar dilemmas under other types of election systems as well (Cox 1997). Tactical voting can occur in proportional representation (PR) systems depending, for example, on whether a party is close nationally to the threshold required for any representation at all in the legislature (for example, in Germany), or close locally to the level required to obtain another seat in a multimember constituency (for example, under the single transferable vote system in Ireland). It can also occur under the single *non*transferable vote, as in Japan before 1994 or in Taiwan (Reed 1990; Cox 1997; Hsieh and Niemi 1998).

If voters have a strong preference for a single party, then "tactical" voting implies that their choice has been constrained and they have been pressured to vote other than for their first preference. But parties in multi-party systems can be viewed as allies as well as enemies. And if voters have a "dual preference" (Miller et al. 1989)—or even a "dual party identification"—then they may view tactical voting more as an opportunity than a constraint.

Ticket-splitting in multiple vote systems

In contrast to FPTP, multiple vote systems widen voters' choices because they can, if they wish, vote for more than one party. In the American phrase, they can "split their ticket." Our purpose here is not to review all of the work on split-ticket voting but to emphasize yet another way in which the electoral system imposes or removes constraints on a voter's behavior.

Various kinds of split-ticket voting are made possible by presidential elections, bicameral legislatures, mixed-member electoral systems, and multi-level governance. Where government is *split* between two separately elected Houses, or between directly elected executives (usually presidents) and legislatures, voters will often cast two or more votes simultaneously – as occurs in the United States and in many Latin American countries.[4] Under *mixed-member systems*, voters are required to cast two votes for a single legislative body. The best known example is the German Bundestag, but mixed-member systems have been growing in popularity and are now used in at least 29 countries covering over a fifth of the world's population—including Japan, New Zealand, post-communist Russia, and (for regional assemblies) post-devolution Britain (Massicotte and Blais 1999: 341; Wattenberg and Shugart 2000). Finally, *multi-level governance* typically requires voters to cast votes for three or four levels of government—national, regional or state, local, and (in Europe) supra-national.

Split-ticket voting has very different magnitudes, sources, and meaning in different countries (Schoen 1999; Banducci, Karp, and Vowles 1998; Curtice and Steed 2000; McAllister and White 2000). In Germany, for example—in complete contrast to the United States—split-ticket voting has nothing to do with the personal attractions of candidates (who are unknown to, and disregarded by, the voters) and mostly depends on coalition preferences. When the FDP was in coalition with the socialist SPD in 1980, 36% of "second" votes for the FDP came from voters who voted SPD with their constituency vote (and only 13% from the CDU/CSU). After the FDP leadership switched sides and went into coalition with the conservative CDU/CSU in 1982–3 however, 58% of "second" votes for the FDP came from voters who voted CDU/CSU with their constituency vote (and a mere 10% from the SPD) (Jesse 1988: 117).

The new electoral system adopted for the Italian Chamber of Deputies after the "*tangentopoli*" scandal provides another example of the dynamics of party-constrained split-ticket voting. The electoral system lifted constraints on voters by giving each voter an opportunity to cast two votes instead of one. But at the same time, party elites reacted by arranging "cartel" deals to field joint candidates in constituencies thereby imposing new constraints on voter choice (Bartolini and d'Alimonte 1998). Voters could vote for their preferred party with their "list" vote but had to switch to their party's coalition partner for their "constituency" vote.

Apart from such coalition pressures and cartel deals, other factors constrain voters' choices in multiple-vote systems. Typically one vote is counted under majoritarian rules, and the other under proportionate (PR) rules. So one choice is constrained by tactical considerations while the other is not. In Germany, Japan, Australia, and Scotland ticket-splitting typically helps the smaller parties in the PR vote but the larger parties in the majoritarian vote (Jesse 1988; Bowler and Denemark 1993; Gallagher 1998c; Miller 1999), though this effect has been less evident in New Zealand (Johnston and Pattie, 1999; Barker and McLeay 2000) and Wales (Jones 1999).

Dual party identities in multi-level systems
"Issue-ownership" theories have been advanced to explain why Democrats or Republicans consistently do better or worse in congressional than presidential elections (Petrocik 1996; Petrocik and Doherty 1996). But by far the best examples of powerful "issue-ownership" effects are provided by multi-level governance, especially when applied to ethnically defined regions.

Voters in ethnic regions of Spain, Britain, and Canada consistently and consciously prefer different parties for regional and national elections. It seems as if voters can cope with the ambiguity of multiple party identifications as easily as they can cope with multiple ethnic identifications (Moreno and Arriba 1996; Brown et al. 1999: 61–2). Averaging across all Spanish elections between 1977 and 1997, for example, regional parties won twice as many votes in regional elections as in national or European elections. They did particularly well in Navarra, Catalonia, and the Basque Country, irrespective of the type of election, but much better in regional than in national elections. In Catalonia, for example, regional parties averaged 58% in Catalan elections but only 32% in national (Spanish) elections.

Moreover, Catalans tend to vote leftist (PSOE) in national elections yet for a conservative regional party (CiU) in regional elections (Hamann 1999: 123)—which makes the discrepancy between their regional and national voting choices all the more remarkable.

Where discrepancies between voting preferences for regional and national elections are large and consistent over time, it makes little sense to regard votes at one level as a reflection of voters' party identifications while treating their votes at the other level as temporary deviations in a "second order" election (Reif and Schmitt 1980). It seems more reasonable to infer that significant numbers of voters may even have developed a "dual party identification." A post-devolution NOP poll in Wales gives some insight into this. It found that 26% would vote for the Welsh Nationalists (Plaid Cymru or PC) in a Welsh election but only 16% in a UK election. Of those who would vote *against* PC in a UK election but *for* PC in a Welsh election, 32% explained they would do so simply because it was "a Welsh election not a British," 21% because it was "a local election," and 27% because PC was "more concerned about Wales" (Jones 1999: 330). These are not explanations of temporary defections so much as discriminating choices.

But the best direct evidence of dual party identification comes from a series of Canadian surveys (Stewart and Clarke 1998). Between 1974 and 1993 the number of Canadians who self-consciously identified with different parties for regional and national elections rose from 17 to 31%. Meanwhile, the number who identified with the same party at both levels declined from 64 to 52% (the rest failing to identify with a party at one or both levels).

Whatever the exact reasons for and the precise interpretation of these dual party-identifications, they provide yet another warning against a purely voter-centered perspective on voting choice. They suggest that not only votes themselves, but even party identifications may be constrained by electoral and party systems. The more votes the system permits, and especially the more simultaneous votes it permits, the greater the incentive to abandon a purely mono-party identification and perhaps develop a dual-party identity. Similarly, the closer parties are locked into quasi-permanent coalition arrangements, the greater the incentive for voters to view them as a composite whole.

Which brings us back to our general theme: the impact of *conditioning and constraint*—as well as more personal factors—on the choices that voters themselves make (or feel that they make). Although there are now calls for more attention to context and institutions as determinants of voter choice (e.g., Scarbrough 2000), this theme is not a new one, not even in its application to party identification. Indeed, the study that first put party identification at the heart of voting research had a chapter on the impact of electoral laws and political systems on the "formal facilitation" of party identification in different states of the United States. (Campbell et al. 1960: ch. 11). But it becomes a more significant theme when viewed over a longer time-scale or from a more global perspective, in which the constraints on voters vary more widely and reveal their power more clearly.

NOTES

1. How to measure partisanship in post-communist democracies has been the subject of considerable debate. Some have emphasized negative identifications (Rose and Mishler 1998; Miller et al. 1998: 162–6). Others have suggested alternatives to self-identification questions altogether (e.g., Miller and Klobucar 2000; Brader and Tucker 2001).

2. A small sample of references covering three countries and a long time span are: Putnam (1966); Cox (1969); McAllister (1987); Huckfeldt et al. (1995); McAllister et al. (2001).

3. One dramatic example of change produced by the public is the imposition in the 1990s of term limits on 19 American state legislatures, 18 of them by referendum (Carey, Niemi, and Powell 2000). Other examples are the recent changes (in opposite directions) in the Italian and New Zealand electoral systems precipitated by popular referenda rather than by dominant elites.

4. For a summary of US research on split-ticket voting and its relation to "divided government" see Niemi and Weisberg (2001: ch. 14). Bean and Wattenberg (1998) conclude that a preference for divided government is not a factor in the United States but that it is a very significant predictor of straight or split-ticket voting in Australia.

9

Political Cleavages, Issues, and Electoral Change

RUSSELL J. DALTON

Electoral politics is the essence of democratic politics. Elections crystallize the political interests existing within a society and provide a mechanism for the public to decide between political options. Although elections are one of the essential and relatively constant features of democracies, the most striking conclusion that emerges from current electoral research is that the underlying bases of electoral choice have changed dramatically. Political cleavages such as class and religion historically structured the content of political and electoral discourse in Western democracies, and thereby partisan alignments and voting choices (Lipset and Rokkan 1967; Lijphart 1981). Over the past generation, these traditional social cleavages have been transformed and weakened as predictors of electoral choice in advanced industrial democracies. In addition, the development of new party systems in Eastern Europe poses an informative and theoretically important comparison to the initial development of Western party systems.

Another transformative force involves the changing bases of ideological conflict in many Western democracies. Citizens in these societies have expanded their interests to include non-economic, quality-of-life issues that represent a new post-material agenda. The growth of environmentalism, the emergence of a women's movement, and demands for increased involvement in the decisions affecting one's life have broadened the boundaries of contemporary politics (Inglehart 1977, 1990). In addition, attention to these new issues has been paralleled by a general growth in issue-based voting, even for "old" issues, such as the size of the welfare state and the overall scope of government (see Chapter 8 above). The evolution of these new patterns of political competition is a distinguishing feature of contemporary electoral politics.

This chapter considers the implications of these changes for the nature of electoral behavior today and in the future. Today, a smaller share of the electorate approaches each election with standing predispositions based on the broad social divisions or partisan identities that once structured electoral competition (Dalton and Wattenberg 2000). Instead, citizens in advanced industrial democracies are using a new calculus to make their electoral decisions. We discuss the role of ideology and issue positions in this calculus and consider how the weight of different issues illustrates the changing nature of electoral competition in contemporary democracies.

The declining role of social cleavages

Modern electoral research began by observing that party competition and voting decisions were structured around the social divisions existing within a polity. In their seminal study, Lipset and Rokkan (1967) explained how ideological and partisan divisions sprang from the social cleavages in the nation. Differences between competing social groups—such as social classes or religious groups—provided the potential basis for political conflict. Given their nature, such cleavages could be expected to persist over long periods of time. In one of the most often-cited conclusions of comparative politics, Lipset and Rokkan (1967: 50) stated "the party systems of the 1960s reflect, with but few significant exceptions, the cleavage structures of the 1920s." In other words, Lipset and Rokkan claimed that Western party systems became "frozen" around the cleavages that existed during their formative periods.

Social cleavages were so powerful for several reasons. The class conflict reflects different ideologies on the nature of politics and economics, and the ideal relationship between these two social systems. Economic conservatives on the right stress individual initiative, accept social and economic inequality, and favor a limited role for government. Socialists and social democrats on the left advocate a more egalitarian society and attribute a larger role to government in finding political solutions for the inequalities produced by the social and economic systems. Similarly, the conflicts between Protestants and Catholics, or between the secular and religious, represent differences in basic value systems. These social conflicts defined the primary ideological bases of politics in Western democracies and thus provided the framework for party competition.

In addition to these ideological elements, there are institutional reasons why social groups provide a structure for party competition (Zuckerman 1982). Social groups enable political parties to formalize a basis of support. Such groups can provide a political and an organizational basis for a party, furnishing members, funds, and the necessary votes at election times. Social democratic parties turn to the labor movement for party workers and electoral support; Christian Democrats recruit their supporters at Sunday mass, and Labour parties recruit at the union hall. For the groups themselves, close ties with a party guarantee representation within the legislative process and/or in the government. Moreover, this alliance pattern provides an important reference structure in orienting both citizens and political elites to the world of politics. When political parties use labels such as "Labour" or "Christian" they are telling certain voters that this party represents people like yourself. Once these institutional frameworks are established, they tend to produce a system of self-reinforcing political alliances.

Early survey research substantiated Lipset and Rokkan's claims on the importance of cleavage-based voting. Researchers found that social cleavages exerted a potent effect on voting, especially class and religious differences (Alford 1963; Lipset and Rokkan 1967; Rose 1974). As a consequence of this stable cleavage basis of electoral politics, Rose and Urwin's (1969, 1970) research on post-war party systems found striking stability in electoral results during the 1950s and 1960s.

Yet, even as this theme of partisan stability became the conventional wisdom of political science, dramatic changes were already beginning to affect these same party systems. The established parties were presented with new demands and new challenges, and evidence of real partisan change became obvious. The major left and right parties could no longer depend to the same degree on a core group of predictable voters as the base of their support. Most party systems in the OECD nations experienced an increase in the number of political parties over the past several decades, as new political contenders entered the electoral arena. There has also been increasing volatility between elections, measured either at the systemic or individual level (Dalton and Wattenberg 2001: ch. 3). A variety of other indicators— split-ticket voting, divided government, and even the delay in voting decisions to later in the campaign—signaled the increasing uncertainty of electoral politics.

Within a decade, the dominant question in electoral research changed from explaining the persistence of established patterns to explaining electoral change (Dalton, Flanagan, and Beck 1984; Crewe and Denver 1985). Although this theme of increasing partisan change was initially debated in the literature (Bartolini and Mair 1990; Mair 1997), the evidence of increasing fluidity and volatility has grown over time (Franklin, Mackie, Valen, et al. 1992; Dalton and Wattenberg 2000).

The class cleavage

Social scientists probably have devoted more attention to the class cleavage than to any other social characteristic as a basis of electoral politics. At a theoretical level, the class cleavage involves some of the most basic questions of power and politics that evolve from Marxian and capitalist views of political development. Empirically, the class cleavage represents the economic and material problems of industrial societies: providing for the economic security of all citizens and ensuring a just distribution of economic rewards. Issues such as unemployment, inflation, social services, tax policies, and government management of the economy reinforce class divisions. Consequently, Lipset (1981: 230, emphasis added) described the class cleavage as one of the most pervasive bases of party support: "On a world scale, the *principal generalization* which can be made is that parties are primarily based on either the lower classes or the middle and upper classes."

As strong and persistent as class voting patterns were, they were not immutable. Nieuwbeerta and De Graaf (1999) have assembled the most comprehensive evidence of class voting trends in 20 advanced industrial democracies, documenting a general erosion in class voting differences for these polities. Figure 9.1 displays the longitudinal trend in class voting for an illustrative set of advanced industrial democracies.[1] The size of the class voting index in Sweden, Britain, and Australia has decreased by almost half across the second half of the 20th century, and in Germany by almost two-thirds. Class voting patterns follow a less regular decline in American congressional elections; the erosion of class voting is more pronounced in presidential elections (Abramson, Aldrich, and Rohde 1999: ch. 5; Stanley and Niemi 1995).

This decline of the traditional middle class/working class cleavage has generated a series of new research controversies in the literature. Some scholars argue that the nature of class alignments in advanced industrial societies is changing and that in its new forms the effect of social class is as pervasive as in the past (Evans 1999). Goldthorpe (1987) proposed a new categorization of social class, incorporating notions of job autonomy and authority relationships into traditional class criteria such as income level and manual labor. Other scholars have created an expanded list of class categories to incorporate new social contexts, such as the middle class salatariat or affluent blue-collar workers (Pappi 1990; Heath et al. 1991; Hout et al. 1995). Others have explored criteria other than employment as potential bases of socioeconomic cleavage, such as an education cleavage separating the information-rich from the information-poor, or conflicts between the public and private sectors (Dunleavy and Husbands 1985). Some of the most innovative recent research tries to define social position by lifestyle characteristics, distinguishing between industrial employees and Yuppies, for example (Delli Carpini and Sigelman 1986; Gluchowski 1987; Pew Center 1998).

The reconceptualization of social class implies that social cues now function in more complex and differentiated ways than in the past. Yet the empirical reality remains: even these more complex class frameworks have only a modest value in explaining how citizens vote. Rose and McAllister (1986: 50–1) compared several of these alternative models to British voting behavior in the 1983 election and find that each explained only a very modest share of the vote. Similarly, Nieuwbeerta (1995; Nieuwbeerta and de Graaf 1999) shows that alternative statistical measures of class voting do not change the fundamental results.

The diminished electoral role of class is reaffirmed by the data in Figure 9.2, which documents the current extent of class polarization in 13

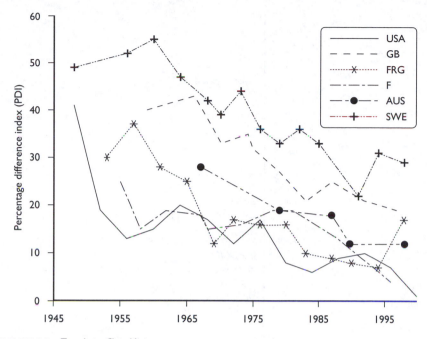

FIGURE 9.1   *Trends in Class Voting*
NOTE: Entries are the Alford Class Voting index, that is, the percentage of the working class preferring a leftist party minus the percentage of the middle class voting for the left. American data are based on congressional elections, except for 1948, which is presidential vote.
SOURCES: Australia (McAllister 1992: 134) and 1998 Australian Election Study; Sweden, Swedish Election Studies; other nations (Dalton 2001: Ch. 8)

advanced industrial democracies, using an expanded measure of social class.[2] Some of the strongest correlations occur in Northern European party systems (Sweden, Britain, and Norway), and the weakest correlations are for the United States, Canada, Japan, and Australia. The weak correlation for Germany occurs because of contrasting patterns of class voting in West and East (Dalton and Bürklin 1996). As Figure 9.1 suggests, these same national rankings may have applied a generation ago, but in all these nations class voting has weakened over time. Present levels of class voting in Sweden, for instance, are a shadow of earlier class polarization.[3] In cross-national terms, the overall effect of social class is now quite modest (average Cramer's V = 0.13). Class-based voting, as conceived of from Marx to Lipset and Rokkan, currently has limited influence in structuring voting choices.

Furthermore, it is important to realize that even when economic issues become salient in contemporary electoral campaigns, these are less often framed in class terms or reinforced by class-based voting choices. Thus, the

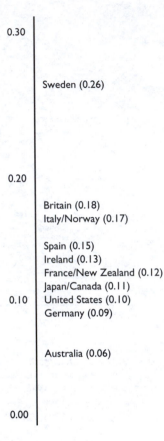

FIGURE 9.2   *The Overall Level of Class Voting*
SOURCE: 1996 International Social Survey Program.
(Values in parentheses are Cramer's V correlations)

class-based rhetoric in many recent campaigns—such as debates about the negative effects of economic globalization, the marginalization of labor, and the spread of "McJobs"—has not revived class voting differences in the United States or other Western democracies.

The religious cleavage

The other major basis for social division in Western party systems has been the religious cleavage in its various forms. As was true with the class cleavage, conflicts over religion defined the structure of elite conflict and the political alliances that existed in the late 19th century. When the modern political parties formed with the extension of mass suffrage, they often allied themselves with specific religious interests: Catholic or Protestant, religious or secular (Lipset and Rokkan 1967). Indeed, parties often proclaimed their religious identity by calling themselves Christian or Christian Democratic parties. Early empirical research on citizen voting behavior underscored the continuing importance of the religious cleavage. Rose and Urwin (1969: 12) examined the social bases of party support in 16 Western democracies. Their often-cited conclusion maintained "religious divisions, not class, are the main social bases of parties in the Western world today."

Despite this evidence of a strong relationship between religious values and partisan preferences, the religious cleavage has followed a pattern of decline similar to the class cleavage. Social modernization disrupted religious alignments in the same way that social class lines have become blurred. Changing lifestyles and religious beliefs and decreased involvement in church activities diminished the church as a focus of social life. Most Western democracies have experienced a steady decline in religious involvement over the past 50 years (Franklin et al. 1992: ch. 1). In the Catholic nations of Western Europe, for instance, frequent church attendance decreased by nearly half in the latter half of the 20th century. Predominantly Protestant countries, such as the nations of northern Europe, began with lower levels of church involvement, but have followed the same downward trend. By definition, this secularization trend means that fewer voters are integrated into religious networks and exposed to the religious cues that can guide the vote.

Also paralleling the class cleavage, conflict between secular and religious forces apparently has moderated over the past several decades. Socialists in many European nations reached a rapprochement with religious groups, especially with the Catholic church in countries with a large Catholic population. The churches also sought to normalize political relations if church interests could be guaranteed as part of the process.

Measuring the present effect of religious cues on voting behavior is more complicated than the analyses of the class cleavage. The class composition of most advanced industrial democracies is similar, but their religious composition is quite varied. Some nations, like Britain or the Scandinavian nations, are predominantly Protestant; the nations of Mediterranean Europe are predominantly Catholic; other nations, such as Germany and the United States, are characterized by religious diversity; and the Japanese case is the most distinct because of its non-Western religious traditions. In addition to the diverse religious composition of these nations, the partisan tendencies of religious denominations also vary cross-nationally (Lipset and Rokkan 1967). In some nations, Catholics have allied with conservative parties; in other nations they are part of a left alliance. This means that the voting cues provided by religious affiliation may differ across national boundaries, in contrast to the consistent working class/middle class pattern of the class cleavage.

The special nature of religious cleavages means that it is more difficult to document the cross-temporal and cross-national trends in ways that are comparable to analyses of social class. The left side of Figure 9.3 describes the current effect of religious denomination on partisan preferences.[4] Where religious voting patterns are uniformly weak, as in the United States, Japan, and Britain, this reflects an ongoing characteristic of the party system rather than the recent erosion in religious voting (Franklin et al. 1992). Voting differences between religious denominations are also relatively modest in nations with significant historical polarization between religious groups, such as in Germany and Canada. Stronger religious effects appear in Italy, but this is based on a relatively small group of non-Catholic voters. Thus, the overall cross-national level of denominational-based voting is fairly modest (average Cramer's V = 0.15).

The right side of Figure 9.3 summarizes the voting differences between those who attend church regularly and those who are not religious. The secular/religious divide has an influence on party preferences that is only slightly greater than the effect of religious denomination (average Cramer's V = 0.17). In both predominanly Catholic or Protestant nations—such as Italy or Sweden—this taps the degree of involvement in a religious network and adherence to religious values. Despite the paucity of explicitly religious issues and the lack of religious themes in most campaigns, religious attachments still influence party choice.

There are some indications that Christian fundamentalism is a growing cleavage in the United States and some other democracies. Employing television and other means of mass communication, evangelical leaders mobilize people on the basis of policy issues dealing with matters of morality and traditional family values (for example, abortion, school prayer, and pornography). There are such periodic fundamentalism revivals in Scandinavia as well. For the United States, Miller and Wattenberg (1984) show that a fundamentalist subset of the electorate constitute a significant part of the Republican coalition, as witnessed by their prominence during the 1992 and 1996 Republican national conventions. Still, longitudinal electoral studies fail to find a significant growth in the relationship between religion and vote choice; the effect of the fundamentalist revival is dwarfed by the ebb and flow of other electoral forces (Wald 1997; Abramson, Aldrich, and Rohde 1999 ch. 5).

Although religiously defined voter groups still differ somewhat in their partisan loyalties, the actual importance of religion as a basis of voting behavior has declined in another sense. Comparisons of voting patterns between religious denominations ignore the compositional change in contemporary electorates because of secularization trends. Voting differences between religious and secular voters have remained fairly constant for the past generation, but secularization is steadily increasing the absolute number of non-religious citizens. Individuals who attend church regularly (like individuals who are embedded in traditional social class networks) are still well integrated into a religious network and maintain distinct voting patterns, but there are fewer of these individuals today. By definition, the growing number of secular voters are not basing their party preferences on

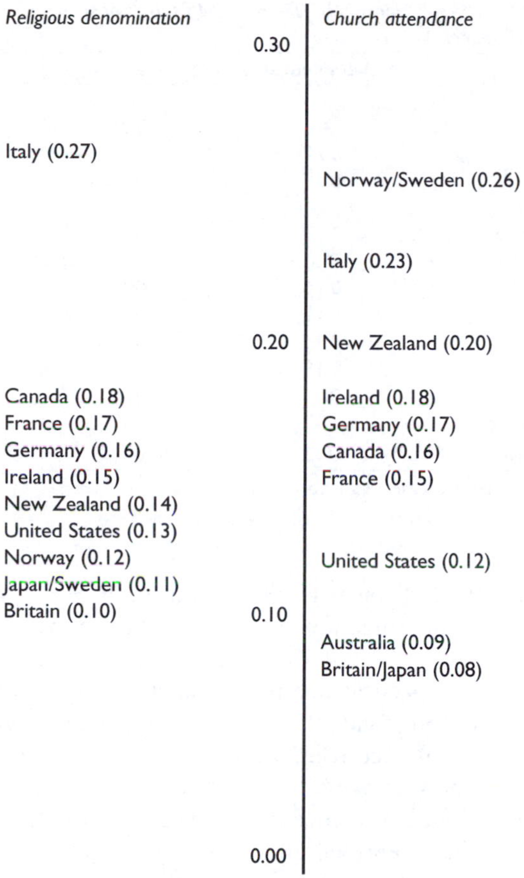

Religious denomination

Italy (0.27)

Canada (0.18)
France (0.17)
Germany (0.16)
Ireland (0.15)
New Zealand (0.14)
United States (0.13)
Norway (0.12)
Japan/Sweden (0.11)
Britain (0.10)

0.30

0.20

0.10

0.00

Church attendance

Norway/Sweden (0.26)

Italy (0.23)

New Zealand (0.20)

Ireland (0.18)
Germany (0.17)
Canada (0.16)
France (0.15)

United States (0.12)

Australia (0.09)
Britain/Japan (0.08)

FIGURE 9.3   *The Overall Level of Religious Voting*
SOURCE: 1996 International Social Survey Program.
(Values in parentheses are Cramer's V correlations)

religious cues. Thus, the changing composition of the electorate is lessening the partisan significance of religious cues by decreasing the number of individuals for whom these cues are relevant.

Other social divisions

The decline of social-based voting is most apparent for the class and religious cleavages, but a similar erosion of influence has occurred for most other sociological characteristics. In most advanced industrial democracies, urban and rural voters display only modest differences in their voting patterns. The average correlation between rural/urban residence and partisan

TABLE 9.1   *The Relationship between Social Characteristics and Party Preferences*

	Urban/rural	Region	Gender
Australia	—	—	0.04
Britain	—	0.24	0.08
Canada	0.21	0.26	0.17
France	0.11	0.23	0.08
Germany	—	0.16	0.08
Ireland	0.25	—	0.16
Italy	0.20	0.24	0.15
Japan	0.14	0.13	0.08
New Zealand	0.11	0.17	0.16
Norway	0.15	0.14	0.12
Spain	0.15	0.30	0.11
Sweden	0.13	0.12	0.12
United States	0.10	0.11	0.13
Average	0.13	0.16	0.12

NOTE: Entries are Cramer's V correlations.

SOURCE: 1996 International Social Survey Program

preference is only 0.13 (Table 9.1). Furthermore, these differences also have narrowed as social modernization has decreased the gap between urban and rural lifestyles.

Regional differences occasionally flare up as a basis of political division. Over the past generation, regional interests have emerged and found partisan representatives in Britain (Scottish National Party and Plaid Cymru), Canada (Bloc Québécois), and Germany (the PDS). In other societies, such as Spain and Italy, sharp regional differences from the past persist to the present, and also have found their representation through regional parties. In most nations, however, region exerts only a minor influence on voting preferences. Table 9.1 reaffirms this point; the average correlation between region and party preferences is 0.16.

There is also increasing discussion of gender as a potential new basis of political cleavage (Jelen, Thomas, and Wilcox 1994; Oskarson 1995). As women have entered the labor force in increasing numbers, and new issues of pay equity and family policies have attracted voter interest, there is a potential for gender-related issues to form a new basis of cleavage. In reality, however, gender differences in voting are fairly modest in most advanced industrial societies; the average Cramer's V in Table 9.1 is only 0.11. Moreover, in half of these nations women are more likely to vote for conservative parties—that is, the gender gap runs in the opposite direction as in the United States. This may reflect the slow evolution of gender preferences from a period when women disproportionately supported parties of the right because of their religious attachments and concern with family issues, to a new preference for leftist parties based on more feminist issue appeals (Studlar, McAllister, and Hayes 1978; Norris 1999a).

One possible exception to the pattern of declining social cleavages involves race and ethnicity, such as the link between blacks and the

Democratic party in the United States (Carmines and Stimson 1989; Tate 1994) or the voting patterns of minority immigrant populations in Europe (Saggar and Heath 1999). Ethnicity has the potential to be a highly polarizing cleavage, because it may involve sharp social differences and strong feelings of group identity. Yet, to the extent that most societies remain ethnically homogeneous or nearly so, the effect of ethnicity as an overall predictor of vote choice is limited.[5]

When all of the evidence is assembled, one of the most widely repeated findings of modern electoral research is the declining value of the sociological model of voting behavior. Franklin and his colleagues (1992) tracked the ability of a set of social characteristics (including social class, education, income, religiosity, region, and gender) to explain partisan preferences. Across 14 Western democracies, they found a marked and fairly consistent erosion in the voting effect of social structure. The rate and timing of this decline varies across nations, but the end-product is the same. In party systems like the United States and Canada, where social-group-based voting was initially weak, the decline has occurred more slowly. In other electoral systems, such as Germany, the Netherlands, and several Scandinavian nations, where sharp social divisions once structured the vote, the decline has been more pronounced. They conclude with the new "conventional wisdom" of comparative electoral research: "One thing that has by now become quite apparent is that almost all of the countries we have studied show a decline ... in the ability of social cleavages to structure individual voting choice" (Franklin et al. 1992: 385).

Explaining the decline in cleavage-based voting

Although the evidence of the decline in cleavage-based voting is generally accepted, scholars disagree on how to interpret this finding. Franklin et al. (1992: ch. 5) argue that the goal of democratic politics is to resolve political divisions that exist within societies. To the extent that social cleavages reflect broad-based and long-standing social and economic divisions within advanced industrial democracies, then the declining electoral relevance of these cleavages signals success in resolving such political divisions. A consensus on the welfare state, for instance, presumably resolves old political conflicts between socioeconomic groups, as an equalization of living conditions may erode urban/rural differences, and so forth.[6]

This interpretation is linked to the earlier "end of ideology" literature, which argued that advanced industrial democracies have moved away from ideological politics in the 1950s and 1960s (Kirchheimer 1966; Beer 1978). Because of spreading affluence and social modernization, some political parties adopted moderate programs in order to attract centrist voters. Socialist parties shed their Marxist programs and adopted more moderate domestic and foreign policy goals. Conservative parties tempered their views and accepted the basic social programs proposed by the left. Socialist parties vied for the votes of the new middle class, and conservative parties sought votes from the working class. Historical analyses of party programs during these decades show a general convergence of party positions on socioeconomic issues (Robertson 1976; Thomas 1979; Caul and Gray 2001). With smaller class-related differences in the parties' platforms, it seemed only natural that class and religious cues would become less important in guiding voting behavior.

Although this is an appealing explanation, especially as Western democracies bask in their new-found self-esteem with the collapse of the Soviet empire, it suffers from the same problem as the earlier end-of-ideology thesis, which had not anticipated the growing polarization and partisan change that has occurred in these same nations. Although Western democracies have made real progress in meeting their long-term social goals, social and political divisions have not ended. During the 1980s Thatcher, Reagan, and Kohl pursued new conservative agendas that stimulated new economic issues. Recurring global recessions periodically renew the focus on economic problems among Western industrial countries, and problems of persisting poverty, the homeless, and crime are still with us. Similarly, current political debates over abortion, homosexual rights, and other moral issues continue to reflect the value differences underlying the religious cleavage.

Furthermore, partisan contrasts on these political controversies have not necessarily ended. Evidence from Germany indicates that the partisan clarity of class cues actually increased over the same period that class voting diminished (Dalton 1992). Recent surveys of the German and American publics show that the public still clearly perceives the partisan leanings of unions, business associations, and religious groups (Dalton 1996b: ch. 7). In short, it does not appear that citizens today are unclear about the class positions of the parties. Rather, these cues are now simply less relevant to voters than they were in previous times.

I believe that three factors explain the decline in the sociological model of voting behavior. First, the ties between individuals and their respective social groups have weakened. Social cues may still be a potent influence on voting behavior for people who are integrated into traditional class or religious networks and who share the values of these milieu, but today far fewer people fit within such clearly defined social categories. This partially reflects a fragmentation of life spaces. Fewer people are integrated into stable and bounded social structures, such as the working class milieu and religious networks that originally furnished the basis of the class and religious cleavages (see also Putnam 2000). Lifestyles have become more individualized and diverse.

This change in lifestyles has also led to greater diversity within the established political parties. For instance, Huckfeldt and Kohfeld (1989) described how the constituency of the US Democratic party is now split along class, racial, and value lines, and similar factional splits exist among groups within the Republican alliance. It is a monumental task to unite such diverse constituencies at election time, and even more difficult to sustain agreement during the governing process. A similar fragmentation of constituencies has affected both social democratic and conservative parties in Europe (Kitschelt 1994).

Second, citizens are less likely today to rely on social group cues even when they perceive these cues. Rising levels of education and political information have generally led to a process of cognitive mobilization, whereby citizens feel better able to make the decisions affecting their lives without habitual reliance on external cues (Dalton 1984; Inglehart 1990). Greater access to information through an expanding electronic media also increases the number and diversity of political cues to which individuals are exposed. In addition, the broadening of political discourse to include a wider range of political issues erodes the value of fixed social characteristics as a guide to electoral choice. Even when economic conflicts are salient—for example, on issues such as tax reform, trade policy, or deficit reduction—social class is a poor guide to determining a voter's positions on these issues. Class cues carry even less value in determining positions on environmental quality, affirmative action, or gay rights. For the majority of the electorate, therefore, social position and the attendant political cues no longer provide a very useful shortcut to political decision-making. Many of these cues are of decreasing relevance to contemporary voters.

Third, once these processes of social change began to blur the lines of political cleavage, on which many of the established parties were based, the parties responded to these developments in a way that reinforced this process. Przeworski and Sprague (1985) showed how the numerical demise of the working class during the 20th century forced social democratic parties to soften their class image and look to new sources of support in the middle class. Similarly, attempts to broaden the sources of political support are occurring among conservative parties as they observe their past social bases of support eroding. In other words, the parties are contributing to the demise of cleavage voting by their need to compensate for the changing social bases of advanced industrial societies.

Social cleavages still shape the partisan loyalties of some voters. But many other voters now find themselves without a clear location in class, religious, or other social groupings—or with multiple locations that press them in alternate directions. The fragmentation of party images further erodes the value of social cues in guiding behavior. Thus, social change is weakening the structure of political cleavages that once framed party competition and provided voters with a simple framework for making their electoral decisions.

The growth of issue voting and new bases of political cleavage

One immediate implication of the decline of long-term partisan predispositions based on social position is that the basis of electoral behavior should shift toward short-term factors, such as candidate image and issue opinions. Another possibility is that performance-based voting increases, such as judging the government by the performance of the economy (Anderson 1995). There is evidence that the new electoral order also includes a shift towards a more candidate-centered politics. Wattenberg (1991) has documented the growing importance of candidate image in Americans' electoral choices, and comparable data are available for other Western democracies (Bean and Mughan 1989; Ansell and Fish 1999). This is an important development that potentially has far-reaching implications for the nature of contemporary electoral politics, but it lies outside of this chapter's coverage (McAllister 1996).

The decline in long-term forces shaping the vote also increases the potential for issue voting. For example, Franklin (1985) showed that the decreasing influence of long-term forces on British voting decisions was counterbalanced by an increased effect of issues on the vote. In reviewing the evidence from their comparative study of voting behavior, Franklin et al. (1992: 400) restate this point, concluding: "If all the issues of importance to voters had been measured and given their due weight, then the rise of issue voting would have compensated more or less precisely for the decline in cleavage politics."

It is important to realize that issue voting can take two forms. In one form, long-standing social issues—such as concerns about social inequality or economic well-being—exert an impact on electoral choice that is not strongly linked to social position or social group cues. For instance, the apparently growing emphasis on economic performance as a basis for voting may illustrate such patterns (Lewis-Beck 1988; Anderson 1995; Lewis-Beck and Paldham 2000). Voters are judging parties on their economic achievements, but such judgments are not based on class or social group positions to the same extent as in the past.

Another form of issue voting is the growth of new political issues, such as the post-material controversies that have emerged onto the agenda of advanced industrial societies (Inglehart 1977, 1990). Environmental protection, women's rights, and quality-of-life issues now attract the attention of a significant number of contemporary voters. These issues expand the boundaries of politics to include areas that were once the prerogative of markets or individual choice. To the extent that longitudinal data are available, they suggest that post-material values gradually have strengthened as a predictor of party preferences in West European democracies (Knutsen 1995; Knutsen and Scarbrough 1995; Palmer 1995).

These new issues arise more readily with the weakening of traditional party ties. With fewer citizens bound to parties by social bonds or psychological attachments, voters can be mobilized by new issues and innovative programs. Post-material issues have other characteristics that contribute to the decline of social-cleavage-based alignments (Knutsen 1987). These issues tend to cut across established cleavage lines, thereby further weakening traditional social bonds. For instance, some members of the middle class who might normally vote conservatively are drawn to the political program of environmentalists. Furthermore, "new politics" issues attract the attention of the same social groups that are weakly integrated into traditional social cleavages—the young, the new middle class, the better educated, and the non-religious.

At first, these new issues were simply added to the political agenda of advanced industrial societies, representing a set of discrete concerns. Gradually, however, advocates of these issues began to articulate a more encompassing view of politics. Environmental issues were framed in terms of a conceptualization of a sustainable society; gender issues and minority programs became part of a larger agenda of human rights; empowerment became a symbol for expanding participation opportunities. Political alliances also developed between social groups and the citizen interest lobbies that developed to represent these issues. New political parties, such as the Greens, formed to promote these new political positions, further eroding the traditional frameworks of party competition.

The combined and interactive effects of these new issue demands is difficult to summarize, especially across a range of advanced industrial societies. In some nations the new issues have reshaped the party system through the creation of new parties and the realignment of the issue positions of old parties. In other cases, there seems to be a cyclical pattern of responsiveness on one set of issues, and then a shift to an alternative agenda without clear resolutions on either front. This is why current electoral research is more successful in documenting this pattern of heightened party and voter volatility than in predicting the development of these trends.

Although the issues of each specific election campaign are often different, we can illustrate how key political issues—both "old politics" and "new politics" issues—are currently related to party choice. Table 9.2 displays the correlations between party choice and three broad issue areas: the government's role in the economy (a class issue), attitudes toward abortion (a religious issue), and post-material values based on Inglehart's value scale.[7] Obviously, this is only a single snapshot of the ebb and flow of issues across specific elections. But snapshots can still illuminate the general cross-national pattern that might transcend specific elections.

Economic and religious issues continue to exert a significant impact on party choice in several nations. In Northern Europe, where class cues are still relatively strong, economic issues carry substantial weight—even greater than for social class itself. And in nations where the abortion issue continues to tap religious controversies, this issue is also strongly related to vote choice.

In other words, even though the social bases of political cleavage have diminished in importance, the issues derived from these cleavages are still influencing voting choices.[8] For instance, the effect of economic issues is strongest when social groups and the parties remain oriented toward this dimension, such as in Scandinavia, Britain, and Australia. But even in nations where class divisions are weak, such as the United States, Canada,

TABLE 9.2   *Correlations between Attitudes and Party Preferences, 1990–1991*

	Economic issues	Abortion attitudes	Post-material values
Austria	0.10	0.14	0.21
Belgium	0.17	0.17	0.13
Britain	0.21	0.07	0.16
Canada	0.13	0.09	0.14
Denmark	0.29	0.18	0.21
Finland	0.25	0.19	0.25
France	0.24	0.13	0.16
Germany	0.16	0.12	0.18
Ireland	0.15	0.14	0.12
Italy	0.15	0.20	0.15
Japan	0.14	0.10	0.21
Netherlands	0.24	0.20	0.22
Norway	0.22	0.19	0.16
Portugal	0.15	0.14	0.13
Spain	0.19	0.22	0.18
Sweden	0.19	0.22	0.14
United States	0.15	0.06	0.11
Average	0.19	0.14	0.17

NOTE: Entries are Cramer's V correlations. Respondents without a party preference are excluded.

SOURCE: 1990 World Values Survey

and Japan, economic issues can have a significant effect on party preferences. The 2000 US presidential election, for example, often evoked the economic rhetoric of prior campaigns, even though the group bases of these positions has become blurred. Similarly, the abortion issue is significantly related to partisanship in Mediterranean Europe and in several nations with a religiously divided electorate (such as Belgium). Despite the long-term erosion of the group bases of both issue conflicts, these long-standing political controversies are embedded in the values of many citizens, and thus remain a significant influence on the vote in many advanced industrial democracies.

Table 9.2 indicates that post-materialism is also related to partisanship (average correlation is 0.17) at almost the same level as economic issues. In several nations—Germany, Austria, and Japan—post-materialism is the strongest single correlate of partisanship. The development of a new basis of partisan cleavage is generally a long and difficult process (Dalton, Flanagan, and Beck 1984: ch. 15). Groups must organize to represent "new politics" voters and mobilize their support. The parties also must develop clear policy images on these issues. Initially, many established parties were hesitant to identify themselves with these issues because the stakes were unclear and many parties found themselves internally divided on such issues. Yet the data presented in Table 9.2, and the longitudinal trends that are available, suggest that the post-material issues are being integrated into the calculus of issue voting. Indeed, the additional influence of these new issue interests may be a major factor explaining the general increase in issue voting over time.

The experiences of new democracies

While our discussion has focused primarily on the experiences of advanced industrial democracies, a new set of democratic party systems in Eastern Europe and elsewhere face the task of developing basic structures of electoral choice. These party systems are now forming the initial political structures that Lipset and Rokkan examined historically for the West. This presents a unique opportunity to study this process scientifically. How do new party attachments take root, how are the relationships between social groups and parties formed, how are party images created, and how do citizens learn the process of electoral choice and representative democracy? The venerable Lipset and Rokkan framework is a valuable starting point for this research, and the Michigan model of party identification may provide a framework for studying how new political identities form.

For the emerging democracies in Central and Eastern Europe, there are reasons to expect that political parties may draw upon the same historic cleavages as those that emerged in Western Europe, albeit in potentially different forms (Lawson, Römmele, and Karasimeonov 1999; Kitschelt et al. 1999). For instance, religious cleavages rapidly emerged in many of these new party systems, as Christian democratic parties formed to represent religious voters. In nations such as Poland, the religious/secular divide was apparent in early electoral results. Economic factors embedded in the transition from a planned to a market economy, and the economic disruptions that accompany this transition, furnish another potential base for mobilizing voters who either benefitted or suffered from the transition (Harper 2000). In a new party system where voters are developing their party identities and preferences, as well as learning about democracy, such social cues can guide voting choice, much as they did for the earlier electorates in Western Europe.

At the same time, the political trajectory of Eastern Europe is much different than the historical paths Lipset and Rokkan charted for Western Europe. For Lipset and Rokkan, autonomous social groups formed to represent societal interests *in advance of* the creation of modern mass parties; thus the parties were inevitably drawn to these social groups as a basis of electoral support. In Eastern Europe, democracy and party systems were created virtually overnight as a consequence of the collapse of communism, and preceded the formation of autonomous social groups that had been prohibited by the communist regimes. In addition, the citizens of Eastern Europe are much more educated and politically sophisticated than the mass publics of the late 1800s and early 1900s, and are thus less likely to defer to the simple voting directives of a parish priest or union official. Furthermore, the creation of party systems in the world of television and mass communication, greater knowledge about electoral politics (at the elite and public levels), and fundamentally different electorates is unlikely to follow the pattern of Western Europe in the early 1900s.

We will not extensively analyze voting alignments in Eastern Europe, but some initial comparisons to Western patterns are illuminating. Table 9.3

describes the levels of class, religious and other social cleavage voting in seven East European party systems. These data are drawn from the 1996 ISSP survey, and come after two or more democratic elections have been held in most of these nations.

There is an apparent similarity between cleavage voting in Eastern Europe and the portrait of voting choice we have described for the advanced industrial democracies. These new party systems do not display high levels of class or religious voting, although there are some exceptions. Religion, for instance, is a relatively sharp basis of polarization in Bulgaria, the Czech Republic, and Latvia; this reflects internal social divisions with a religious and often regional basis. Church attendance is also a significant predictor of vote choice in several nations. Overall, however, the cleavage correlations in the East average only slightly higher than in the West—and we have stressed the limited role of these influences in the West based on similar correlations. It may be that such cleavages in the East will strengthen further as voters turn to them to simplify their choices and as these cleavage choices become more politically meaningful. But it is also possible that the patterns of electoral choice in many new democracies may be drawn towards the same short-term factors—candidate images and issue positions—that have recently gained prominence in the electoral politics of many advanced industrial democracies.

The apparent East–West similarities in the weakness of social cleavage voting is thus only superficial. Advanced industrial democracies are experiencing an evolution in the patterns of electoral choice that flow from the breakdown of long-standing alignments and party attachments, the development of a more sophisticated electorate, and efforts to move beyond the restrictions of representative democracy. The new electoral forces in Eastern European democracies are trying to develop a stable political base following the democratic transition, and social cleavages by themselves do not appear to be generating much structure. Certainly, further analysis is necessary to track the evolution of voting alignments over time and to define the nature of political alliances,[9] but such group cues have not yet emerged as a powerful factor in structuring voting choice in these new systems.

Conclusion

If Western party systems were ever "frozen," it is clear that they are no longer so. Contemporary electoral politics is now characterized by a greater fluidity in the vote, greater volatility in electoral outcomes, and even a growing turnover in the number and types of parties represented (Dalton and Wattenberg 2000). The gathering winds of electoral change that first appeared in the early 1980s have now grown in force.

We have traced these changes to two broad trends in the electoral politics of advanced industrial societies. First, there has been an erosion in the ability of social cleavages (and the social characteristics derived from these

TABLE 9.3 *Social Cleavages and Party Preferences in Eastern Europe*

	Class	Denomination	Church attendance	Rural/urban	Region	Gender
Bulgaria	0.15	0.29	0.12	0.19	0.16	0.13
Czech Republic	0.15	0.24	0.24	0.15	0.14	0.12
Hungary	0.12	0.09	0.21	0.13	0.17	0.14
Latvia	0.12	0.23	0.10	0.19	0.18	0.14
Poland	0.20	0.19	0.21	0.33	0.13	0.11
Russia	0.10	0.10	0.13	0.16	0.12	0.14
Slovenia	0.17	0.22	0.29	0.25	0.15	0.21
Average	0.15	0.19	0.19	0.20	0.15	0.14

NOTE: Entries are Cramer's V correlations.

SOURCE: 1996 International Social Survey Program

cleavages) to explain electoral choice. The weakening of class and religious alignments has been accompanied by an apparent erosion in long-term partisan commitments and enduring feelings of party identification (Dalton 2001). Second, concomitant with this trend has been the growth of short-term factors, such as issues and candidate images, as a basis of electoral choice. Indeed, we should consider these as complementary trends and not just coincidental; the erosion of social cleavages created more "free-floating" voters who might be mobilized on the basis of candidate images or issue appeals, and the changing nature of citizen issue interests spurred the erosion of fixed social cleavages.

Our findings thus lead to several predictions about the changing nature of electoral behavior in these democracies. An increased weight of short-term factors as predictors of voting choice means that electoral volatility is likely to be a continuing characteristic of contemporary electoral politics. For a time, issues and candidate images may create an equilibrium that endures across a set of elections. By their very nature, these factors are more labile and susceptible to exogenous forces. Some US commentators foresaw a new democratic era following Clinton's victory in 1992, and then a new era of Republic ascendancy in 1994, then a Democratic rebound in 1996, followed by the Bush presidency in 2000. John Major and Helmut Kohl appeared to face certain defeat in 1992 and 1994, respectively, only to emerge from these elections with their majorities intact—then to lose in the next election. Rather than the failures of survey research to be able to predict outcomes, one might cite these cases as illustrations of the inherent volatility of contemporary electoral politics. As electoral research has developed in its scientific skill, the phenomena we are trying to predict have become less predictable. The issue-based and candidate-based voting choices of today are intrinsically less stable and more difficult to predict than were the group-based cleavages of the past.

The shift to issue and candidate voting is likely to increase the evaluative content of elections. Parties will be judged more often by their leadership and the policies they advocate. On the one hand, this might be a welcome trend because it suggests an increase in democratic responsiveness, or implies that electorates are developing some of the characteristics identified with theories of rational democratic choice. Issues and candidates, not party identifications and lifelong social traits, are becoming more important as predictors of voting. On the other hand, we cannot be certain that the content of these evaluations will necessarily be more rational. Some voters will be drawn to candidates or issue positions for well-reasoned principles; others might be drawn by superficial media campaigns and oversimplified electioneering. We might see this development as containing the potential for candidates to advocate more populist appeals that link them to the average citizen, but there is also a potential for demagogic leaders to exploit the public. Indeed, the political framework of the group-based party systems may have provided a method for ensuring electoral responsiveness and accountability that is lacking in electorates focused on short-term considerations (Kirchheimer 1966).

The proliferation of issue interests also raises questions about how to develop coherent government programs in a fragmented political context. Tensions between old left and new left have created considerable instability in many Western party systems over the past two decades, and this is now being amplified by heightened tensions between old right and new right constituencies. Governments that function in a multidimensional political space with shifting emphases on each dimension face major difficulties in finding any political equilibrium. The fixed system of cleavage structures and party alignments solved this paradox by constraining electoral choice. Modern governments may face increasing difficulty in generating a political consensus in favor of any policy in this new context.

In the end, the degree of change in electoral politics will be dependent on the choices that parties and candidates make in responding to these new forces. How democracies choose will determine whether these new forces of electoral change ultimately enrich or weaken the democratic process.

NOTES

1. The figure presents the Alford index of class voting. To maximize the comparability of these analyses, we focus on the left/right voting patterns of the working class versus the combined middle class (old and new). The Alford index measures class voting as the simple difference between the percentage of the working class voting for the left and the percentage of the middle class voting left.
2. Our analyses rely on Cramer's V as a measure of relationships. It is important to note that Cramer's V does not make any predictive assumptions about the patterns of relationship; for instance, that higher social status leads to conservative voting. It simply measures the amount of party differences independent of a theoretically expected pattern. If we imposed such theoretical constraints, the influence of most predictors would be even weaker. The partisan measure is based on a question about voting choice: "If there were a general election tomorrow, which party would you vote for?"

The source of these data is the 1996 International Social Survey Program. These data are available from the Inter-university Consortium for Political and Social Research at the University of Michigan. We measured social class by the occupation of the respondent coded into the following categories: (1) government, (2) professional/managerial, (3) technical/clerk, (4) service/sales, (5) farming, (6) worker, and (7) other occupations. In Britain, Italy, Japan, and Sweden a subjective measure of social class is used because the standard occupation codes were not available.

3. The national rankings are also very similar to those from 1990–91 presented in the previous edition of this chapter (Dalton 1996b).

4. Religious denomination was coded into the following categories: (0) no religion, (1) Catholic, (2) Jewish, (3) Muslim, (4) Protestant, (5) Eastern orthodox, and (6) Other; church attendance was coded as: (1) weekly, (2) 2–3 times a month, (3) monthly, (4) several times a year, (5) less often, and (6) never or no religion.

5. The Cramer's V correlations for ethnicity in the three nations with a significant racial minority are quite modest, often because the minorities represent a small proportion of the voting public: United States = 0.12, Britain = 0.06, Sweden = 0.09.

6. Supporting this position, Nieuwbeerta (1995) finds that the strength of class polarization in voting is inversely related to the extent of the welfare state in a nation.

7. The economic measure is a simple additive combination of positions on four issue dimensions: income inequality, government ownership of economic enterprises, state responsibility for individual well-being, and government responsibility for providing jobs. The abortion issue measures support for abortion under four different conditions. The post-material values index is based on Inglehart's 12-item battery.

8. The issue correlations are normally stronger than for social characteristics and partisanship because issue positions are more psychologically proximate to the voting choice (and thus are intervening variables) and partially because the effect of social cleavages has weakened, which allows for attitudinal factors to increase in importance.

9. Cramer's V correlation only describes the overall differences in voting patterns by social characteristics without imposing any theoretical structure on these relationships, such as the "standard" finding that the middle class votes for the right and the working class for the left. There is repeated evidence that the patterns of social cleavage may also differ across East European party systems because the communist historical and economic experience created different cleavages lines. This requires more extensive analysis of the patterns underlying the Cramer's V correlations.

10

Consolidating Democracies

LARRY DIAMOND

In the past quarter century, no global trend has been more powerful and transformative than the expansion of democratic forms of government in the world. It is one thing to inaugurate a democracy, however, and quite another to maintain it in stable fashion. For the long run, the stable functioning of democracy requires a process that has been termed "democratic consolidation." This chapter assesses the global challenge of consolidating democracies, showing how these differences are patterned by region and by country size. It then proceeds to assess the varied progress toward democratic consolidation, as revealed by a wealth of public opinion data from the post-communist states, Latin America, Africa, and two East Asian countries, showing what the people think of their democracies. These data demonstrate that beneath the surface of global democratic progress lie a number of tensions, vulnerabilities, and deep-seated problems in the functioning of democracy and in the way that democracy is perceived and evaluated by its citizens. Such problems must be addressed with a comprehensive agenda of reform and institution-building if democracy is to become truly consolidated.

The global democratic trend

Since the inauguration in 1974 of what Samuel Huntington (1991) dubbed the "third wave" of democratization, the number of democracies in the world has tripled (Table 10.1). Of course, when the Portuguese military overthrew the Salazar–Caetano dictatorship in 1974, no one had an inkling of the breathtaking political transformation that would sweep the world within a generation. Indeed, the pace of democratic transformation was quite slow in the 1970s, confined mainly to Southern Europe and a few Latin American countries. During the 1980s, the wave washed over Asia, restoring or inaugurating democracy in the Philippines, Korea, Taiwan,

TABLE 10.1 *Trends in Electoral Democracies, 1974: 1988–2000*

Year	Number of democracies	Number of countries	Democracies as a percentage of all countries	Annual rate of increase in democracies (%)
1974	39	142	27.5	
1988	66	167	39.5	
1990	76	165	46.1	
1991	91	183	49.7	19.7
1992	99	186	53.2	8.1
1993	108	190	56.8	8.3
1994	114	191	59.7	5.3
1995	117	191	61.3	2.6
1996	118	191	61.8	0.9
1997	117	191	61.3	−0.9
1998	117	191	61.3	0
1999	120	192	62.5	2.6
2000	120	192	62.5	0

NOTE: Figures for 1990–2000 are for the end of the calendar year. Figures for 1974 estimate the number of democracies in the world in April 1974, at the end of the inception of the third wave.

SOURCES: Freedom House, *Freedom in the World: The Annual Survey of Political Rights and Civil Liberties, 1900–91, … 1999–2000* (New York: Freedom House, 1991 …); and *Journal of Democracy* 12 (1), 2001

Thailand, and Pakistan, among other countries. It swept throughout the Americas, leaving virtually the entire Western Hemisphere with freely elected governments by 1990. Yet, by the late 1980s, most countries still had authoritarian regimes. At the end of 1988, only about two in every five regimes were democratic, and almost one-third of these democracies were in countries with populations of less than one million.

The dramatic events of 1989 changed everything. The collapse of communism in Eastern Europe, dramatically symbolized by the popular uprisings and the tearing down of the Berlin Wall, not only expanded the number of democracies in Europe. It also generated diffusion and demonstration effects that brought down the Soviet communist regime, split apart the Soviet Empire, and undermined the remaining Soviet client states and Marxist regimes in the third world. These impacts were felt with particular force on the African continent. There, two key developments in February of 1990 (shortly after the fall of the Wall)—the release of Nelson Mandela and the unbanning of the African National Congress in South Africa, and the National Conference that effectively seized power from the dictatorship in Benin—initiated a wave of political transitions.

Huntington shows that both previous waves of democratic expansion were followed by "reverse waves," in which the number of democratic breakdowns considerably exceeded the number of transitions to democracy. These were bleak periods (1922–42, 1958–75) for peace and human rights in the world. Even if one accepts Huntington's theory and periodization of "waves," it does not necessarily follow theoretically that a wave of democratic expansion *must* be followed by a reverse wave. It is possible that global democratic expansion could pause in a state of equilibrium for some extended period of time, before it resumes again.

Remarkably, a quarter-century after the inception of the third wave of democratization (in 1974), there is no sign yet that the world has entered a "third reverse wave." Not only are there more democracies than ever before, but also there have been very few "high profile" democratic reversals. In fact, during the first 25 years of the third wave, there were only three blatant reversals of democracy in countries with more than 20 million people: the military coup in Nigeria at the end of 1983, the 1989 military coup in Sudan, and the 1991 military coup in Thailand. The former two coups occurred in Africa (where the majority of democratic breakdowns have taken place during the third wave), and these two coups happened *before* the third wave of democratization reached the African continent in 1991. The Thai coup was a major setback for democracy in Southeast Asia, but it did not last. In little more than a year, the country's military leaders felt compelled to convene national elections to legitimize their rule, and their insistence on installing a non-elected army commander as prime minister triggered massive demonstrations that brought down the authoritarian project. Just 17 months after the February 1991 coup, democracy was restored to Thailand with the election of the first non-military prime minister since the mid-1970s.

The October 1999 military coup in Pakistan may portend a more ominous trend. The principal causes of democratic breakdown in Pakistan—the abuse of executive power, human rights, and the rule of law; growing ethnic and religious violence; and economic failure and injustice—are not unique to Pakistan. Increasingly, these problems afflict many other emerging democracies in the world, such as Russia, Brazil, Turkey, Nigeria, and the Philippines.

In the coming decade, it is not likely that we will see a dramatic expansion in the number of democracies in the world, that is, a fourth wave, or a re-ignition of the now stalled third wave. Most of the remaining non-democracies are in regions (particularly the Arab Middle East, Central Asia, and sub-Saharan Africa) and countries whose conditions (authoritarian cultures, low incomes, and long histories of ethnic and regional conflict) are not propitious for democratization. This does not mean that democratic transitions cannot occur in particular countries—and in surprising ways—but it suggests that in the near term, the chances for a broad succession of democratic breakthroughs are low. Rather, the principal challenge facing democracy in the world over the next decade is to consolidate the considerable number of new democracies that have come into being over the past two decades, or that have become destabilized during this period.

Conceptual issues

Democracies—in the minimal sense, "electoral" democracies—share at least one broad, essential requirement. The principal positions of political power in the country are filled through regular, free, and fair elections between competing parties, and it is possible for an incumbent government to be turned out of office in those elections. However, the standard for electoral democracy—what constitutes "free and fair"—is more ambiguous than is often appreciated. Electoral fraud is endemic in Nigeria, despite the renewal of a competitive party system. There was also evidence of outright fraud in the March 2000 election that confirmed Vladimir Putin in the presidency of Russia. But even short of fraud, Putin had such massive advantages of incumbency and support from crony capitalists that opposition parties virtually conceded his election in advance.

However we judge them, elections are only one dimension of democracy. The quality of democracy also depends on its levels of freedom, pluralism, justice, and accountability. The deeper level of *liberal democracy* requires the following:

- Freedom of belief, expression, organization, demonstration, and other civil liberties, including protection from political terror and unjustified imprisonment.
- A rule of law under which all citizens are treated equally and due process is secure.
- Political independence and neutrality of the judiciary and of other institutions of "horizontal accountability" that check the abuse of power, such as electoral administration, the audit, and the central bank.
- An open, pluralistic civil society, which affords citizens multiple, ongoing channels for expression and representation of their interests and values, in independent associations and movements and in the mass media as well.
- Freedom of cultural, religious, ethnic, and other minorities to speak their languages, practice their cultures, and express their identities.
- Civilian control over the military (Dahl 1971: 1–3, 1989: 220–2; Linz and Stepan 1996: 3–15; Diamond 1999: 10–12; O'Donnell 1999).

To be viable, these dimensions of liberal democracy require several other institutions, including a constitution that is supreme in law and in public esteem, a state bureaucracy that is capable and professional, and a party system with some degree of institutionalization and linkage to societal interests (Linz and Stepan 1996; Weingast 1997; Mainwaring 1998). Particularly in societies with deep ethnic or nationality cleavages, liberal democracy requires an electoral system that can manage and transcend the country's divisions, a constitutional structure that limits majoritarian power, and a federal system or other means to devolve power to lower levels of authority and give territorial minorities a sense of security (Diamond 1999: 93–160; Lijphart 1999; Stepan 1999).

We also need to consider how stable and firmly rooted democracies are. Democracies are "consolidated" when all significant political elites, parties, and organizations, as well as an overwhelming majority of the mass public, are firmly committed to the democratic constitutional system and regularly comply with its rules and constraints. Consolidation thus requires a broad normative and behavioral consensus on the desirability of democracy in general and on the legitimacy of the specific constitutional system in place in the country (Linz and Stepan 1996: 5–7; Diamond 1999: 65–73). In a consolidated democracy, the norms, procedures, and expectations of democracy are so internalized that actors routinely, instinctively conform to the rules of the game (both written and unwritten). This is what Rustow (1970) refers to as "habituation." "It is the deep, unquestioned, routinized commitment to democracy and its procedures at the elite and mass levels that produces a crucial element of consolidation, a reduction in the uncertainty of democracy, regarding not so much the outcomes as the rules and methods of political competition" (Diamond 1999: 65). Democracy is genuinely, organically stable, hence consolidated, when all political actors capable of mobilizing any significant power or popular following not only obey the rules and norms of democracy but trust that their adversaries (real and potential) will do so as well (Whitehead 1989).

How the people view democracy

One indispensable indicator of the health and stability of a democracy and the degree to which it is consolidated derives from public opinion data. How the people assess and value their political system, and the principles of democracy and freedom more generally, can tell us much about whether democracy is consolidated in a country. Surveys of public opinion alone cannot tell us whether a democracy is consolidated, for consolidation also involves the behavior of the mass public (for example in elections, and in other social actions) and the beliefs and behavior of elites and major parties and organizations as well. However, if democracy does not have widespread popular support, it cannot be considered consolidated, no matter how favorable the other indicators.

For democratic consolidation, the most important dimension of public opinion is the level of support for democracy *as a political system or regime*. Essentially, this involves a belief in the legitimacy of democracy, that it is the best form of government for society, or at least better than any alternative that citizens can imagine (Linz 1978: 16; Lipset 1981: 64). System support, however, has multiple dimensions. Building on the work of David Easton, Pippa Norris and her colleagues have distinguished five different objects of political support that form a continuum (Norris 1999b: 9–13, 16–21). The most diffuse levels are the *political community*, or the nation-state and its specific boundaries, and the core *regime principles* or values of the political system. The latter dimension taps beliefs about the legitimacy of democracy, as measured in the surveys discussed below by support for alternative regime forms and by the belief that democracy is always the best type of system for the country. At the intermediate level are evaluations of *regime performance*, how the political system functions in practice. A classic measure for this, employed in several of the regional surveys below, is the degree of satisfaction with the way democracy is working in the country. Performance is also tapped to some extent by measures of regime "approval" (although these measures overlap somewhat ambiguously with the legitimacy dimension). A fourth, more specific, political object is composed of the different *regime institutions*. This is often measured (as in the surveys below) by assessing levels of public trust or confidence in major political institutions, such as parliament, the president, the courts, the military, and political parties. Finally, one can assess support for *political actors*, but to the extent this measures support for individual political leaders (rather than politicians more generally), such information tells us little of value about the legitimacy of democracy and its progress toward consolidation. Hence, this level of assessment is omitted from the analysis below.

Support for democracy has been measured repeatedly in surveys of post-communist Europe and Latin America in recent years, and more recently in surveys of Korea, Taiwan, and a number of African states. While the measures used are not always strictly comparable to one another, they do permit some cross-regional comparisons, as well as comparisons within regions and within countries, over time. We can begin by examining the extent to which post-communist publics in these countries give a positive rating to the working of two different systems: "the former communist regime" and the "current system of governing with free elections and many parties." Because these two questions pertain to "how our system of government works," they straddle the boundary between *regime principles* and *regime performance*. As we see in Table 10.2, the publics in Central and Eastern Europe (CEE) are (on this intermediate level) much more supportive of democracy than are the former Soviet publics, in this case Russia, Ukraine, and Belarus. Whereas clear majorities (often over 60%) in each of the seven CEE countries have approved of the way the current multiparty system works, the overall percentage in the post-Soviet heartland has never been much more than a third. At the same time, retrospective approval of the previous communist system is much higher in the post-Soviet states than in the CEE ones—by an average of 30 percentage points in the most recent survey.[1] Overall, more than two-thirds of these post-Soviet publics look back favorably (perhaps wistfully) on the old communist regimes, whereas only about two in five citizens in post-communist Europe do so.

However, there has been a recent downward trend (between 1995 and 1998) in the CEE states in approval of the democratic system's performance. This is likely due to protracted economic difficulties in many countries, such as Romania (where approval of the current economic system in 1998 was only 23%, compared to 40% in Hungary and Slovenia and 61% in Poland). Economically, most people think they (and their families) were better off under communism, but while the average thinking so (in 1998) was 56% in the seven CEE states (and about that in Russia), it was 79% in

TABLE 10.2   *Support for the Current Regime in Post-Communist States*

Country	1991	Percentage expressing approval			
	1991	1992	1993	1995	1998
Czech Republic	71	71	78	77	56
Slovakia	50	58	62	61	50
Hungary	57	43	51	50	53
Poland	52	56	69	76	66
Slovenia	49	68	55	66	51
Bulgaria	64	55	58	66	58
Romania	69	68	60	61	55
Russia		14	36	26	36
Belarus		35	29	35	48
Ukraine		25	24	33	22

NOTE: The question asked was "Here is a scale for ranking how government works. The top, plus 100, is the best; the bottom, minus 100, the worst. Where on this scale would you put our present system of governing with free elections and many parties?" Approval is indicated by a placement above zero.

SOURCES: Mishler and Rose (1998: Table 2), Rose and Haerpfer (1998: 49–50), Rose (1999: Table 4.1)

Belarus and 90% in Ukraine (Rose and Haerpfer 1998: 47). The other factor that may be depressing approval is the widespread perception of corruption in the region. "Across post-communist Europe, Barometer surveys find an average of 72 percent believe that their new regime is more corrupt than its predecessor;" and in every post-communist country surveyed a majority of the public believes the national government is corrupt (Rose 2001: 101). As we will see, these proportions bear a striking resemblance to the views of Latin American publics. While people are well capable of separating their views of politicians or of regime performance from their assessment of regime principles, these perceptions of corruption do reflect a trend of growing cynicism about politics and politicians that appears to impede the consolidation of many new democracies.

Two others questions are particularly useful for evaluating public support for democracy at the level of *regime principles*. One examines support for imaginable alternative, undemocratic regimes (a return to Communist rule, rule by the army, closing down parliament in favor of a "strong leader who can decide things quickly," and a return to monarchy). Rejection of all these authoritarian alternatives indicates robust support for democracy as a form of government. Such support is lacking in Russia, Belarus, and Ukraine, where, in 1998, an average of only 36% of the public opposed all authoritarian alternatives (Table 10.3). By contrast, in the states of post-communist Europe, strong majorities (ranging from 56 to 78%) oppose all authoritarian alternatives.

As Richard Rose (2001) shows, the crucial divide among the post-communist states is not purely between Europe as opposed to the former Soviet Union. This heavily overlaps with the divide between those states with levels of civil and political freedom roughly comparable to the European

TABLE 10.3   *Rejection of All Authoritarian Alternatives in Post-Communist States*

Country	Percentage rejecting authoritarian alternatives		
	1993	**1995**	**1998**
Czech Republic	79	82	75
Slovakia	67	70	57
Hungary	72	69	68
Poland	57	63	67
Slovenia	58	68	78
Bulgaria	44	55	56
Romania	60	61	60
Russia	n.a.	n.a.	39
Belarus	35	30	46
Ukraine	37	23	24

NOTE: The question asked was "Our present system of government is not the only one that this country has had. Some people say that we would be better off if the country was governed differently. What do you think? Please tell for each point whether you strongly agree, somewhat agree, somewhat disagree, or strongly disagree: 1) We should return to Communist rule. 2) The army should govern the country. 3) Best to get rid of Parliament and elections and have a strong leader who can quickly decide everything. 4) A return to monarchy would be better." "Rejection" is indicated by somewhat or strong disagreement with all four items.

SOURCES: See Table 10.2; Rose and Haerpfer (1998: question 24)

Union and those that lag well behind. Among the ten countries rated "free" by Freedom House, an average of 63% reject all authoritarian alternatives (and 55% approve of the current system). Among the six others, only 43% reject all authoritarian alternatives (and only about a third approve of the current system) (Rose 2001: 99). This is indicative of a more general problem. "The great obstacle to the completion of democracy in post-communist Europe is the absence of the rule of law" (Rose 2001: 94). This absence is particularly glaring in the less-than-free states, which are also the ones with the highest external perceptions of corruption, as measured by Transparency International.

Both the public opinion data and independent measures of the actual operation of these systems (in terms of democracy, freedom, and transparency) point in the same direction. The post-communist states are sharply diverging in two directions. One set is increasingly drawn into the gravitational pull of a wider Europe, and looks to integration into the European Union and NATO. This set, which includes Central Europe and the Baltic states, is much freer and less corrupt. Most of these states are now broadly liberal democracies. With the recent defeat of the quasi-dictator Slobodan Milosevic in the 2000 presidential election, Serbia is moving toward this more progressive and liberal European group, as Croatia began doing two or three years before. The other set contains the post-Soviet states that are slipping backwards, away from democracy and the rule of law. These are the more repressive and corrupt of the post-communist states (including not only Russia and Ukraine but also in large measure Georgia and Armenia), where democracy is increasingly shallow or beleaguered, or gone altogether (as in Belarus and the Kyrgyz Republic). The problem is not simply a growing divergence between *electoral* democracy and *liberal* democracy. The spreading erosion of liberty and accountability and the increasing centralization of power in countries such as Russia and Ukraine are exacting a heavy toll on the electoral dimension of democracy as well.

Latin America

Within Latin America as well, there is significant variation in support for democratic *regime principles* (as measured by the question of whether "democracy is preferable to any other kind of government" or sometimes "an authoritarian government can be preferable"). Several features of the time series data for Latin America are noteworthy.[2] First, only two small countries have levels of support for democracy comparable to the levels— well over 70% in Spain, Portugal, and Greece—which are indicative of firm democratic consolidation. These are Costa Rica and Uruguay, where support for democracy exceeds 80% and the willingness to entertain the authoritarian option is at 10% or less. The only other country where 70% or more of the public consistently support democracy is Argentina. By this measure, some other countries have made progress or appear reasonably supportive, but others have regressed. Particularly striking are the very low level of support for democracy in Brazil; the rather high levels of consideration for authoritarian rule in Mexico, Paraguay, Brazil, Colombia, and Venezuela; and the deterioration in support for democracy in Colombia (Table 10.4).

The malaise of democracy in the Andean region and in some other parts of Latin America is driven by dissatisfaction with the way democracy is working, and underlying that, concern about corruption, poor economic performance, and a general lack of responsiveness on the part of politicians. One response that has remained virtually unchanged over the past four years in Latin America is the assessment of the trend with respect to corruption. When asked whether it has increased a little or a lot, remained the same, or decreased a little or a lot in the past 12 months, an astonishing 75% of Latin Americans said in 2000 that corruption has increased *a lot*. Another 10% said corruption has increased a little and less than 5% perceived any decline.[3] Even in countries with strong support for democracy, such as Costa Rica, Uruguay, and Argentina, most people think corruption has increased a lot. As with the post-communist states, much of this perception may be the ironic consequence of greater freedom to report political wrongdoing (and the attendant press sensationalism).

As for economic performance, several countries remained mired in economic crisis, and even where the economy is growing overall (as in Brazil) severe problems of inequality leave huge swaths of the population excluded from its benefits. The disgust with democratic politicians in Ecuador, where

TABLE 10.4   *Democratic Legitimacy in Latin America*

Country	Year	Percentage agree		
		Democracy is preferable	Sometimes authoritarianism is preferable	It doesn't matter to people like me
Costa Rica	2000	83	7	8
	1996	80	6	6
Uruguay	2000	84	9	6
	1996	80	9	8
Argentina	2000	71	16	11
	1996	71	15	11
Chile	2000	57	19	22
	1996	54	19	23
Brazil	2000	39	24	28
	1996	50	24	21
Paraguay	2000	48	39	13
	1996	59	26	13
Venezuela	2000	61	24	10
	1996	62	19	13
Colombia	2000	50	23	20
	1996	60	20	18
Mexico	2000	45	34	19
	1996	53	23	17
Latin America	2000	60	17	17
average	1996	61	17	17

NOTES: The question asked was "Which of the following statements do you agree with most? 1) Democracy is preferable to any other form of government. 2) In certain situations, an authoritarian government can be preferable to democracy. 3) It doesn't matter to people like me whether we have a democratic or non-democratic government."

SOURCES: Lagos (1996, 2001); Informe de Prensa: Latinobarómetro 1999/2000, Santiago, http://www.latinobarometro.cl/Infopre00nr.htm. Additional data from Marta Lagos. Latin America average is for all 17 countries surveyed.

indigenous organizations and sections of the military joined to seize power briefly in January 2000, can be attributed at least in part to severe economic crisis. In 1999, social spending fell by half and the minimum salary by a quarter while unemployment doubled in a country with the third worst distribution of income in the region (Lucero 2001).

The political malaise in Latin America is vividly conveyed by the low levels of satisfaction with the way democracy is working (Table 10.5). On average, only 37% of Latin Americans in 2000 were satisfied with the working of democracy. This is similar to the average levels among the highly cynical post-communist publics, but compares unfavorably to the 53% among EU countries (1997–1999), 45% in Korea (2000), and 59% in Taiwan (1999). Only in three countries were majorities of the Latin American public satisfied with the working of democracy in 2000, and the extremely low levels of satisfaction in Brazil (18%), Ecuador (23%), and Paraguay (12%) are indicative of a crisis of democratic confidence.

TABLE 10.5   *Satisfaction with Democracy in Latin America*

	Percentage satisfied			
	1996	1997	1998	1999–2000
Costa Rica	51	68	54	61
Uruguay	52	54	68	69
Argentina	34	42	49	46
Chile	27	37	32	35
Brazil	20	23	27	18
Venezuela	30	35	35	55
Colombia	16	40	24	27
Peru	28	21	17	24
Ecuador	34	31	33	23
Paraguay	22	16	24	12
Latin America average	27	41	37	37

NOTES: The question asked was "In general, would you say that you are very satisfied, fairly satisfied, not very satisfied, or not at all satisfied with the way democracy works in [name of country]?"

SOURCES: See Table 10. 4

East Asia and Africa

At the level of regime principles, support for democracy is lower in Korea and Taiwan, where (in response to the same question asked in Latin America) only a little more than half of each public says democracy is always best. Particularly striking is the substantial proportion of Koreans (almost one-third in 1998 and 1999) who say that sometimes an authoritarian regime may be preferable. On the other hand, satisfaction with democracy is higher in Korea, and particularly in Taiwan, where three in five are satisfied. The data from Korea and Taiwan paint an ambiguous picture. Neither democracy is in danger of collapse. But support for democracy in Korea declined significantly in the wake of the November 1997 financial collapse and a string of high-profile corruption scandals. Moreover, on some measures of regime principles, such as the ten-point scale by which Koreans judge how "suitable" democracy is for their country, support for democracy has declined perceptibly in the past three years in Korea and is outpaced by the level of support for democracy in Taiwan. Koreans are torn. They reject authoritarian alternatives about as often as the more democratic post-communist publics, yet when forced to weigh democracy against economic security, their commitment wavers. And about seven in ten Koreans seem willing to tolerate illegal actions by the president in a crisis (Chu, Diamond, and Shin, 2001a, b).

Even more striking by way of comparison are the African data. Five of the six African countries analyzed by Bratton and Mattes (2001) show levels of support for democracy (on the regime principle of "democracy is always best"), higher than the Latin American average. In the context of its long history of stable democratic functioning without interruption, the

82% support level in Botswana is evidence of democratic consolidation. The same level (81%) in Nigeria more likely reflects the broad revulsion with predatory military rule and the euphoria of the recent transition back to civilian rule. The 71% figure in Zimbabwe reflects the strength of opposition to Robert Mugabe's repressive and corrupt regime. The even higher figure in Ghana (76%) can now be read as a harbinger of the extraordinary opposition victory in the December 2000 presidential election. Even among those who say that democracy is "not working," "democracy is supported by large majorities in Zimbabwe (74%) and Botswana (65%) as well as by substantial majorities in Malawi (59%) and Zambia (54%)" (Mattes et al. 2000: 12). Moreover, very large majorities in five of the six African countries (except Namibia) also reject authoritarian alternatives such as military and one-party rule.

One reason why support for democracy is so high in these African countries is that people are satisfied with the way democracy is working. Except in Zimbabwe, where there has been no democracy for some time, satisfaction ranges from 54 to 84%, much higher than in Latin America. Bratton and Mattes (2001: 119) find that in Africa (as elsewhere) "popular support for democracy has a strong instrumental component. Citizens extend support to a democratic regime in good part because they are satisfied with its performance in delivering desired goods and services." Yet, one in five Africans surveyed supports democracy despite dissatisfaction with its performance. Moreover, asked if they would prefer democracy or a "strong leader who does not have to bother with elections" when "democracy does not work," substantial majorities in several countries still chose democracy as "always best" (Mattes et al. 2000: 13).

The high levels of support for democracy in these African countries cannot be dismissed as deriving from a vacuous or specious understanding of democracy. Large majorities in each country are able to attach a meaning to democracy, and most of these (about seven in ten) define democracy in terms of political procedures, not substantive outcomes. Indeed, "popular African conceptions of democracy are, perhaps unexpectedly, quite *liberal*," with the open-ended responses citing "civil liberties and personal freedoms more frequently than any other meanings (34%)" (Bratton and Mattes 2001: 110). Where democracy has stood the longest, Botswana, the identification of democracy with civil and political rights is most frequent (55%).

The meaning of the data

There is a cautionary message in the public opinion data. The road to democratic consolidation is longer and more complicated than was often blithely assumed a decade ago when many of these new democracies were taking shape. There is no imminent threat to democracy in Korea and Taiwan, and no democracy has ever broken down in a society even approaching their level of per capita income. However, at the level of mass public beliefs, values, and evaluations, democracy has yet to be consolidated in either country, and indeed has probably moved in the reverse direction in Korea. The democratic ambivalence of Korea and Taiwan is evidenced as well in the political crises and stalemates each country has experienced since the rotation of presidential power to opposition parties in 1998 in Korea and 2000 in Taiwan. Neither system has been able to construct a sustainable, democratic working relationship between executive and legislature, government and opposition. Elsewhere, most of Latin America is stuck somewhere between democratic stability and crisis, with only three countries showing overwhelming mass support for democracy. In Central and Eastern Europe it is mainly an external factor—the enormous attraction of the EU, with its clear political conditionality—that is propelling these systems toward consolidation, though not without some signs of regression, anxiety, and institutional deformity. In a number of countries, public opinion is much more supportive of democracy than are the elites or the institutional actors. This is particularly so in Africa, where, with the exception of Botswana, the high levels of public support for democracy do not indicate consolidation. Yet these levels do constitute a positive sign, and in Ghana they may well herald a new era of sustainable democracy.

The evidence from these and other public opinion studies underscores the crucial importance of regime performance in fostering or stunting the growth of democratic legitimacy. We are still a very long way from being able to determine very clearly and satisfactorily what generates sustainable support for democracy. But the recent data add to our sense that both economic and political performance matter. A sharp economic downturn can diminish support for democracy when misrule appears to be the cause, at least in part. And people will blame the government for bad economic times, whether it deserves that blame or not. The key is whether they will go on to blame *the system of government*. The capacity for throwing the incumbents out has eclipsed that judgment for some time in many countries. However, the declines in democratic support in Colombia, Venezuela, and elsewhere in Latin America suggest that if economic difficulties go on for long enough—and especially if they are deemed to derive from broader problems of governance, such as corruption and abuse of power—the system of government will begin to be blamed.

One of the key problems in much of Latin America is that trust in institutions is very low. Overall in the region, only 28% express trust in parliament, only 20% trust in parties, 35% in the courts, and 38% in the president. In fact, low levels of institutional trust are a problem in most of the emerging democracies. Trust in parties and parliament especially is low almost everywhere, and the relatively low trust in the courts epitomizes the weakness of the rule of law. Among 11 post-communist countries surveyed by the "New Democracies Barometer" in 1998, on average only 29% of citizens trusted in the courts. The highest proportion was Romania (40%), and in Russia, surveyed separately, only a quarter of the people trust the courts. Trust in parties is even lower, as only one in every eight post-communist citizens express confidence in political parties. It is not hard to see why political parties have so much difficulty mobilizing broad bases of support for painful but necessary structural reforms when they are so distrusted and disliked by the public. Against these miserable levels of public confidence, the data from Korea and Taiwan look relatively encouraging, yet even in those two countries, very few political institutions are trusted by more than half the public.

These skeptical—if not overtly cynical—assessments of democratic institutions and how they perform overall retard the process of legitimation. Causal analysis of the data from Korea and Taiwan suggests that political factors are more important than economic ones in shaping support for democracy. The more satisfied people are with the way democracy works, the more they trust key political institutions, and in particular the more they perceive the system to be democratic, the more likely they are to support democracy. The African survey data also contain some indications that perceptions of the degree to which the system is functioning democratically may be important in affecting support for the political system. And Rose and his colleagues have shown the perception of greater freedom to be a significant determinant of support for post-communist democracies, while political factors in general outweigh economic ones (Rose, Mishler, and Haerpfer 1999).

Freedom is important but it is not sufficient. If democracies are to be seen to deliver on the political promise of democracy, they must deliver a rule of law in a second sense as well, not just *permitting* citizens to express themselves and live their lives, but also *restraining* government officials from abusing power. We do not have nearly enough data specifically measuring how citizens perceive corruption and what factors shape their perceptions. The data we have demonstrate widespread and growing cynicism about corruption in public life, even though actual levels of corruption in some countries may well be lower than when the press was less free to report it and the institutions of investigation and horizontal accountability less active. If democracy is going to be consolidated at the level of mass public beliefs and values, there will need to be much more dramatic progress in controlling corruption in politics and government and improving responsiveness and accountability more generally. The growing accumulation of public opinion data only reinforces this fundamental point: the challenge of democratic consolidation remains substantially one of providing effective democratic governance.

Improving governance

To be effective and stable, a democratic state must be legitimate, and to sustain popular legitimacy, it must be a "self-restraining state" (Schedler, Diamond, and Plattner 1999). Common to all the troubled democracies is the need for more powerful, state institutions to check the abuse of power by other state institutions and actors and to ensure that state officials comply with the law, the constitution, and norms of good governance.

The most important institution in this regard is the judicial system. With a few exceptions, the legal systems of many emerging democracies are understaffed, underpaid, underfunded, ill equipped, inefficient, and much too susceptible to political direction and constraint. In the most troubled cases, such as Russia, Ukraine, Turkey, Brazil, Mexico, Colombia, or Nigeria, corruption warps the administration of justice, despite the presence of some courageous individual judges. This is why mass publics have so little confidence in their judiciaries.

Comprehensive reforms are needed to modernize and professionalize the judiciary and to insulate its appointment, remuneration, administration, and supervision from political influence. This requires giving judges long terms, even life tenure, decent salaries, and autonomous means for the financing of the judicial branch (administered by the Supreme Court or by an independent judicial council). It further means entrusting to judicial councils made up of judges, retired judges, lawyers, law professors, the bar association, and other non-political (or less political) actors in civil society, primary say over the appointment of new judges, the elevation of judges to higher courts, and the disciplining of the profession. Particularly in Latin America and the post-communist states, legal codes need extensive revision (Domingo 1999). In short, the quest for more effective and independent judicial systems requires reinforcement from complementary institutions, demand from below, and support from the outside.

A genuine rule of law requires an overlapping, reinforcing system of agencies of horizontal accountability. This involves creation, or empowerment, of a number of other complementary institutions that are truly independent of partisan politics, such as a counter-corruption commission, human rights commission, ombudsman, auditor-general, and national electoral commission. A counter-corruption commission should receive annually declarations of assets from all elected officials and other high office-holders; make those declarations publicly available and scrutinize and investigate them; bring charges for bribery, embezzlement, influence-peddling, and other wrongdoing; and prosecute violations before a court or special tribunal. A human rights commission should receive citizen complaints about violations of rights that are guaranteed under the constitution and international and regional covenants. It must have the legal authority and obligation to investigate those complaints, make its reports public, compensate victims, and recommend removal or punishment of offending state actors. Citizens must have the further opportunity to register complaints about ill treatment and abuse of power by various state agencies with an ombudsman's commission that will similarly investigate wrongdoing, report publicly, and recommend redress. An auditor-general should have the authority to audit the accounts of any state agency on suspicion of any wrongdoing, and on a periodic basis otherwise, and its findings must be made available to parliament and the public. The national electoral administration must enable *vertical accountability* to work to turn rotten incumbents out of office. It must ensure that opposing parties and candidates can campaign freely, with reasonable access to the media, and that citizens can vote freely and have their ballots counted fairly and accurately.

Many emerging democracies have some or all of these other institutions of horizontal accountability, but typically they do not function very effectively. This is for the same reason that judicial systems do not: they are politically staffed or constrained, and they lack the resources and authority to do a serious job. All of these institutions need to be empowered. They need a huge infusion of human capital—training for judges, lawyers, prosecutors, paralegals, accountants, and technical and research support staff. And they need other, "harder" infusions of capital: more money for higher salaries, computers, and other equipment. Most of all they need the political incentive and authority to exercise their functions. As with the judiciary, this requires some institutional means to insulate them from political interference in appointments, supervision, administration, and funding.

Strengthening state institutions alone will not develop a rule of law or control corruption. There must also be a strong societal demand for reform. An effective reform strategy requires strengthening the capacity of professional and civic associations, think tanks, the mass media, and independent interest groups (including trade unions and business chambers) for several purposes. First, these actors in civil society must mobilize vigorously to generate broad societal demand for institutional reforms. Second, these organizations and media can provide an additional and independent arena for monitoring government performance, thus checking and reinforcing the conduct of the relevant formal agencies of horizontal accountability. Investigative media are vitally important. Third, civil society organizations and mass media need to educate citizens about their democratic rights and responsibilities, so that they can defend their rights and use and support the institutions of horizontal accountability. Fourth, civil society actors, such as legal aid organizations and human rights groups, can help citizens, particularly the poor and the marginalized, to make use of these institutions of accountability. Fifth, in these direct ways and through their own internal functioning, civil society organizations and independent media can help arrest the descent into the fragmented, cynical world of the uncivic community. They do this by generating a different set of expectations based on cooperation and respect for law and state authority, properly exercised (Putnam et al. 1993; Gyimah-Boadi 1997; Schmitter 1997; Diamond 1999).

The challenges to the peace and integrity of the nation-state are diverse, but all derive in one way or another from the feeling of some groups that they are excluded from a fair share of power and resources, or are otherwise victimized by the groups that control the central state. Big and ethnically diverse countries such as India, Nigeria, Indonesia, Russia, and Turkey cannot hold together democratically unless aggrieved groups and regions feel they have a stake—and a safe, dignified place—in the nation-state. The challenge of constructing this is far too complex to survey even briefly, but everywhere there are at least two requirements. First, every group deserves the right to use its culture and language and have its group identity respected and protected in the larger system. Second, territorially based groups—such as the Kurds of southeastern Turkey and the Ogonis and other minorities of Nigeria's oil-rich delta—need real political autonomy if they are to surrender aspirations for total independence. This need not always mean a fully federal system, but it must grant aggrieved regions a constitutionally embedded right to some meaningful self-government, including the ability to mobilize and use a good share of their own resources for their own development. Affected countries cannot achieve a stable, liberal democracy until they resolve their ethnic and regional insurgencies by negotiating some devolution of power (Horowitz 1985; Diamond and Plattner 1994; Diamond 1999: 149–54; Ergil 2000).

Better governance means improving the performance and integrity of the state, but in a democracy that cannot be accomplished without politics. Many of the reforms that are needed to invigorate horizontal accountability, manage regional conflicts, strengthen the state, and liberalize the economy require legislative action. In a country plagued with multiple crises of governance, mobilizing a sustainable coalition for reform is a maddeningly difficult but quintessentially political task—as the reform president, Fernando Henrique Cardoso, has discovered in Brazil (Cardoso 1996).

In a democracy, crafting a coalition for reform must involve political parties. It is political parties that in the end must bargain, coalesce, and produce the votes for reform in parliament. Political parties must be involved in mobilizing popular support in society, and in linking the grievances of citizens and the demands of interest groups to an agenda for institutional reform. The crises of governance are ones of state- and nation-building, but they cannot be resolved democratically without reforming and rebuilding political parties, and regenerating some measure of civic respect for and confidence in them. This means enhancing their organizational coherence and capacity, instituting means for them to cultivate and communicate with concrete interest and regional constituencies, democratizing and making more transparent their internal governance and means of finance, and fortifying their autonomy through (at least partial) public financing of parties and election campaigns (Mainwaring 1998; Diamond and Gunther 2001).

The situation is not without hope. From Thailand to Brazil, from Korea to Argentina, reform is at least on the agenda. And the crises of governance also threaten authoritarian regimes, as in China, Iran, and Egypt. However, as Indonesia is now discovering, regime transition driven by an implosion of governance does not leave a very favorable legacy for a new democracy. International actors have a crucial role to play in pressing the necessary reform agenda, in supporting civil society actors who see the need for reform, and in providing the financial and technical resources needed to help construct and enable the necessary institutions. An international vision for reform, with distinct institution-building targets and country priorities, could transform an increasingly precarious global situation. Alternatively, a failure of will or lack of clear vision could squander an unparalleled opportunity to build a truly democratic world.

NOTES

1. The difference would be even greater if Hungary were set aside, given that its much softer "goulash" communism does not evoke the same repressive, authoritarian memories that the other systems do.
2. For the country data on this measure for the years 1996, 1998, and 2000, see Lagos (2001: Table 1, p. 139).
3. Data provided by Marta Lagos from the Latinobarómetro. The percentages saying corruption has "increased a lot" were 75% in 1996, 79% in 1997 and again in 1998, and 75% in 2000.

Bibliography

Aardal, Bernt, and Henrik Oscarsson. 2000. "The Myth of Increasing Personalisation of Politics: Party Leader Effects on Party Choice in Sweden and Norway 1979–98." Paper presented at the annual meeting of the American Political Science Association, Washington, DC.

Aardal, Bernt, Anders Todal Jenssen, Henrik Oscarsson, Risto Sänkiaho, and Erika Säynässalo. 1998. "Can Ideology Explain the EU Vote?" In *To Join or Not to Join: Three Nordic Referendums on Membership in the European Union*, ed. Anders Todal Jenssen, Pertti Pesonen, and Mikael Gilljam. Oslo: Scandinavian University Press.

Abramson, Paul, John Aldrich, and David Rohde. 1999. *Change and Continuity in the 1996 and 1998 Elections*. Washington, DC: CQ Press.

Abramson, Paul R., John H. Aldrich, Phil Paolino, and David Rohde. 1992. "Sophisticated Voting in the 1988 Presidential Primaries." *American Political Science Review* 86: 55–70.

Aldrich, John. 1995. *Why Parties? The Origin and Transformation of Party Politics in America*. Chicago: University of Chicago Press.

Alford, Robert. 1963. *Party and Society: The Anglo-American Democracies*. Chicago: Rand McNally.

Allswang, John M. 2000. *The Initiative and Referendum in California, 1898–1998*. Stanford, CA: Stanford University Press.

Almond, Gabriel A., and Sidney Verba. 1963. *The Civic Culture*. Princeton, NJ: Princeton University Press.

Almond, Gabriel A., G. Bingham Powell, Jr, and Robert J. Mundt. 1993. *Comparative Politics: A Theoretical Framework*. New York: HarperCollins.

Alvarez, R. Michael, and Jonathan Nagler. 2000. "A New Approach for Modeling Strategic Voting in Multiparty Elections." *British Journal of Political Science* 30: 57–75.

Andersen, Robert. 2000. "Reporting Public Opinion Polls: The Media and the 1997 Canadian Election." *International Journal of Public Opinion Research* 12: 285–98.

Anderson, Christopher. 1995. *Blaming the Government: Citizens and the Economy in Five European Democracies*. Armonk, NY: M.E. Sharpe.

Anderson, Christopher J. 2000. "Economic Voting and Political Context: A Comparative Perspective." *Electoral Studies* 19: 151–70.

Ansell, Christopher, and Steven Fish. 1999. "The Art of Being Indispensable: Noncharismatic Personalism in Contemporary Political Parties." *Comparative Political Studies* 32: 283–312.

Ansolabehere, Stephen, and Shanto Iyengar. 1995. *Going Negative: How Political Advertisements Shrink and Polarize the Electorate*. New York: Free Press.

Ayres, B. Drummond, Jr 1995. "Easier Voter Registration Doesn't Raise Participation." *New York Times* 3 December.

Bagdikian, Ben. 1997. *The Media Monopoly*. Boston, MA: Beacon Press.

Balsom, Dennis, and J.B. Jones, eds. *Road to the National Assembly for Wales*. Cardiff: University of Wales Press.

Banducci, Susan, Jeffrey Karp, and Jack Vowles. 1998. "Vote Splitting Under MMP." In *Voter's Victory? New Zealand's First Election under Proportional Representation*, ed. Jack Vowles, Peter Aimer, Susan Banducci, and Jeffrey Karp. Auckland: Auckland University Press.

Banks, Arthur S., and Thomas C. Muller, eds. 1999. *Political Handbook of the World*. Binghamton, NY: CSA Publications.

Barker, Fiona, and Elizabeth McLeay. 2000. "How Much Change? An Analysis of the Initial Impact of Proportional Representation on the New Zealand Parliamentary Party System." *Party Politics* 6: 131–54.

Barnes, Samuel, Max Kaase, et al. 1979. *Political Action: Mass Participation in Five Western Democracies*. Beverly Hills, CA: Sage.

Bartels, Larry M. 1993. "Messages Received: The Political Impact of Media Exposure." *American Political Science Review* 87: 267–85.

Bartels, Larry M. 2000. "Partisanship and Voting Behavior, 1952–1996." *American Journal of Political Science* 44: 35–50.

Barthélemy, Joseph. 1912. *L'Organisation du suffrage et l'expérience belge*. Paris: M. Jiard et É. Brière.

Bartle, John. 2000. "More Evidence on a New Measure of Party Identification." Paper presented at the annual meeting of EPOP (Elections, Parties and Opinion Polls Group of the Political Studies Association), Edinburgh.

Bartolini, Stefano. 1984. "Institutional Constraints and Party Competition in the French Party System." *West European Politics* 7: 103–27.

Bartolini, Stefano, and Roberto d'Alimonte. 1995. "Il Sistema Partitico: Una Transizione Difficile." In *Maggioritario Ma Non Troppo*, ed. Stefano Bartolini and Roberto D'Alimonte. Bologna: Il Mulino.

Bartolini, Stefano, and Roberto d'Alimonte. 1998. "Majoritarian Miracles and the Question of Party System Change." *European Journal of Political Research* 34: 151–69.

Bartolini, Stefano, and Peter Mair. 1990. *Identity, Competition, and Electoral Availability: The Stabilisation of European Electorates, 1885–1985*. Cambridge: Cambridge University Press.

Bean, Clive, and Anthony Mughan. 1989. "Leadership Effects in Parliamentary Elections in Australia and Britain." *American Political Science Review* 83: 1165–79.

Bean, Clive S., and Martin P. Wattenberg. 1998. "Attitudes Towards Divided Government and Ticket-Splitting in Australia and the United States." *Australian Journal of Political Science* 33: 25–36.

Beck, Nathaniel, and Jonathan N. Katz. 1995. "What To Do (and What Not To Do) with Time-Series—Cross-Section Data in Comparative Perspective." *American Political Science Review* 89: 634–47.

Beer, Samuel. 1978. *The British Political System*. New York: Random House.

Beeson, Trevor as Rapporteur for the British Council of Churches Working Party. 1974. *Discretion and Valour: Religious Conditions in Russia and Eastern Europe*. Glasgow: Collins Fontana.

Bell, Daniel. 1973. *The Coming of Post-Industrial Society: A Venture in Social Forecasting*. New York: Basic Books.

Bell, D.V.J., and F. Fletcher, eds. 1991. *Reaching the Voter: Constituency Campaigning in Canada*. Toronto: Dundurn.

Berelson, Bernard, Paul F. Lazarsfeld, and William N. McPhee. 1954. *Voting*. Chicago: University of Chicago Press.

Best, Heinrich, and Maurizio Cotta, eds. 2000. *Parliamentary Representatives in Europe, 1848–2000: Legislative Recruitment and Careers in Eleven European Countries*. Oxford: Oxford University Press.

Betz, Hans-Georg. 1994. *Radical Right-Wing Populism in Western Europe*. Basingstoke: Macmillan.

Bianco, Alessandro, and Gianluca Gardini. 1999. "The Funding of Political Parties in Italy." In *The Funding of Political Parties: Europe and Beyond*, ed. Keith D. Ewing. Bologna: Cooperativa Libraria Universitaria Editrice Bologna.

Bille, Lars. 1990. "Denmark: The Oscillating Party System." In *Understanding Party System Change in Western Europe*, ed. Peter Mair and Gordon Smith. London: Cass.

Bille, Lars. 1992. "Denmark." In *Party Organizations: A Data Handbook on Party Organization in Western Democracies, 1960–90*, ed. Richard S. Katz and Peter Mair. London: Sage.

Bille, Lars. 2001. "Democratizing a Democratic Procedure: Myth or Reality? Candidate Selection in Western European Parties, 1960–90." *Party Politics* 7: 363–80.

Bjørklund, Tor. 1982. "The Demand for Referendum: When Does It Arise and When Does It Succeed?" *Scandinavian Political Studies* 5: 237–59.

Black, Jerome H. 1978. "The Multicandidate Calculus of Voting: Application to Canadian Federal Elections." *American Journal of Political Science* 22: 609–38.

Blais, André. 1988. "The Classification of Electoral Systems." *European Journal of Political Research* 16: 99–110.

Blais, André. 1991. "The Debate over Electoral Systems." *International Political Science Review* 12: 239–60.

Blais, André. 1993. "Rethinking our Electoral System: The Case for Majority Run-Off Elections." *Inroads* 2: 124–31.

Blais, André, and Ken Carty. 1987. "The Impact of Electoral Formulae on the Creation of Majority Governments." *Electoral Studies* 5: 209–18.

Blais, André, and Ken Carty. 1991. "The Psychological Impact of Electoral Laws: Measuring Duverger's Elusive Factor." *British Journal of Political Science* 21: 79–93.

Blais, André, and Stéphane Dion. 1990. "Electoral Systems and the Consolidation of New Democracies." In *Democratic Transition and Consolidation in Southern Europe, Latin America and Southeast Asia*, ed. Diane Ethier. London: Macmillan.

Blais, André, and A. Dobrzynska. 1990. "Turnout in Electoral Democracies." *European Journal of Political Research* 33: 239–61.

Blais, André, and Louis Massicotte. 1997. "Electoral Formulas: A Macroscopic Perspective." *European Journal of Political Research* 32: 107–29.

Blais, André, and Richard Nadeau. 1996. "Measuring Strategic Voting: A Two-Step Procedure." *Electoral Studies* 15: 39–52.

Blais, André, Louis Massicotte, and Agnieszka Dobrzynska. 1997. "Direct Presidential Elections: A World Summary." *Electoral Studies* 16: 441–55.

Blais, André, Richard Nadeau, Elisabeth Gidengil, and Neil Nevitte. 2001. "Measuring Strategic Voting in Multiparty Plurality Elections." *Electoral Studies* 20: 343–52.

Blake, Donald E., and R.K. Carty. 1999. "The Adoption of Membership Votes for Choosing Party Leaders." *Party Politics* 5: 211–24.

Blaustein, Albert P., and Gilbert P. Flanz. n.d. *Constitutions of the Countries of the World*. Dobbs Ferry, NY: Oceana Publications.

Blondel, Jean. 1968. "Party Systems and Patterns of Government in Western Democracies." *Canadian Journal of Political Science* 1: 180–203.

Blumler, Jay. 1983. *Communicating to Voters: Television in the First European Parliamentary Elections*. London: Sage.

Blumler, Jay, and Michael Gurevitch. 1995. *The Crisis of Public Communication*. London: Routledge.

Blumler, Jay G., and Denis McQuail. 1968. *Television in Politics: Its Uses and Influence*. London: Faber.

Blumler, Jay G., Jack M. McLeod, and Karl Erik Rosengren. 1992. *Comparatively Speaking: Communication and Culture Across Space and Time*. London: Sage.

Bogart, Leo. 1995. *Commercial Culture: The Media System and the Public Interest.* New York: Oxford University Press.

Bowler, Shaun, and David Denemark. 1993. "Split Ticket Voting in Australia: Dealignment and Inconsistent Votes Reconsidered." *Australian Journal of Political Science* 28: 19–37.

Bowler, Shaun, and Todd Donovan. 1998. *Demanding Choices: Opinion, Voting, and Direct Democracy.* Ann Arbor, MI: University of Michigan Press.

Bowler, Shaun, and Bernard Grofman, eds. 2000. *Elections in Australia, Ireland, and Malta under the Single Transferable Vote. Reflections on an Embedded Institution.* Ann Arbor, MI: University of Michigan Press.

Bowler, Shaun, Todd Donovan, and Caroline J. Tolbert, eds. 1998. *Citizens as Legislators: Direct Democracy in the United States.* Columbus, OH: Ohio State University Press.

Boy, Daniel, and Nonna Mayer. 2000. "Cleavage Voting and Issue Voting in France." In *How France Votes,* ed. Michael S. Lewis-Beck. New York: Chatham House.

Boyd, Richard. 1981. "The Decline of US Voter Turnout: Structural Explanations." *American Politics Quarterly* 9: 133–59.

Boyer, Patrick. 1992. *The People's Mandate: Referendums and a More Democratic Canada.* Toronto: Dundurn.

Brace, Paul, and Barbara Hinckley. 1992. *Follow the Leader.* New York: Basic Books.

Brader, Ted, and Joshua A. Tucker. 2001. "The Emergence of Mass Partisanship in Russia, 1993–1996." *American Journal of Political Science* 45: 69–83.

Brams, Steven J., and Peter C. Fishburn. 1982. *Approval Voting.* Boston, MA: Birkhauser.

Bratton, Michael, and Robert Mattes. 2001. "How People View Democracy: Africans' Surprising Universalism." *Journal of Democracy* 12: 107–21.

Broder, David. 2000. *Democracy Derailed.* New York: Harcourt.

Brown, Alice, David McCrone, Lindsay Paterson, and Paula Surridge. 1999. *The Scottish Electorate: The 1997 General Election and Beyond.* London: Macmillan.

Bryant, Jennings, and Dolf Zillmann. 1994. *Media Effects.* Hillsdale, NJ: Lawrence Erlbaum.

Budge, Ian. 1996. *The New Challenge of Direct Democracy.* Cambridge: Polity Press.

Burnham, Walter Dean. 1965. "The Changing Shape of the American Political Universe." *American Political Science Review* 59: 7–28.

Butler, David, and Bruce E. Cain. 1992. *Congressional Redistricting: Comparative and Theoretical Perspectives.* New York: Macmillan.

Butler, David, and Austin Ranney, eds. 1994. *Referendums around the World: The Growing Use of Direct Democracy.* London: Macmillan.

Butler, David, and Donald Stokes. 1974. *Political Change in Britain: The Evolution of Electoral Choice,* 2nd ed. London: Macmillan.

Cain, Bruce E. 1978. "Strategic Voting in Britain." *American Journal of Political Science* 22: 639–55.

Cairns, Alan C. 1968. "The Electoral System and the Party System in Canada, 1921–1965." *Canadian Journal of Political Science* 1: 55–80.

Campbell, Angus, Philip E. Converse, Warren E. Miller, and Donald E. Stokes. 1960. *The American Voter.* New York: Wiley.

Campbell, James A. 2000. *The American Campaigns: US Presidential Elections and the National Vote.* College State, TX: Texas A&M Press.

Capdevielle, Jacques, Elisabeth Dupoirier, and Colette Ysmal. 1988. "Tableau des électorats en mars 1978." In *France de gauche, vote à droite?* ed. Jacques Capdevielle et al. Paris: Fondation Nationale des Sciences Politiques.

Capoccia, Giovanni. 2000. *Defending Democracy: Reactions to Extremist Parties in Interwar European Democracies.* PhD Thesis, European University Institute, Florence.

Cardoso, Fernando Henrique. 1996. "In Praise of the Art of Politics." *Journal of Democracy* 7: 7–19.

Carey, John M., Richard G. Niemi, and Lynda W. Powell. 2000. *Term Limits in the State Legislatures*. Ann Arbor, MI: University of Michigan Press.

Carmines, Edward, and James Stimson. 1989. *Issue Evolution: Race and the Transformation of American Politics*. Princeton, NJ: Princeton University Press.

Carty, Kenneth, and Monroe Eagles. 1999. "Do Local Campaigns Matter? Campaign Spending, the Local Canvass and Party Support in Canada." *Electoral Studies* 18: 69–87.

Carty, Kenneth, William Cross, and Lisa Young. 2000. *Rebuilding Canadian Party Politics*. Vancouver: University of British Columbia Press.

Caul, Miki, and Mark Gray. 2001. "From Platform Declarations to Policy Outcomes." In *Parties without Partisans: Political Change in Advanced Industrial Democracies*, ed. Russell Dalton and Martin Wattenberg. Oxford: Oxford University Press.

Center for the Study of Direct Democracy, University of Geneva. http://c2d.unige.ch.

Chu, Yun-han, Larry Diamond, and Doh Chull Shin. 2001a. "How People View Democracy: Halting Progress in Korea and Taiwan." *Journal of Democracy* 12(3): 122–36.

Chu, Yun-han, Larry Diamond, and Doh Chull Shin. 2001b. "Growth and Equivocation in Support for Democracy: Korea and Taiwan in Comparative Perspective." *Studies in Public Policy* 345, Center for the Study of Public Policy, University of Strathclyde.

Clarke, Harold D., and Allan Kornberg. 1994. "The Politics and Economics of Constitutional Choice: Voting in Canada's 1992 National Referendum." *Journal of Politics* 56: 940–62.

Clarke, Harold D., and Allan Kornberg. 1996. "Choosing Canada?: The 1995 Quebec Sovereignty Referendum." *PS: Political Science and Politics* 29: 676–82.

Clarke, Harold D., Jane Jenson, Lawrence LeDuc, and Jon H. Pammett. 1996. *Absent Mandate: Canadian Electoral Politics in an Era of Restructuring*, 3rd ed. Toronto: Gage.

Cohen, Jacob, and Patricia Cohen. 1983. *Applied Multiple Regression/Correlation Analysis for the Behavioral Sciences*, 2nd ed. Hillsdale, NJ: Erlbaum.

Coleman, Stephen, ed. 1999. *Televised Election Debates*. London: Routledge.

Converse, Philip E. 1969. "Of Time and Partisan Stability." *Comparative Political Studies* 2: 139–71.

Converse, Philip E. 1974. "Comment on Burnham's 'Theory and Voting Research'." *American Political Science Review* 68: 1024–27.

Coppedge, Michael. 1992. "Deinstitutionalization of Latin American Party Systems." Paper presented at the XVII International Congress of the Latin American Studies Association, Los Angeles, September.

Cox, Gary W. 1997. *Making Votes Count: Strategic Coordination in the World's Electoral Systems*. Cambridge: Cambridge University Press.

Cox, Kevin R. 1969. "The Voting Decision in a Spatial Context." *Progress in Geography* 1: 81–117.

Crewe, Ivor. 1981. "Electoral Participation." In *Democracy at the Polls: A Comparative Study of Competitive National Elections*, ed. David Butler and Howard Penniman. Washington, DC: American Enterprise Institute.

Crewe, Ivor. 1992. "Changing Votes and Unchanging Voters." *Electoral Studies* 11: 335–45.

Crewe, Ivor, and David T. Denver, eds. 1985. *Electoral Change in Western Democracies*. New York: St Martin's.

Crewe, Ivor, Neil Day, and Anthony Fox. 1991. *The British Electorate 1963–87: A Compendium of Data from the British Election Studies*. Cambridge: Cambridge University Press.

Crisp, Brian F., and Maria Escobar-Lemmon. 1998. "A Conceptual Model of Nomination Procedures." Mimeo.

Cronin, Thomas. 1989. *Direct Democracy: The Politics of Initiative, Referendum and Recall.* Cambridge, MA: Harvard University Press.

Curtice, John, and Michael Steed. 2000. "And Now for the Commons? Lessons From Britain's First Experience of Proportional Representation." In *British Elections and Parties Review*, vol. 10, ed. Philip Cowley, David Denver, Andrew Russell, and Lisa Harrison. London: Frank Cass.

Czudnowski, Moshe M. 1975. "Political Recruitment." In *Handbook of Political Science*, vol. 2, ed. Fred I. Greenstein and Nelson W. Polsby. Reading, MA: Addison–Wesley.

Daalder, Hans. 1983. "The Comparative Study of European Parties and Party Systems: An Overview." In *Western European Party Systems: Continuity and Change*, ed. Hans Daalder and Peter Mair. London: Sage.

Daalder, Hans. 1992. "A Crisis of Party?" *Scandinavian Political Studies* 15: 269–87.

Dahl, Robert A. 1966. "Patterns of Opposition." In *Political Oppositions in Western Democracies*, ed. Robert A. Dahl. New Haven, CT: Yale University Press.

Dahl, Robert A. 1971. *Polyarchy: Participation and Opposition.* New Haven, CT: Yale University Press.

Dahl, Robert A. 1989. *Democracy and its Critics.* New Haven: Yale University Press.

Dalton, Russell. 1984. "Cognitive Mobilization and Partisan Dealignment in Advanced Industrial Democracies." *Journal of Politics* 46: 264–84.

Dalton, Russell. 1992. "Two German Electorates?" In G. Smith et al. *Developments in German Politics*. London: Macmillan.

Dalton, Russell. 1996a. *Citizen Politics in Western Democracies*, 2nd ed. Chatham, NJ: Chatham House.

Dalton, Russell. 1996b. "Political Cleavages, Issues, and Electoral Change." In *Comparing Democracies*, ed. Lawrence LeDuc, Richard G. Niemi, and Pippa Norris. Thousand Oaks, CA: Sage.

Dalton, Russell. 1999. "Political Support in Advanced Industrial Democracies." In *Critical Citizens: Global Support for Democratic Governance*, ed. Pippa Norris. Oxford: Oxford University Press.

Dalton, Russell. 2001. "The Decline of Party Identification." In *Parties without Partisans: Political Change in Advanced Industrial Democracies*, ed. Russell J. Dalton and Martin P. Wattenberg. Oxford: Oxford University Press.

Dalton, Russell, and Wilhelm Bürklin. 1996. "The Social Bases of the Vote." In *Germans Divided*, ed. Russell Dalton. New York and Oxford: Berg.

Dalton, Russell, and Martin Wattenberg, eds. 2001. *Parties without Partisans: Political Change in Advanced Industrial Democracies.* Oxford: Oxford University Press.

Dalton, Russell J., Paul Beck, and Robert Huckfeldt. 1998. "Partisan Cues and the Media: Information Flows in the 1992 Presidential Election." *American Political Science Review* 92: 111–26.

Dalton, Russell, Scott Flanagan, and Paul Beck, eds. 1984. *Electoral Change in Advanced Industrial Democracies.* Princeton, NJ: Princeton University Press.

Dalton, Russell J., Kazuhisa Kawakami, Holli A. Semetko, Hiroshisa Suzuki, and Katrin Voltmer. 1998. "Partisan Cues in the Media: Cross-National Comparisons of Election Coverage." Paper presented at the annual meeting of the Midwest Political Science Association, Chicago.

Darcy, Robert, Susan Welch, and Janet Clark. 1994. *Women, Elections, and Representation.* Lincoln, NE: Nebraska University Press.

Darcy, Robert, and Michael Laver. 1990. "Referendum Dynamics and the Irish Divorce Amendment." *Public Opinion Quarterly* 54: 4–20.

Davidson, Chandler, and Bernard Grofman, eds. 1994. *Quiet Revolution in the South.* Princeton, NJ: Princeton University Press.

Davis, Richard. 1999. *The Web of Politics.* Oxford: Oxford University Press.

Davis, Richard, and Diana Owen. 1998. *New Media and American Politics.* New York: Oxford University Press.

Dearing, John W., and Everett M. Rogers. 1996. *Agenda-Setting.* London: Sage.

de Guchteneire, Paul, Lawrence LeDuc, and Richard G. Niemi. 1985. "A Compendium of Survey Studies of Elections around the World." *Electoral Studies* 4: 159–74.

de Guchteneire, Paul, Lawrence LeDuc and Richard G. Niemi. 1991. "A Compendium of Survey Studies of Elections around the World, Update 1." *Electoral Studies* 10: 231–43.

Delli Carpini, Michael, and Scott Keeter. 1996. *What Americans Know About Politics and Why It Matters.* New Haven, CT: Yale University Press.

Delli Carpini, Michael, and Lee Sigelman. 1986. "Do Yuppies Matter? Competing Explanations of Their Political Distinctiveness." *Public Opinion Quarterly* 50: 502–18.

Denver, David. 1988. "Britain: Centralized Parties with Decentralized Selection." In *Candidate Selection in Comparative Perspective: The Secret Garden of Politics,* ed. Michael Gallagher and Michael Marsh. London: Sage.

Denver, David, and Gordon Hands. 1997. *Modern Constituency Electioneering.* London: Frank Cass.

Denver, David, James Mitchell, Charles Pattie, and Hugh Bochel. 2000. *Scotland Decides.* London: Frank Cass.

Derbyshire, J. Dennis, and Ian Derbyshire. 1999. *Political Systems of the World.* Oxford: Helicon Publishing.

Deutsch, Karl W. 1964. "Social Mobilization and Political Development." *American Political Science Review* 55: 493–514.

De Winter, Lieven. 1988. "Belgium: Democracy or Oligarchy?" In *Candidate Selection in Comparative Perspective: The Secret Garden of Politics,* ed. Michael Gallagher and Michael Marsh. London: Sage.

Diamond, Larry. 1992. "Economic Development and Democracy Reconsidered." In *Reexamining Democracy: Essays in Honor of Seymour Martin Lipset.* Newbury Park, CA: Sage.

Diamond, Larry. 1996. "Is the Third Wave of Democracy Over?" *Journal of Democracy* 7(3): 20–37.

Diamond, Larry. 1999. *Developing Democracy: Toward Consolidation.* Baltimore, MD: Johns Hopkins University Press.

Diamond, Larry, and Richard Gunther, eds. 2001. *Political Parties and Democracy.* Baltimore: Johns Hopkins University Press.

Diamond, Larry, and Marc F. Plattner, eds. 1994. *Nationalism, Ethnic Conflict, and Democracy.* Baltimore, MD: Johns Hopkins University Press.

Domingo, Pilar. 1999. "Judicial Independence and Judicial Reform in Latin America." In *The Self-Restraining State: Power and Accountability in New Democracies,* ed. Andreas Schedler, Larry Diamond, and Marc F. Plattner. Boulder, CO: Lynne Rienner.

Downs, Anthony. 1957. *An Economic Theory of Democracy.* New York: Harper.

Dunleavy, Patrick, and Christopher T. Husbands. 1985. *British Democracy at the Crossroads: Voting and Party Competition in the 1980s.* London: Allen and Unwin.

Dunleavy, Patrick, and Helen Margetts. 1995. "Understanding the Dynamics of Electoral Reform." *International Political Science Review* 16: 9–30.

Duverger, Maurice. 1951. *Les Partis politiques.* Paris: Seuil.

Duverger, Maurice. 1954, 1959. *Political Parties: Their Organization and Activity in the Modern State.* London: Methuen; New York: Wiley.

Entman, Robert, and Andrew Rojecki. 2000. *The Black Image in the White Mind: Media and Race in America.* Chicago: University of Chicago Press.

Epstein, Leon D. 1964. "A Comparative Study of Canadian Parties." *American Political Science Review* 58: 46–59.

Epstein, Leon D. 1980. *Political Parties in Western Democracies*, 2nd ed., New Brunswick, NJ: Transaction Books.

Epstein, Leon D. 1986. *Political Parties in the American Mold*. Madison, WI: University of Wisconsin Press.

Ergil, Dogu. 2000. "The Kurdish Question in Turkey." *Journal of Democracy* 11: 122–35.

Europa World Year Book. 2000. London: Europa Publications.

Evans, Geoffrey, ed. 1999. *The End of Class Politics? Class Voting in Comparative Context*. New York: Oxford University Press.

Evans, Geoffrey, and Pippa Norris. 1999. *Critical Elections: British Parties and Voters in Long-term Perspective*. London: Sage.

Evans, Geoffrey, Anthony Heath, and Clive Payne. 1999. "Class: Labour as a Catch-All Party?" In *Critical Elections: British Parties and Voters in Long-term Perspective*, ed. Geoffrey Evans and Pippa Norris. London: Sage.

Eysenck, Hans J. 1954, 1999. *The Psychology of Politics*. London: Routledge and Kegan Paul; New Brunswick, NJ: Transaction Books.

Fidrmuc, Jan. 2000. "Economics of Voting in Postcommunist Countries." *Electoral Studies* 19: 199–217.

Fiorina, Morris. 1981. *Retrospective Voting in American National Elections*. New Haven, CT: Yale University Press.

Fisichella, Dominico. 1984. "The Double-Ballot as a Weapon Against Anti-System Parties." In *Choosing an Electoral System: Issues and Alternatives*, ed. Arend Lijphart and Bernard Grofman. New York: Praeger.

Flanagan, Scott C., and Russell J. Dalton. 1984. "Parties under Stress: Realignment and Dealignment in Advanced Industrial Societies." *West European Politics* 7: 7–23.

Flanagan, Scott C., Shinsaku Kohei, Ichiro Miyake, Bradley M. Richardson, and Joji Watanuki. 1991. *The Japanese Voter*. New Haven, CT: Yale University Press.

Flickinger, Richard, and Donley Studler. 1992. "Explaining Declining Turnout in Western European Elections." *West European Politics* 15: 1–16.

Foley, Michael. 1993. *The Rise of the British Presidency*. Manchester: Manchester University Press.

Franklin, Mark. 1985. *The Decline of Class Voting in Britain*. Oxford: Oxford University Press.

Franklin, Mark, and Wolfgang Hirczy de Mino. 1998. "Separated Powers, Divided Government and Turnout in US Presidential Elections." *American Journal of Political Science* 42: 316–26.

Franklin, Mark N., and Thomas T. Mackie. 1983. "Familiarity and Inertia in the Formation of Governing Coalitions in Parliamentary Democracies." *British Journal of Political Science* 13: 275–98.

Franklin, Mark, Patrick Lyons, and Michael Marsh. 2000. "The Tally of Turnout: Understanding Cross-National Turnout Decline Since 1945." Paper presented at the annual meeting of the American Political Science Association, Washington, DC.

Franklin, Mark, Tom Mackie, Henry Valen, et al. 1992. *Electoral Change: Responses to Evolving Social and Attitudinal Structures in Western Countries*. New York: Cambridge University Press.

Franklin, Mark, Michael Marsh, and Christopher Wlezien. 1996. "Attitudes Toward Europe and Referendum Votes: A Response to Siune and Svensson." *Electoral Studies* 13: 117–21.

Franklin, Mark, Cees van der Eijk and Michael Marsh. 1995. "Referendum Outcomes and Trust in Government: Public Support for Europe in the Wake of Maastricht." *West European Politics* 18: 101–17.

Franklin, Mark, Cees van der Eijk, and Erik Oppenhuis. 1996. "The Institutional Context: Turnout." In *Choosing Europe? The European Electorate and National*

Politics in the Face of Union, Cees van der Eijk and Mark Franklin, et al. Ann Arbor: University of Michigan Press.

Freedom House. 1999. *Democracy's Century: A Survey of Global Change in the 20th Century*. www.freedomhouse.org

Freedom House. 2000. *Freedom in the World*.

Gallagher, Michael. 1988a. "Introduction." In *Candidate Selection in Comparative Perspective: The Secret Garden of Politics*, ed. Michael Gallagher and Michael Marsh. London: Sage.

Gallagher, Michael. 1988b. "Conclusion." In *Candidate Selection in Comparative Perspective: The Secret Garden of Politics*, ed. Michael Gallagher and Michael Marsh. London: Sage.

Gallagher, Michael. 1998c. "The Political Impact of Electoral System Change in Japan and New Zealand 1996." *Party Politics* 4: 203–28.

Gallagher, Michael, and Michael Marsh, eds. 1988. *Candidate Selection in Comparative Perspective: The Secret Garden of Politics*. London: Sage.

Gallagher, Michael, and Pier Vincenzo Uleri, eds. 1996. *The Referendum Experience in Europe*. London: Macmillan.

Galligan, Brian. 1990. "The 1988 Referendums and Australia's Record on Constitutional Change." *Parliamentary Affairs* 43: 497–506.

Gerber, Elisabeth. 1999. *The Populist Paradox*. Princeton, NJ: Princeton University Press.

Gidengil, Elisabeth, André Blais, Richard Nadeau, and Neil Nevitte. 2000. "Are Party Leaders Becoming More Important to Vote Choice in Canada?" Paper presented at the annual meeting of the American Political Science Association, Washington, DC.

Gluchowski, Peter. 1987. "Lebensstile und Wandel der Wählerschaft in der Bundesrepublik Deutschland." *Aus Politik und Zeitgeschichte* 21: 18–32.

Gluchowski, Peter M., and Ulrich von Wilamowitz-Moellendorff. 1998. "The Erosion of Social Cleavages in Western Germany, 1971–97." In *Stability and Change in German Elections*, ed. Christopher J. Anderson and Carsten Zelle. Westport, CT: Praeger.

Goldthorpe, John. 1987. *Social Mobility and Class Structure in Modern Britain*. Oxford: Clarendon Press.

Gramberg, Donald, and Sören Holmberg. 1988. "Preferences, Expectations and Voting in Sweden's Referendum on Nuclear Power." *Social Science Quarterly* 67: 379–91.

Gray, Mark, and Miki Caul. 2000. "Declining Voter Turnout in Advanced Industrialized Democracies, 1950 to 1997." *Comparative Political Studies* 33: 1091–122.

Grofman, Bernard, William Koetzle, and Thomas Brunell. 1997. "An Integrated Perspective of the Three Potential Sources of Partisan Bias: Malapportionment, Turnout Differences, and the Geographic Distribution of the Party Vote." *Electoral Studies* 16: 457–70.

Gundelach, Peter, and Karen Siune, eds. 1992. *From Voters to Participants*. Århus: Institute for Political Science, University of Aarhus.

Gunther, Richard. 1989. "Electoral Laws, Party Systems, and Elites: The Case of Spain." *American Political Science Review* 83: 835–59.

Gunther, Richard, and Anthony Mughan, eds. 2000. *Democracy and the Media: A Comparative Perspective*. New York: Cambridge University Press.

Gyimah-Boadi, E. 1997. "Civil Society in Africa." In *Consolidating the Third Wave Democracies: Themes and Perspectives*, ed. Larry Diamond, Marc F. Plattner, Yun-han Chu, and Hung-mao Tien. Baltimore, MD: Johns Hopkins University Press.

Haggard, Stephan. 2000. "The Politics of the Asian Financial Crisis." *Journal of Democracy* 11: 130–44.

Hamann, Kerstin. 1999. "Federalist Institutions, Voting Behavior, and Party Systems in Spain." *Publius: The Journal of Federalism* 29: 111–37.

Hamon, Francis. 1995. *Le Référendum: Étude comparative.* Paris: LGDJ.

Harper, Marcus. 2000. "Economic Voting in Post-Communist Eastern Europe." *Comparative Political Studies* 33: 1191–227.

Harrison, Lawrence E., and Samuel P. Huntington, eds. 2001. *Culture Matters: How Values Shape Human Progress.* New York: Basic Books.

Hazan, Reuven Y. 1997a. "The 1996 Intra-Party Elections in Israel: Adopting Party Primaries." *Electoral Studies* 16: 95–102.

Hazan, Reuven Y. 1997b. "Executive–Legislative Relations in an Era of Accelerated Reform: Reshaping Government in Israel." *Legislative Studies Quarterly* 22: 329–50.

Hazan, Reuven Y. 1999. "Yes, Institutions Matter: The Impact of Institutional Reform on Parliamentary Members and Leaders in Israel." *Journal of Legislative Studies* 5: 303–26.

Hazan, Reuven Y., and Paul Pennings, eds. 2001. "Democratizing Candidate Selection: Causes and Consequences." Special issue of *Party Politics* vol. 7, no. 3.

Hazan, Reuven Y., and Gideon Rahat. 2000. "Representation, Electoral Reform and Democracy: Theoretical and Empirical Lessons from the 1996 Elections in Israel." *Comparative Political Studies* 33: 1310–36.

Heath, Anthony, and Bridget Taylor. 1999a. "New Sources of Abstention?" In *Critical Elections: British Parties and Voters in Long-term Perspective*, ed. Geoffrey Evans and Pippa Norris. London: Sage.

Heath, Anthony, and Bridget Taylor. 1999b. "Were the Scottish and Welsh Referendums Second Order Elections?" In *Scotland and Wales: Nations Again?* ed. Bridget Taylor and Katarina Thomson. Cardiff: University of Wales Press.

Heath, Anthony, Roger Jowell, and John Curtice. 1985. *How Britain Votes.* Oxford: Pergamon.

Heath, Anthony, Iain McLean, Bridget Taylor, and John Curtice. 1999. "Between First and Second Order: A Comparison of Voting Behaviour in European and Local Elections in Britain." *European Journal of Political Research* 35: 389–414.

Heath, Anthony, John Curtice, Roger Jowell, Geoff Evans, Julia Field, and Sharon Witherspoon. 1991. *Understanding Political Change: The British Voter 1964–1987.* London: Pergamon.

Hirczy, Wolfgang. 1992. *Electoral Participation.* Ann Arbor, MI: University Microfilms (University of Houston PhD Dissertation).

Hirczy, Wolfgang. 1995. "Explaining Near-Universal Turnout: The Case of Malta." *European Journal of Political Research* 27: 255–72.

Hirczy de Mino, Wolfgang, and John C. Lane. 2000. "Malta: STV in a Two-Party System." In *Elections in Australia, Ireland, and Malta under the Single Transferable Vote*, ed. Shaun Bowler and Bernard Grofman. Ann Arbor, MI: University of Michigan Press.

Holbrook, Thomas M. 1996. *Do Campaigns Matter?* Thousand Oaks, CA: Sage.

Hopkin, Jonathan. 2001. "Bringing the Members Back In? Democratising Candidate Selection in Britain and Spain." *Party Politics* 7: 343–61.

Horowitz, Donald. 1985. *Ethnic Groups in Conflict.* Berkeley, CA: University of California Press.

Hout, Michael, Clem Brooks, and Jeff Manza et al. 1995. "The Democratic Class Struggle in the United States, 1948–1992." *American Sociological Review* 60: 805–28.

Hout, Michael, Jeff Manza, and Clem Brooks. 1999. "Classes, Unions and the Realignment of US Presidential Voting, 1952–92." In *The End of Class Politics? Class Voting in Comparative Context*, ed. Geoffrey Evans. Oxford: Oxford University Press.

Hovland, Carl. 1959. "Reconciling Conflicting Results Derived from Experimental and Survey Studies of Attitude Change." *American Psychologist.* 14: 8–17.

Hsieh, John Fuh-sheng, and Richard G. Niemi. 1998. "Can Duverger's Law Be Extended to SNTV? The Case of Taiwan's Legislative Yuan Elections." *Electoral Studies* 18: 101–16.

Huckfeldt, Robert, and Carol Kohfeld. 1989. *Race and the Decline of Class in American Politics*. Urbana, IL: University of Illinois Press.

Huckfeldt, Robert, and John Sprague. 1995. *Citizens, Politics, and Social Communications*. Cambridge: Cambridge University Press.

Huckfeldt, Robert, Paul Allen Beck, Russell J. Dalton, and Jeffrey Levine. 1995. "Political Environments, Cohesive Social Groups, and the Communication of Public Opinion." *American Journal of Political Science* 39: 1025–54.

Hughes, Colin. 1994. "Australia and New Zealand." In *Referendums Around the World: The Growing Use of Direct Democracy*, ed. David Butler and Austin Ranney. London: Macmillan.

Huntington, Samuel P. 1991. *The Third Wave: Democratization in the Late Twentieth Century*. Oklahoma: University of Oklahoma Press.

Ignazi, Piero. 1992. "The Silent Counter-Revolution: Hypotheses on the Emergence of Extreme Right-Wing Parties in Europe." *European Journal of Political Research* 22: 3–34.

Ignazi, Piero. 1994. *L'Estrema Destra in Europa*. Bologna: Il Mulino.

Inglehart, Ronald. 1977. *The Silent Revolution: Changing Values and Political Styles Among Western Publics*. Princeton, NJ: Princeton University Press.

Inglehart, Ronald. 1990. *Culture Shift in Advanced Industrial Society*. Princeton, NJ: Princeton University Press.

Inglehart, Ronald. 1998. *Modernization and Postmodernization*. Princeton, NJ: Princeton University Press.

Initiative and Referendum Institute, USA. www.iandrinstitute.org

International Institute for Democracy and Electoral Assistance (IDEA). www.idea.int

International Institute for Democracy and Electoral Assistance (IDEA). 2002. *Handbook on Funding of Parties and Election Campaigns*. Stockholm: International Institute for Democracy and Electoral Assistance.

Iyengar, Shanto, and Donald Kinder. 1987. *News That Matters: Agenda-Setting and Priming in a Television Age*. Chicago: University of Chicago Press.

Iyengar, Shanto, and A.F. Simon. 2000. "New Perspectives and Evidence on Political Communication and Campaign Effects." *Annual Review of Psychology* 51: 149–69.

Jackman, Robert. 1987. "Political Institutions and Voter Turnout in the Industrial Democracies." *American Political Science Review* 81: 405–23.

Jackman, Robert, and Ross A. Miller. 1995. "Voter Turnout in the Industrial Democracies during the 1980s." *Comparative Political Studies* 27: 467–92.

Jahn, Detlef, and Ann-Sofie Storsved. 1995. "Legitimacy Through Referendum: The Nearly Successful Domino Strategy of the EU Referendums in Austria, Finland, Sweden and Norway." *West European Politics* 18: 18–37.

Jahn, Detlef, Pertti Pesonen, Tore Slaatta, and Leif Åberg. 1998. "The Actors and the Campaigns." In *To Join or Not to Join: Three Nordic Referendums on Membership in the European Union*, ed. Anders Todal Jenssen, Pertti Pesonen, and Mikael Gilljam. Oslo: Scandinavian University Press.

Jelen, Ted, Sue Thomas, and Clyde Wilcox. 1994. "The Gender Gap in Nordic Voting Behavior." In *Nordic Women in Politics*, ed. Lauri Karvonen and Per Selle. Aldershot: Dartmouth.

Jenkins, Lord. 1998. *The Report of the Independent Commission on the Voting System*. London: HMSO.

Jensen, Klaus Bruhn, ed. 1998. *News of the World: World Cultures Look at Television News*. London: Routledge.

Jenssen, Anders Todal, Pertti Pesonen, and Mikael Gilljam, eds. 1998. *To Join or Not to Join: Three Nordic Referendums on Membership in the European Union*. Oslo: Scandinavian University Press.

Jesse, Eckhard. 1988. "Split-Voting in the Federal Republic of Germany: An Analysis of the Federal Elections from 1953 to 1987." *Electoral Studies* 7: 109–24.

Johnston, Richard, André Blais, Henry E. Brady, and Jean Crête. 1992. *Letting the People Decide: Dynamics of a Canadian Election*. Montreal: McGill–Queen's University Press.

Johnston, Richard, André Blais, Elisabeth Gidengil, and Neil Nevitte. 1996. *The Challenge of Direct Democracy: The 1992 Canadian Referendum*. Montreal: McGill–Queens University Press.

Johnston, Ron, and Charles Pattie. 1999. "Constituency Campaign Intensity and Split-Ticket Voting: New Zealand's First Election Under MMP 1996." *Political Science* 51: 164–81.

Jones, J. Barry. 1999. "The First Welsh National Assembly Election." *Government and Opposition* 34: 323–33.

Jones, Mark P. 1995a. "A Guide to the Electoral Systems of the Americas." *Electoral Studies* 14: 5–21.

Jones, Mark P. 1995b. *Electoral Laws and the Survival of Presidential Democracies*. Notre Dame, IN: University of Notre Dame Press.

Jowell, Roger, Sharon Witherspoon, and L. Brook, eds. 1987. *British Social Attitudes*. Aldershot: Gower.

Just, Marion, Ann Creigler, Dean Alger, Montague Kern, Darrell West, and Timothy Cook. 1996. *Crosstalk: Citizens, Candidates and the Media in a Presidential Campaign*. Chicago: University of Chicago Press.

Kaase, Max. 1994. "Is there Personalisation in Politics? Candidates and Voting Behavior in Germany." *International Political Science Review* 15: 211–30.

Kahn, Kim Fridkin. 1996. *The Political Consequences of Being a Woman: How Stereotypes Influence the Content and Impact of Statewide Campaigns*. New York: Columbia University Press.

Kaid, Lynda Lee, and Christina Holtz-Bacha. 1995. *Political Advertising in Western Democracies*. Thousand Oaks, CA: Sage.

Karatnycky, Adrian. 2000. "The 1999 Freedom House Survey: A Century of Progress." *Journal of Democracy* 11(1): 187–200.

Katz, Richard S. 1980. *A Theory of Parties and Electoral Systems*. Baltimore, MD: Johns Hopkins University Press.

Katz, Richard S. 1997. *Democracy and Elections*. New York: Oxford University Press.

Katz, Richard S. 2001. "The Problems of Candidate Selection and Models of Party Democracy." *Party Politics* 7: 277–96.

Katz, Richard S., and Robin Kolodny. 1994. "Party Organization as an Empty Vessel: Parties in American Politics." In *How Parties Organize: Change and Adaptation in Party Organizations in Western Democracies*, ed. Richard S. Katz and Peter Mair. London: Sage.

Katz, Richard S., and Peter Mair, eds. 1992. *Party Organizations: A Data Handbook on Party Organizations in Western Democracies, 1960–90*. Newbury Park, CA: Sage.

Katz, Richard S., and Peter Mair, eds. 1995. "Changing Models of Party Organization and Party Democracy: The Emergence of the Cartel Party." *Party Politics* 1: 5–28.

King, Anthony. 1977. *Britain Says YES*. Washington, DC: American Enterprise Institute.

Kirchheimer, Otto. 1966. "The Transformation of the Western European Party Systems." In *Political Parties and Political Development*, ed. Joseph LaPalombara and Myron Weiner. Princeton, NJ: Princeton University Press.

Kitschelt, Herbert. 1994. *The Transformation of European Social Democracy*. New York: Cambridge University Press.

Kitschelt, Herbert et al. 1999. *Post-communist Party Systems: Competition, Representation, and Inter-party Cooperation*. New York: Cambridge University Press.

Klapper, Joseph T. 1960. *The Effects of the Mass Media*. Glencoe, IL: Free Press.

Kleinnijenhuis, Jan, and Jan A. de Ridder. 1998. "Issue News and Electoral Volatility: A Comparative Analysis of Media Effects during the 1994 Election Campaigns in Germany and the Netherlands." *European Journal of Political Research* 33: 413–37.

Knack, Stephen. 1999. "Drivers Wanted: Motor Voter and the Election of 1996." *PS: Political Science & Politics* 32: 237–43.

Knutsen, Oddbjorn. 1987. "The Impact of Structural and Ideological Cleavages on West European Democracies." *British Journal of Political Science* 18: 323–52.

Knutsen, Oddbjorn. 1995. "Party Choice." In Jan Van Deth and Elinor Scarbrough, ed. *The Impact of Values*. New York: Oxford University Press.

Knutsen, Oddbjorn, and Elinor Scarbrough. 1995. "Cleavage Politics." In *The Impact of Values*, ed. J. Van Deth and E. Scarbrough. New York: Oxford University Press.

Kobach, Kris. 1993a. *The Referendum: Direct Democracy in Switzerland*. Aldershot: Dartmouth.

Kobach, Kris. 1993b. "Recent Developments in Swiss Direct Democracy." *Electoral Studies* 12: 342–65.

Kolodny, Robin, and Richard S. Katz. 1992. "The United States." In *Party Organizations: A Data Handbook on Party Organizations in Western Democracies, 1960–90*, ed. Richard S. Katz and Peter Mair. London: Sage.

Koole, Ruud, and Hella van de Velde. 1992. "Netherlands." In *Party Organizations: A Data Handbook on Party Organization in Western Democracies, 1960–90*, ed. Richard S. Katz and Peter Mair. London: Sage.

Kriesi, Hanspeter. 1993. *Citoyenneté et démocratie directe*. Zürich: Seismo.

Kristjánsson, Svanur. 1998. "Electoral Politics and Governance: Transformation of the Party System in Iceland, 1970–1996." In *Comparing Party System Change*, ed. Paul Pennings and Jan-Erik Lane. London: Routledge.

Laakso, M., and Rein Taagepera. 1979. "Effective Number of Parties: A Measure with Application to West Europe." *Comparative Political Studies* 12: 3–27.

Lagos, Marta. 1996. "The Latinobarómetro: Media and Political Attitudes in South America." Paper presented at the annual meeting of the American Political Science Association, San Francisco.

Lagos, Marta. 2001. "How People View Democracy: Between Stability and Crisis in Latin America." *Journal of Democracy* 12(1): 137–45.

Lakeman, Enid. 1974. *How Democracies Vote: A Study of Electoral Systems*. London: Faber and Faber.

Lalljee, Mansur, and Geoffrey Evans. 1998. "Political Talk and the Stability and Consistency of Political Orientation." *British Journal of Social Psychology* 37: 203–12.

Lau, Richard R., Lee Sigelman, Caroline Heldman, and Paul Babbitt. 1999. "The Effects of Negative Political Advertisements: A Meta-Analytic Assessment." *American Political Science Review* 94: 851–76.

Laver, Michael. 1989. "Party Competition and Party System Change." *Journal of Theoretical Politics* 1: 301–24.

Laver, Michael, and Norman Schofield. 1990. *Multiparty Government: The Politics of Coalition in Western Europe*. Oxford: Oxford University Press.

Lawson, Kay, Andrea Römmele, and Georgi Karasimeonov, eds. 1999. *Cleavages, Parties, and Voters: Studies from Bulgaria, the Czech Republic, Hungary, Poland, and Romania*. Westport, CT: Praeger.

Lazarsfeld, Paul F., Bernard Berelson, and Hazel Gaudet. 1944, 1948. *The People's Choice: How the Voter Makes Up His Mind in a Presidential Campaign.* New York: Columbia University Press.

LeDuc, Lawrence. 2000. "Referendums and Elections: How Do Campaigns Differ?" Paper presented at the European Consortium for Political Research Joint Sessions Workshops, University of Copenhagen.

LeDuc, Lawrence. 2001. "Democratizing Party Leadership Selection." *Party Politics* 7: 323–41.

LeDuc, Lawrence. Forthcoming. *Understanding Referendums: Direct Democracy in Theory and Practice.* Toronto: Broadview Press.

LeDuc, Lawrence and Jon H. Pammett. 1995. "Referendum Voting: Attitudes and Behaviour in the 1992 Constitutional Referendum." *Canadian Journal of Political Science* 28: 3–33.

Lerner, Daniel. 1958. *The Passing of Traditional Society: Modernizing the Middle East.* New York: Free Press.

Lewis-Beck, Michael. 1988. *Economics and Elections.* Ann Arbor, MI: University of Michigan Press.

Lewis-Beck, Michael. 1997. "Who's the Chef? Economic Voting Under a Dual Executive." *European Journal of Political Research* 31: 315–25.

Lewis-Beck, Michael, ed. 2000. *How France Votes.* New York: Chatham House.

Lewis-Beck, Michael S., and Martin Paldam, ed. 2000. *Economics and Elections.* Special issue of *Electoral Studies* vol.19, no. 2/3.

Lichter, Robert S. 2001. "Substance and Fairness in US TV News." *The Harvard International Journal of Press/Politics* 6.

Lijphart, Arend. 1977. *Democracy in Plural Societies.* New Haven, CT: Yale University Press.

Lijphart, Arend. 1981. "Political Parties." In David Butler et al. *Democracy at the Polls.* Washington, DC: American Enterprise Institute.

Lijphart, Arend. 1994a. *Electoral Systems and Party Systems: A Study of Twenty-Seven Democracies, 1945–1990.* Oxford: Oxford University Press.

Lijphart, Arend. 1994b. "Democracies: Forms, Performance, and Constitutional Engineering." *European Journal of Political Research* 25: 1–17.

Lijphart, Arend. 1999. *Patterns of Democracy: Government Forms and Performance in Thirty-Six Countries.* New Haven, CT: Yale University Press.

Lijphart, Arend, Rafael Lopez Pintor, and Yasumori Sone. 1986. "The Limited Vote and the Single Nontransferable Vote: Lessons from Japanese and Spanish Examples." In *Electoral Laws and Their Political Consequences*, ed. Bernard Grofman and Arend Lijphart. New York: Agathon Press.

Linz, Juan J. 1978. *The Breakdown of Democratic Regimes: Crisis, Breakdown, and Reequilibration.* Baltimore, MD: Johns Hopkins University Press.

Linz, Juan J., and Alfred Stepan. 1996. *Problems of Democratic Transition and Consolidation: Southern Europe, South America, and Post-Communist Europe.* Baltimore, MD: Johns Hopkins University Press.

Lipset, Seymour Martin. 1959. "Some Social Requisites of Democracy: Economic Development and Political Legitimacy." *American Political Science Review* 53: 69–105.

Lipset, Seymour Martin. 1960, 1981. *Political Man: The Social Bases of Politics.* Garden City, NY: Doubleday; Baltimore, MD: Johns Hopkins University Press.

Lipset, Seymour Martin, and Stein Rokkan. 1967. "Cleavage Structures, Party Systems and Voter Alignments." In *Party Systems and Voter Alignments*, ed. Seymour Martin Lipset and Stein Rokkan. New York: Free Press.

Listhaug, Ola, Sören Holmberg, and Risto Sänkiaho. 1998. "Partisanship and EU Choice." In *To Join or Not to Join: Three Nordic Referendums on Membership in the European Union*, ed. Anders Todal Jenssen, Pertti Pesonen, and Mikael Gilljam. Oslo: Scandinavian University Press.

Lodge, Milton, Kathleen M. McGraw, and Patrick Stroh. 1989. "An Impression-driven Model of Candidate Evaluation." *American Political Science Review* 83: 399–419.

Lodge, Milton, and Marco R. Steenbergen, with Shawn Brau. 1995. "The Responsive Voter: Campaign Information and the Dynamics of Candidate Evaluation." *American Political Science Review* 89: 309–26.

Longley, Lawrence D., and Reuven Y. Hazan, eds. 2000. *The Uneasy Relationship Between Parliamentary Members and Leaders*. London: Frank Cass.

Lowenthal, Abraham. 2000. "Latin America at the Century's Turn." *Journal of Democracy* 11(2): 41–55.

Lowery, Shearon A., and Melvin L. deFleur. 1995. *Milestones in Mass Communications Research*. New York: Longman.

Lucero, José Antonio. 2001. "Crisis and Contention in Ecuador." *Journal of Democracy* 12(2): 59–73.

Lull, James, and Stephen Hinerman, eds. 1997. *Media Scandals*. Cambridge: Polity Press.

Lupia, Arthur. 1992. "Busy Voters, Agenda Control, and the Power of Information." *American Political Science Review* 86: 390–403.

Lupia, Arthur. 1994. "Shortcuts versus Encyclopedias: Information and Voting Behavior in California's Insurance Reform Elections." *American Political Science Review* 88: 63–76.

Luther, Kurt Richard, and Kris Deschouwer. 1999. "'Prudent Leadership' to Successful Adaptation? Pillar Parties and Consociational Democracy Thirty Years On." In *Party Elites in Divided Societies: Political Parties in Consociational Democracies*, eds. Kurt Richard Luther and Kris Deschouwer. London: Routledge.

Mackie, Thomas, and Richard Rose. 1991. *The International Almanac of Electoral History*. Washington, DC: CQ Press.

MacKuen, Michael, Robert S. Erikson, and James A. Stimson. 1992. "Peasants or Bankers? The American Electorate and the U.S. Economy." *American Political Science Review* 86: 597–611.

Magleby, David. 1988. "Taking the Initiative: Direct Legislation and Direct Democracy in the 1980s." *PS: Political Science & Politics* 21: 600–11.

Magleby, David. 1994. "Direct Legislation in the American States." In *Referendums Around the World: The Growing Use of Direct Democracy*, ed. David Butler and Austin Ranney. London: Macmillan.

Mainwaring, Scott. 1998. "Party Systems in the Third Wave." *Journal of Democracy* 9(3): 67–81.

Mainwaring, Scott and Timothy R. Scully, eds. 1995a. *Building Democratic Institutions: Party Systems in Latin America*. Stanford, CA: Stanford University Press.

Mainwaring, Scott and Timothy R. Scully. 1995b. "Introduction: Party Systems in Latin America." In *Building Democratic Institutions: Party Systems in Latin America*, eds. Scott Mainwaring and Timothy R. Scully. Stanford, CA: Stanford University Press.

Mair, Peter, ed. 1990. *The West European Party System*. Oxford: Oxford University Press.

Mair, Peter, 1994. "Party Organizations: From Civil Society to the State." In *How Parties Organize: Change and Adaptation in Party Organizations in Western Democracies*, Richard S. Katz and Peter Mair. London: Sage.

Mair, Peter, 1997. *Party System Change*. Oxford: Clarendon Press.

Mair, Peter, 2001. "The Freezing Hypothesis." In *Party Systems and Voter Alignments Revisited*, ed. Lauri Karvonen and Stein Kuhnle. London: Routledge.

Mair, Peter, and Tomokazu Sakano. 1998. "Japanese Political Realignment in Perspective: Change or Restoration?" *Party Politics* 4: 77–201.

Mair, Peter, and Ingrid van Biezen. 2001. "Party Membership in Twenty European Democracies, 1980–2000." *Party Politics* 7: 5–21.

Margolis, Michael, and David Resnick. 2000. *Politics as Usual: The Cyberspace "Revolution."* Thousand Oaks, CA: Sage.

Markus, Gregory B. 1992. "The Impact of Personal and National Economic Conditions on Presidential Voting, 1956–1988." *American Journal of Political Science* 36: 829–34.

Marsh, Michael. 1993. "Introduction: Selecting the Party Leader." *European Journal of Political Research* 24: 229–31.

Martin, Pierre. 1997. *Les systèmes électoraux et les modes de scrutin.* Paris: Montchrestien.

Massicotte, Louis. 2000. "Second Chamber Elections." In *International Encyclopedia of Elections*, ed. Richard Rose. Washington, DC: CQ Press.

Massicotte, Louis, and André Bernard. 1985. *Le scrutin au Québec: un miroir déformant.* Montréal: Hurtubise HMH.

Massicotte, Louis, and André Blais. 1999. "Mixed Electoral Systems. A Conceptual and Empirical Survey." *Electoral Studies* 18: 341–66.

Massicotte, Louis, André Blais, and Antoine Yoshinaka. 2001. *Establishing the Rules of the Game: Election Laws in Democracies.* Montreal: Typescript.

Matland, Richard E. 1998. "Women's Representation in National Legislatures: Developed and Developing Countries." *Legislative Studies Quarterly* 23: 109–25.

Mattes, Robert, Michael Bratton, Yul Derek Davids, and Cherrel Africa. 2000. "Public Opinion and the Consolidation of Democracy in Southern Africa: An Initial Review of Key Findings of the Southern African Democracy Barometer." *The Afrobarometer Series*, no. 1, July.

Mazzoleni, Gianpietro. 1987. "Media Logic and Party Logic in Campaign Coverage: The Italian General Election of 1983." *European Journal of Communication* 2: 81–103.

McAllister, Ian. 1987. "Social-Context, Turnout and the Vote—Australian and British Comparisons." *Political Geography Quarterly* 6: 17–30.

McAllister, Ian. 1992. *Political Behavior: Citizens, Parties and Elites in Australia.* Melbourne: Longman.

McAllister, Ian. 1996. "Leaders." In *Comparing Democracies,* ed. Lawrence LeDuc, Richard G. Niemi, and Pippa Norris. Thousand Oaks, CA: Sage.

McAllister, Ian. 2000. "Elections without Cues: The 1999 Australian Republic Referendum." Unpublished paper, Research School of Social Sciences, Australian National University.

McAllister, Ian, and Stephen White. 2000. "Split Ticket Voting in the 1995 Russian Duma Elections." *Electoral Studies* 19: 563–76.

McAllister, Ian, Ron J. Johnston, Charles J. Pattie, Helena Tunstall, Danny F. Dorling, and David J. Rossiter. 2001. "Class Dealignment and the Neighbourhood Effect: Miller Revisited." *British Journal of Political Science* 31: 41–59.

McChesney, Robert W. 1999. *Rich Media, Poor Democracy.* Urbana, IL: University of Illinois Press.

McDonald, Michael P., and Samuel L. Popkin. 2001. "The Myth of the Vanishing Voter." *American Political Science Review* 95.

McKean, Margaret, and Ethan Scheiner. 2000. "Japan's New Electoral System: La (*sic*) plus ça change …" *Electoral Studies* 19: 447–77.

McQuail, Denis, and Karen Siune. 1998. *Media Policy: Convergence, Concentration and Commerce.* London: Sage.

McRobie, Alan, ed. 1993. *Taking It to the People: The New Zealand Electoral Referendum Debate.* Christchurch: Hazard Press.

Medding, Peter Y. 2000. "From Government by Party to Government Despite Party." In *Parties, Elections and Cleavages: Israel in Comparative and*

Theoretical Perspective, ed. Reuven Y. Hazan and Moshe Maor. London: Cass.

Mendelsohn, Matthew, and Andrew Parkin, eds. 2000. *Referendum Democracy: Citizens, Elites and Deliberation in Referendum Campaigns*. London: Macmillan.

Merrill, John C. 1995. *Global Journalism: Survey of International Communication*. New York: Longman.

Mickiewicz, Ellen. 2000. *Changing Channels: Television and the Struggle for Power in Russia*, rev. ed. Durham, NC: Duke University Press.

Miller, Arthur H., and Thomas F. Klobucar. 2000. "The Development of Party Identification in Post-Soviet Societies." *American Journal of Political Science* 44: 667–86.

Miller, Arthur H., and Martin P. Wattenberg. 1984. "Politics and the Pulpit." *Public Opinion Quarterly* 48: 301–17.

Miller, Arthur H., Gwyn Erb, William M. Reisinger, and Vicki L. Hesli. 2000. "Emerging Party Systems in Post-Soviet Societies: Fact or Fiction?" *Journal of Politics* 62: 455–90.

Miller, Warren E. 1976. "The Cross-National Use of Party Identification as a Stimulus to Political Inquiry." In *Party Identification and Beyond: Representations of Voting and Party Competition*, ed. Ian Budge, Ivor Crewe, and Dennis Farlie. London: Wiley.

Miller, Warren E., and J. Merrill Shanks. 1996. *The New American Voter*. Cambridge, MA: Harvard University Press.

Miller, William L. 1978. "Social Class and Party Choice in England: A New Analysis." *British Journal of Political Science* 8: 257–84.

Miller, William L. 1991. *Media and Voters: The Audience, Content and Influence of Press and Television at the 1987 General Election*. Oxford: Oxford University Press.

Miller, William L. 1999. "The First Elections to the Scottish Parliament." *Government and Opposition* 34: 299–322.

Miller, William L., and Stephen White. 1998. "Political Values Underlying Partisan Cleavages in Former Communist Countries." *Electoral Studies* 17: 197–216.

Miller, William L., Annis May Timpson, and Michael Lessnoff. 1996. *Political Culture in Contemporary Britain: People and Politicians, Principles and Practice*. Oxford: Oxford University Press.

Miller, William L., Stephen White, and Paul Heywood. 1996. "Measuring and Interpreting the Trends in Public Opinion during the 1993 Russian Election Campaign." *Public Opinion Quarterly* 60: 106–27.

Miller, William L., Stephen White, and Paul Heywood. 1998. *Values and Political Change in Postcommunist Europe*. London: Macmillan.

Miller, William L., David Broughton, Niels Sonntag, and Duncan McLean. 1989. "Political Change in Britain During the 1987 Campaign." In *Political Communications: The General Election Campaign of 1987*, ed. Ivor Crewe and Martin Harrop. Cambridge: Cambridge University Press.

Mishler, William, and Richard Rose. 1998. "Five Years after the Fall: Trajectories of Support for Democracy in Post-Communist Europe." Studies in Public Policy 298, Center for the Study of Public Policy, University of Strathclyde.

Mitra, Subrata K., and V.B. Singh. 1999. *Democracy and Social Change in India A Cross-sectional Analysis of the Indian Electorate*. Delhi: Sage.

Mitchell, Glenn, and Christopher Wlezien. 1995. "The Impact of Legal Constraints on Voter Registration, Turnout, and the Composition of the American Electorate." *Political Behavior* 17: 179–202.

Mochmann, Ekkehard, Ingvill C. Oedegaard, and Reiner Mauer. 1998. *Inventory of National Election Studies in Europe 1945–1995*. Bergisch Gladbach: Edwin Ferger Verlag.

Molinar, Juan. 1991. "Counting the Number of Parties: An Alternative Index." *American Political Science Review* 85: 1383–91.

Morel, Laurence. 1993. "Party Attitudes Toward Referendums in Western Europe." *West European Politics* 16: 225–43.

Morel, Laurence. 1996. "France: Towards a Less Controversial Use of the Referendum." In *The Referendum Experience in Europe*, ed. Michael Gallagher and Pier Vincenzo Uleri. London: Macmillan.

Moreno, Luis, and Ana Arriba. 1996. "Dual Identity in Autonomous Catalonia." *Scottish Affairs* 17: 78–97.

Morlino, Leonardo. 1998. *Democracy between Consolidation and Crisis: Parties, Groups, and Citizens in Southern Europe.* Oxford: Oxford University Press.

Mowlana, Hamid. 1997. *Global Information and World Communication*, 2nd ed. London: Sage.

Mudde, C.E. 2000. *The Ideology of the Extreme Right*. Manchester: Manchester University Press.

Mughan, Anthony. 1995. "Television and Presidentialism: Australian and US Legislative Elections Compared." *Political Communication* 12: 327–42.

Müller, Wolfgang C. 1992. "Austria." In *Party Organizations: A Data Handbook on Party Organization in Western Democracies, 1960–90*, ed. Richard S. Katz and Peter Mair. London: Sage.

Nadeau, Richard, and Richard G. Niemi. 1999. "Rating the Chancellors and Their Budgets." *Political Studies* 46: 857–76.

Nadeau, Richard, Richard G. Niemi, and Timothy Amato. 2000. "Elite Economic Forecasts, Economic News, Mass Economic Expectations and Voting Intentions in Great Britain." *European Journal of Political Research* 38: 135–70.

Nadeau, Richard, Richard G. Niemi, and Antoine Yoshinaka. 2001. "A Cross-National Analysis of Economic Voting: Taking Account of the Political Context across Time and Nations." *Electoral Studies* 20.

Neto, Octario Amorim, and Gary W. Cox. 1997. "Electoral Institutions, Cleavage Structures, and the Number of Parties." *American Journal of Political Science* 41: 149–74.

Nevitte, Neil, André Blais, Elisabeth Gidengil, and Richard Nadeau. 1999. *Unsteady State: The 1997 Canadian Federal Election*. Toronto: Oxford University Press.

Newman, Bruce, I., ed. 1999. *Handbook of Political Marketing*. Thousand Oaks, CA: Sage.

Newman, Roland, and Shelley Cranshaw. 1973. "Towards a Closed Primary Election in Britain." *Political Quarterly* 44: 447–52.

Niemi, Richard. 1984. "The Problem of Strategic Behavior under Approval Voting." *American Political Science Review* 78: 952–58.

Niemi, Richard G., and Herbert F. Weisberg, 2001. *Controversies in Voting Behavior*, 4th ed. Washington, DC: CQ Press.

Niemi, Richard, Jeffrey S. Hill, and Bernard Grofman. 1985. "The Impact of Multimember Districts on Party Representation in State Legislatures." *Legislative Studies Quarterly* 10: 441–55.

Niemi, Richard G., Linda W. Powell, and Patricia L. Bicknell. 1986. "The Effects of Congruity between Community and District on Salience of US House Candidates." *Legislative Studies Quarterly* 11: 187–203.

Nieuwbeerta, Paul. 1995. *The Democratic Class Struggle in Twenty Countries, 1945–90*. Amsterdam: Thesis Publishers.

Nieuwbeerta, Paul, and Nan Dirk de Graaf. 1999. "Traditional Class Voting in 20 Postwar Societies." In *The End of Class Politics?,* ed. Geoffrey Evans. New York: Oxford University Press.

Nieuwbeerta, Paul, and Wout Ultee. 1999. "Class Voting in Western Industrialized Countries, 1945–1990: Systematizing and Testing Explanations." *European Journal of Political Research* 35: 123–60.

Norpoth, Helmut. 1996. "The Economy." In *Comparing Democracies: Elections and Voting Behavior in Global Perspective*, ed. Lawrence LeDuc, Richard G. Niemi, and Pippa Norris. Thousand Oaks, CA: Sage.

Norris, Pippa. 1996. "Legislative Recruitment." In *Comparing Democracies: Elections and Voting in Global Perspective*, ed. Lawrence LeDuc, Richard G. Niemi, and Pippa Norris. Thousand Oaks, CA: Sage.

Norris, Pippa, ed. 1997. *Passages to Power: Legislative Recruitment in Advanced Democracies*. Cambridge: Cambridge University Press.

Norris, Pippa. 1999a. A Gender-Generation Gap. In *Critical Elections: British Parties and Voters in Long-Term Perspective*, ed. Geoffrey Evans and Pippa Norris. London: Sage.

Norris, Pippa. 1999b. "Introduction: The Growth of Critical Citizens?" In *Critical Citizens: Global Support for Democratic Governance*. Oxford: Oxford University Press.

Norris, Pippa. 2000a. "Electoral Systems and Ethnic Conflict: Testing Consociational Theories in 12 Old and New Democracies." Paper presented at the International Political Science Association World Congress, Quebec City, August.

Norris, Pippa. 2000b. *A Virtuous Circle: Political Communications in Post-Industrial Societies*. New York: Cambridge University Press.

Norris, Pippa. 2001. *Digital Divide? Civic Engagement, Information Poverty and the Internet Worldwide*. New York: Cambridge University Press.

Norris, Pippa, ed. 2002. "Britain Votes 2001." *Parliamentary Affairs*, special issue, in press.

Norris, Pippa, John Curtice, David Sanders, Margaret Scammell, and Holli Semetko. 1999. *On Message: Communicating the Campaign*. London: Sage.

Obler, Jeffrey. 1974. "Intraparty Democracy and the Selection of Parliamentary Candidates: The Belgian Case." *British Journal of Political Science* 4: 163–85.

O'Donnell, Guillermo. 1999. "Horizontal Accountability in New Democracies." In *The Self-Restraining State: Power and Accountability in New Democracies*, ed. Andreas Schedler, Larry Diamond, and Marc F. Plattner. Boulder, CO: Lynne Rienner.

O'Donnell, Guillermo, Philippe Schmitter, and Lawrence Whitehead. 1987. *Transitions from Authoritarian Rule*. Baltimore, MD: Johns Hopkins University Press.

OECD. 2000. *OECD Information and Technology Outlook*. Paris: OECD.

Oppenhuis, Erik. 1995. *Voting Behavior in the European Community: A Comparative Analysis of Electoral Participation and Party Choice*. University of Amsterdam PhD dissertation.

Ordeshook, Peter C., and Olga V. Shvetsova. 1994. "Ethnic Heterogeneity, District Magnitude and the Number of Parties." *American Journal of Political Science* 38: 100–23.

Oskarson, Maria. 1995. 'Gender Gaps in Nordic Voting Behavior. In *Women in Nordic Press*, ed. Lauri Karvonen and Per Selle. Aldershot: Dartmouth.

Østergaard, Vernt Stubbe, ed. 1997. *The Media in Western Europe*, 2nd ed. London: Sage.

Page, Benjamin, and Robert Y. Shapiro. 1992. *The Rational Public: Fifty Years of Trends in Americans' Policy Preferences*. Chicago: University of Chicago Press.

Palmer, Harvey D. 1995. "Effects of Authoritarian and Libertarian Values on Conservative and Labour Party Support in Great Britain." *European Journal of Political Research* 27: 273–92.

Palmer, Harvey D. 1999. "Making Sense of the Noise in Personal Financial Evaluations: Reconsidering the Evidence of Pocketbook Economic Voting." Unpublished paper, University of Mississippi.

Pammett, Jon H., and Lawrence LeDuc. 1998. "Attitudes Toward Sovereignty and the Vote Decision in the 1995 Quebec Referendum." Paper presented at the annual meeting of the Canadian Political Science Association, Ottawa.

Pammett, Jon H., Harold D. Clarke, Jane Jenson, and Lawrence LeDuc. 1983. "Political Support and Voting Behaviour in the Quebec Referendum." In *Political Support in Canada: The Crisis Years*, ed. Allan Kornberg and Harold D. Clarke. Durham, NC: Duke University Press.

Panebianco, Angelo. 1988. *Political Parties: Organization and Power*. Cambridge: Cambridge University Press.

Papadopoulos, Yannis. 1998. *Démocratie directe*. Paris: Economica.

Pappi, Franz Urban. 1990. Klassenstruktur und Wählerverhalten im sozialen Wandel. In *Wahlen und Wähler: Analysen aus Anlass der Bundestagswahl 1987*, ed. Max Kaase and Hans-Dieter Klingemann. Opladen: Westdeutscher Verlag.

Parodi, Jean-Luc. 1978. "Note sur une règle peu connue du deuxième tour en régime majoritaire bipolaire." *Revue française de science politique* 28: 21–7.

Patterson, Thomas E. 1993. *Out of Order*. New York: Knopf.

Patterson, Thomas, and Robert McClure. 1976. *The Unseeing Eye: The Myth of Television Power in National Elections*. New York: Putnam.

Pattie, Charles, and Ron Johnston. 2001. "Talk as a Political Context: Conversation and Electoral Change in British Elections 1992–1997." *Electoral Studies* 20: 17–40.

Pedersen, Mogens N. 1979. "The Dynamics of European Party Systems: Changing Patterns of Electoral Volatility." *European Journal of Political Research* 7: 1–26.

Pedersen, Mogens N. 1988. "The Defeat of All Parties: The Danish Folketing Election of 1973." In *When Parties Fail: Emerging Alternative Organizations*, ed. Kay Lawson and Peter H. Merkl. Princeton, NJ: Princeton University Press.

Pesonen, Pertti. 1998. "Voting Decisions." In *To Join or Not to Join: Three Nordic Referendums on Membership in the European Union*, eds. Anders Todal Jenssen, Pertti Pesonen, and Mikael Gilljam. Oslo: Scandinavian University Press.

Petrocik, John R. 1996. "Issue-Ownership in Presidential Elections, With a 1980 Case Study." *American Journal of Political Science* 40: 825–50.

Petrocik, John R., and Joseph Doherty. 1996. "The Road to Divided Government: Paved without Intention." In *Divided Government: Change, Uncertainty, and the Constitutional Order*, ed. Peter F. Galderisi with Roberta Q. Hertzberg and Peter McNamara. Lanham, MD: Rowman and Littlefield.

Pew Center for People and the Press. 1999. *Retro-Politics: The Political Typology*. www.people-press.org/typo99rpt.htm

Pew Center for People and the Press. 2000. "Endnotes on Campaign 2000." www.people-press.org/endnote00rpt.htm

Piven, Frances, and Richard Cloward. 1977. *Poor People's Movements: Why they Succeed, How They Fail*. New York: Vintage.

Plassner, Fritz, Christian Scheucher, and Christian Senft. 1999. "Is There a European Style of Political Marketing?" In *The Handbook of Political Marketing*, ed. Bruce I. Newman. Thousand Oaks, CA: Sage.

Poguntke, Thomas. 1996. "Anti-Party Sentiment—Conceptual Thoughts and Empirical Evidence: Explorations into a Minefield." *European Journal of Political Research* 29: 319–44.

Powell, G. Bingham, Jr. 1980. "Voting Turnout in Thirty Democracies: Partisan, Legal and Socio-Economic Influences." In *Electoral Participation: A Comparative Analysis*, ed. Richard Rose. London: Sage.

Powell, G. Bingham, Jr. 1982. *Contemporary Democracies: Participation, Stability and Violence*. Cambridge, MA: Harvard University Press.

Powell, G. Bingham, Jr. 1986. "American Voter Turnout in Comparative Perspective." *American Political Science Review* 80: 17–43.

Powell, G. Bingham, Jr. 1989. "Constitutional Design and Citizen Electoral Control." *Journal of Theoretical Politics* 1: 107–30.

Powell, G. Bingham, Jr. 2000. *Elections as Instruments of Democracy: Majoritarian and Proportional Visions*. New Haven, CT: Yale University Press.

Powell, G. Bingham, Jr, and Georg S. Vanberg. 2000. "Election Laws, Disproportionality and Median Correspondence: Implications for Two Visions of Democracy." *British Journal of Political Science* 30: 383–411.

Powell, G. Bingham, Jr, and Guy D. Whitten. 1993. "A Cross-National Analysis of Economic Voting: Taking Account of the Political Context." *American Journal of Political Science* 37: 391–414.

Powers, Denise V., and James H. Cox. 1997. "Echoes from the Past: The Relationship between Satisfaction with Economic Reforms and Voting Behavior in Poland." *American Political Science Review* 91: 617–33.

Pryce, Sue. 1997. *Presidentializing the Premiership*. Houndmills: Macmillan.

Przeworski, Adam, and John Sprague. 1985. *Paper Stones: A History of Electoral Socialism*. Chicago: University of Chicago Press.

Putnam, Robert. 1966. "Political Attitudes and the Local Community." *American Political Science Review* 50: 640–54.

Putnam, Robert. 2000. *Bowling Alone: The Collapse and Revival of American Community*. New York: Simon and Schuster.

Putnam, Robert D., with Robert Leonardi and Raffaella Y. Nanetti. 1993. *Making Democracy Work: Civic Traditions in Modern Italy*. Princeton, NJ: Princeton University Press.

Qvortrup, Mads. 1998. "Voter Knowledge and Participation: A Comparative Study of Referendums in Denmark and Switzerland." *Representation* 35: 255–64.

Rae, Douglas W. 1967. *The Political Consequences of Electoral Laws*. New Haven, CT: Yale University Press.

Radcliff, Benjamin. 1992. "The Welfare State, Turnout and the Economy: A Comparative Analysis." *American Political Science Review* 86: 444–54.

Rahat, Gideon, and Reuven Y. Hazan. 2001. "Candidate Selection Methods: An Analytical Framework." *Party Politics* 7: 297–322.

Rahat, Gideon, and Neta Sher-Hadar. 1999. "The 1996 Party Primaries and Their Political Consequences." In *Elections in Israel 1996*, ed. Asher Arian and Michal Shamir. Albany, NY: State University of New York Press.

Ranney, Austin. 1981. "Candidate Selection." In *Democracy at the Polls: A Comparative Study of Competitive National Elections*, ed. David Butler, Howard R. Penniman, and Austin Ranney. Washington: American Enterprise Institute.

Reed, Steven R. 1990. "Structure and Behaviour: Extending Duverger's Law to the Japanese Case." *British Journal of Political Science* 20: 335–56.

Reif, Karlheinz, and Hermann Schmitt. 1980. "Nine Second-Order National Elections: A Conceptual Framework for the Analysis of European Election Results." *European Journal of Political Research* 8: 3–44.

Reif, Karlheinz. 1985. "Ten Second Order National Elections." In *Ten European Elections*, ed. Karlheinz Reif. Aldershot: Gower.

Reynolds, Andrew, and Ben Reilly. 1997. *The International IDEA Handbook of Electoral System Design*. Stockholm: International Institute for Democracy and Electoral Assistance.

Riker, William H. 1986. "Duverger's Law Revisited." In *Electoral Laws and their Political Consequences*, ed. Bernard Grofman and Arend Lijphart. New York: Agathon Press.

Robertson, David. 1976. *A Theory of Party Competition*. New York: Wiley.

Rokkan, Stein. 1968. "The Growth and Structuring of Mass Politics in Smaller European Democracies." *Comparative Studies in Society and History* 10: 173–210.

Rose, Richard, ed. 1974. *Electoral Behavior*. New York: Free Press.

Rose, Richard, ed. 1984. "Electoral Systems: A Question of Degree or of Principle?" In *Choosing an Electoral System: Issues and Alternatives*, ed. Arend Lijphart and Bernard Grofman. New York: Praeger.

Rose, Richard, ed. 1999. "New Russia Barometer Trends Since 1992." Studies in Public Policy 320, Center for the Study of Public Policy, University of Strathclyde.

Rose, Richard, ed. 2000. *International Encyclopedia of Elections*. Washington, DC: CQ Press.

Rose, Richard, ed. 2001. "How People View Democracy: A Diverging Europe." *Journal of Democracy* 12(1): 93–105.

Rose, Richard, and Christian Haerpfer. 1998. "New Democracies Barometer V: A 12-Nation Survey." Studies in Public Policy 306, Center for the Study of Public Policy, University of Strathclyde.

Rose, Richard, and Ian McAllister. 1986. *Voters Begin to Choose: From Closed-class to Open Elections in Britain*. Beverly Hills, CA: Sage.

Rose, Richard, and William Mishler. 1998. "Negative and Positive Party Identification in Post-Communist Countries." *Electoral Studies* 17: 217–34.

Rose, Richard, and Derek Urwin. 1969. "Social Cohesion, Political Parties and Strains in Regimes." *Comparative Political Studies* 2: 7–67.

Rose, Richard, and Derek Urwin. 1970. "Persistence and Change in Western Party Systems Since 1945." *Political Studies* 18: 287–319.

Rose, Richard, William Mishler, and Christian Haerpfer. 1999. *Democracy and Its Alternatives: Understanding Post-communist Societies*. Baltimore, MD: Johns Hopkins University Press.

Rose, Richard, Neil Munro, and Stephen White. 2001. "Voting in a Floating Party System: The 1999 Duma Election." *Europe-Asia Studies* 53: 419–43.

Rosenstone, Steven J., and John Mark Hansen. 1993. *Mobilization, Participation, and Democracy in America*. New York: Macmillan.

Rostow, W.W. 1961. *The Stages of Economic Growth*. Cambridge: Cambridge University Press.

Rourke, John T., Richard P. Hiskes, and Cyrus Zirakzadeh. 1992. *Direct Democracy and International Politics: Deciding International Issues Through Referendums*. Boulder, CO: Lynne Rienner.

Rule, Wilma. 1992. "Multimember Legislative Districts: Minority and Anglo Women's and Men's Recruitment Opportunity." In *United States Electoral Systems: Their Impact on Women and Minorities*, ed. Wilma Rule and Joseph F. Zimmerman. New York: Praeger.

Rule, Wilma. 1994. "Women's Underrepresentation and Electoral Systems." *PS: Political Science & Politics* 27: 689–93.

Rule, Wilma, and Pippa Norris. 1992. "Anglo and Minority Women's Underrepresentation in Congress: Is the Electoral System the Culprit?" In *United States Electoral Systems: Their Impact on Women and Minorities*, ed. Wilma Rule and Joseph F. Zimmerman. New York: Praeger.

Rustow, Dankwart. 1970. "Transitions to Democracy: Toward a Dynamic Model." *Comparative Politics* 2: 337–63.

Sage, G.H. 1999. "Justice Do It! The Nike Transnational Advocacy Network: Organization, Collective Actions, and Outcomes." *Sociology of Sport Journal* 16: 206–35.

Saggar, Shamit, and Anthony Heath. 1999. "Race: Towards a Multicultural Electorate?" In *Critical Elections: British Parties and Voters in Long-term Perspective*, ed. Geoffrey and Pippa Norris. Thousand Oaks, CA: Sage.

Sanders, David. 1999. "Conservative Incompetence, Labour Responsibility and the Feelgood Factor: Why the Economy Failed to Save the Conservatives in 1997." *Electoral Studies* 18: 251–70.

Sanders, David, David Marsh, and Hugh Ward. 1993. "The Electoral Impact of Press Coverage of the British Economy, 1979–87." *British Journal of Political Science* 23: 175–210.

Sankoff, David, and Koula Mellos. 1972. "The Swing Ratio and Game Theory." *American Political Science Review* 66: 551–4.

Sankoff, David, and Koula Mellos. 1973. "La régionalisation électorale et l'amplification des proportions." *Canadian Journal of Political Science* 6: 380–98.

Sartori, Giovanni. 1966. "European Political Parties: The Case of Polarized Pluralism." In *Political Parties and Political Development*, ed. Joseph LaPalombara and Myron Weiner. Princeton, NJ: Princeton University Press.

Sartori, Giovanni. 1970. "The Typology of Party Systems: Proposals for Improvement." In *Mass Politics: Studies in Political Sociology*, ed. Erik Allardt and Stein Rokkan. New York: Free Press.

Sartori, Giovanni. 1973. "What is 'Politics'?" *Political Theory* 1: 5–26.

Sartori, Giovanni. 1976. *Parties and Party Systems: A Framework for Analysis*. Cambridge: Cambridge University Press.

Sartori, Giovanni. 1987. *The Theory of Democracy Revisited*. Chatham, NJ: Chatham House.

Scarbrough, Elinor. 2000. "The British Election Study and Electoral Research." *Political Studies* 48: 391–414.

Scarrow, Susan. 1996. *Parties and their Members: Organizing for Victory in Britain and Germany*. Oxford: Oxford University Press.

Scarrow, Susan. 1999. "Parties and the Expansion of Direct Democracy: Who Benefits?" *Party Politics* 5: 341–62.

Scarrow, Susan. 2000. "Parties without Members? Party Organizations in a Changing Electoral Environment." In *Parties without Partisans*, ed. Russell J. Dalton and Martin P. Wattenberg. Oxford: Oxford University Press.

Scarrow, Susan, Paul Webb, and David Farrell. 2001. "From Social Integration to Electoral Contestation: The Changing Distribution of Power within Political Parties." In *Parties without Partisans: Political Change in Advanced Industrial Democracies*, ed. Russell J. Dalton and Martin P. Wattenberg. Oxford: Oxford University Press.

Schattschneider, E.E. 1942. *Party Government*. New York, Farrar and Rinehart.

Schattschneider, E.E. 1960. *The Semi-Sovereign People*. New York: Holt, Rinehart and Winston.

Schedler, Andreas, Larry Diamond, and Marc F. Plattner, eds. 1999. *The Self-Restraining State: Power and Accountability in New Democracies*. Boulder, CO: Lynne Rienner.

Schickler, Eric, and Donald Green. 1997. "The Stability of Party Identification in Western Democracies." *Comparative Political Studies* 30: 450–83.

Schmitt, Herman, and Sören Holmberg. 1995. "Political Parties in Decline?" In *Citizens and the State*, ed. Hans-Dieter Klingemann and Dieter Fuchs. Oxford: Oxford University Press.

Schmitt-Beck, Rüdiger. 1996. "Mass Media, the Electorate and the Bandwagon: A Study of Communication Effects on Vote Choice in Germany." *International Journal of Public Opinion Research* 8: 266–91.

Schmitter, Philippe. 1997. "Civil Society East and West." In *Consolidating the Third Wave Democracies: Themes and Perspectives*, ed. Larry Diamond, Marc. F. Plattner, Yun-han Chu, and Hung-mao Tien. Baltimore, MD: Johns Hopkins University Press.

Schoen, Harold. 1999. "Split-Ticket Voting in German Federal Elections, 1953–90: An Example of Sophisticated Balloting?" *Electoral Studies* 18: 473–96.

Schumpeter, Joseph A. 1952. *Capitalism, Socialism and Democracy*, 4th ed. London: George Allen & Unwin

Semetko, Holli, Jay G. Blumler, Michael Gurevitch, and David H. Weaver. 1991. *The Formation of Campaign Agendas*. Hillsdale, NJ: Lawrence Erlbaum.

Setälä, Maija. 1999. *Referendums and Democratic Government*. New York: St Martin's.

Seyd, Ben. 1998. "Regulating the Referendum." *Representation* 35: 191–9.

Shabad, Goldie, and Kazimierz M. Slomczynski. 1999. "Political Identities in the Initial Phase of Systemic Transformation in Poland: A Test of the Tabula Rasa Hypothesis." *Comparative Political Studies* 32: 690–723.

Shiratori, Rei. 1988. "Japan: Localism, Factionalism and Personalism." In *Candidate Selection in Comparative Perspective: The Secret Garden of Politics*, ed. Michael Gallagher and Michael Marsh. London: Sage.

Shoemaker, Pamela J., and Stephen D. Reese. 1996. *Mediating the Message*, 2nd ed. New York: Longman.

Shugart, Matthew Soberg. 1995. "The Electoral Cycle and Institutional Sources of Divided Presidential Government." *American Political Science Review* 89: 327–43.

Shugart, Matthew Soberg, and John M. Carey. 1992. *Presidents and Assemblies: Constitutional Design and Electoral Dynamics*. Cambridge: Cambridge University Press.

Shugart, Matthew Soberg, and Martin P. Wattenberg, eds. 2001. *Mixed-Member Electoral Systems: The Best of Both Worlds?* New York: Oxford University Press.

Siegel, M., and L. Biener. 1997. "Evaluating the Impact of Statewide Anti-Tobacco Campaigns: The Massachusetts and California Tobacco Control Programs." *Journal of Social Issues* 53: 147–68.

Simpson, Alan. 1992. *Referendums: Constitutional and Political Perspectives*. Victoria University of Wellington, Department of Political Science.

Sinnott, Richard. 1995. *Irish Voters Decide: Voting Behaviour in Elections and Referendums Since 1918*. Manchester: Manchester University Press.

Sisk, Timothy D. 1995. "Electoral System Choice in South Africa: Implications for Intergroup Moderation." *Nationalism and Ethnic Politics* 1: 178–204.

Siune, Karen, and Wolfgang Truetzschler. 1992. *Dynamics of Media Politics: Broadcast and Electronic Media in Western Europe*. London: Sage.

Siune, Karen, Palle Svensson, and Ole Tonsgaard. 1994. "The European Union: Why the Danes said NO in 1992 but YES in 1993." *Electoral Studies* 13: 107–15.

Smith, Anthony. 1981. "Mass Communications." In *Democracy at the Polls*, ed. David Butler, Howard R. Penniman, and Austin Ranney. Washington, DC: American Enterprise Institute.

Smith, Anthony, ed. 1998. *Television: An International History*, 2nd ed. Oxford: Oxford University Press.

Somit, Albert, Rudolf Wildenmann, Bernhard Boll, and Andrea Römmele, eds. 1994. *The Victorious Incumbent: A Threat to Democracy?* Aldershot: Dartmouth.

Spafford, Duff. 1970. "The Electoral System of Canada." *American Political Science Review* 64: 168–76.

Stanley, Harold W., and Richard G. Niemi. 1995. *Vital Statistics of American Politics*, 4th ed. Washington, DC: CQ Press.

Stanley, Harold W., and Richard G. Niemi. 1999. "Party Coalitions in Transition: Partisanship and Group Support, 1952–96." In *Reelection 1996: How Americans Voted*, ed. Herbert F. Weisberg, and Janet M. Box-Steffensmeier. Chatham, NJ: Chatham House.

Stepan, Alfred. 1999. "Federalism and Democracy: Beyond the US Model." *Journal of Democracy* 10(4): 19–34.

Stepan, Alfred, and Cindy Skach. 1993. "Constitutional Frameworks and Democratic Consolidation: Parliamentarism versus Presidentialism." *World Politics* 46: 1–22.

Stewart, Marianne C., and Harold D. Clarke. 1998. "The Dynamics of Party Identification in Federal Systems: The Canadian Case." *American Journal of Political Science* 42: 97–116.

Stokes, Susan C. 1996. "Introduction: Public Opinion and Market Reforms – The Limits of Economic Voting." *Comparative Political Studies* 29: 499–519.

Strøm, Kaare. 1990. *Minority Government and Majority Rule*. Cambridge: Cambridge University Press.

Studlar, D., Ian McAllister, and B. Hayes. 1978. "Explaining the Gender Gap in Voting: A Cross-national Analysis." *Social Science Quarterly* 79: 779–98.

Suksi, Markku. 1993. *Bringing in the People: A Comparison of Constitutional Form and Practices of the Referendum*. Dordrecht: Nijhoff.

Sussman, Leonard R. 2000. "Censor Dot Gov: The Internet and Press Freedom 2000." *Freedom House Press Freedom Survey 2000*. www.freedomhouse.org/pfs2000/sussman.html

Swanson, David L., and Paolo Mancini. 1996. *Politics, Media, and Modern Democracy: An International Study of Innovations in Electoral Campaigning and Their Consequences*. Westport, CT: Praeger.

Taagepera, Rein. 1986. "Reformulating the Cube Law for Proportional Representation Elections." *American Political Science Review* 80: 489–504.

Taagepera, Rein, and Matthew Soberg Shugart. 1989. *Seats and Votes: The Effects and Determinants of Electoral Systems*. New Haven, CT: Yale University Press.

Tate, Katherine. 1994. *From Politics to Protest*. Cambridge, MA: Harvard University Press.

Taylor, Peter J., and R.J. Johnston. 1979. *Geography of Elections*. New York: Penguin.

Teixeira, Ruy. 1992. *The Disappearing American Voter*. Washington, DC: Brookings.

Tingsten, Herbert. 1937. *Political Behavior*. London: King.

Thomas, John Clayton. 1979. "The Changing Nature of Partisan Divisions in the West: Trends in Domestic Policy Orientations in Ten Party Systems." *European Journal of Political Research* 7: 397–413.

Thurber, James, and Candice J. Nelson, eds. 2000. *Campaign Warriors: Political Consultants in Elections*. Washington, DC: Brookings.

Thurber, James, Candice J. Nelson, and David A. Dulio, eds. 2000. *Crowded Airwaves: Campaign Advertising in Elections*. Washington, DC: Brookings.

Toka, Gabor. 1998. "Party Appeals and Voter Loyalties in New Democracies." *Political Studies* 46: 589–610.

Tonsgaard, Ole. 1992. "A Theoretical Model of Referendum Behaviour." In *From Voters to Participants*, ed. Peter Gundelach and Karen Siune. Århus: Institute for Political Science, University of Aarhus.

Toole, James. 2000. "Government Formation and Party System Stabilization in East Central Europe." *Party Politics* 6: 441–61.

Topf, Richard. 1995. "Electoral Participation." In *Citizens and the State*, ed. Hans-Dieter Klingemann and Dieter Fuchs. Oxford: Oxford University Press.

Tracey, Michael. 1998. *The Decline and Fall of Public Service Broadcasting*. Oxford: Oxford University Press.

Tsebelis, George. 1990. "Elite Interaction and Constitutional Building in Consociational Democracies." *Journal of Theoretical Politics* 2: 5–29.

USIA. 2000. "Central Asians Differ on Islam's Political Role, but Agree on a Secular State." *USIA: Opinion Analysis* (Washington: USIA) 6th July.

Uslaner, Eric M. 1989. "Multiple Party Identifiers in Canada: Participation and Affect." *Journal of Politics* 51: 993–1003.

Valen, Henry. 1988. "Norway: Decentralization and Group Representation." In *Candidate Selection in Comparative Perspective: The Secret Garden of Politics*, ed. Michael Gallagher and Michael Marsh. London: Sage.

van den Bergh, George. 1955. *Unity in Diversity: A Systematic Critical Analysis of All Electoral Systems*. London: B.T. Batsford.

van der Brug, Wouter, Meindert Fennema, and Jean Tillie. 2000. "Anti-Immigrant Parties in Europe: Ideological or Protest Vote?" *European Journal of Political Research* 37: 77–102.

van der Eijk, Cees. 2000. "The Netherlands." In *Democracy and the Media: A Comparative Perspective*, ed. Richard Gunther and Anthony Mughan. New York: Cambridge University Press.

van der Eijk, Cees, Mark Franklin et al. 1996. *Choosing Europe? The European Electorate and National Politics in the Face of Union*. Ann Arbor, MI: University of Michigan Press.

van der Eijk, Cees, and Kees Niemöller. 1983. *Electoral Change in the Netherlands*. Amsterdam: CT Press.

van der Eijk, Cees, Mark Franklin, and Michael Marsh. 1995. "What Voters Teach Us About Europe-Wide Elections: What Europe-Wide Elections Teach Us About Voters." *Electoral Studies* 14: 149–66.

van Egmond, Marcel, Nan Dirk de Graaf, and Cees van der Eijk. 1998. "Electoral Participation in the Netherlands: Individual and Contextual Influences." *European Journal of Political Research* 34: 281–300.

Verba, Sidney, and Norman Nie. 1972. *Participation in America: Political Democracy and Social Equality*. New York: Harper & Row.

Verba, Sidney, Norman Nie, and Jae-on Kim. 1978. *Participation and Political Equality: A Seven-Nation Comparison*. New York: Cambridge University Press.

Verba, Sidney, Kay Schlozman, and Henry Brady. 1995. *Voice and Equality: Civic Voluntarism in American Politics*. Cambridge, MA: Harvard University Press.

Vowles, Jack and Peter Aimer, eds. 1994. *Double Decision: The 1993 Election and Referendum in New Zealand*. Victoria: University of Wellington Press.

Wald, Kenneth. 1997. *Religion and Politics in America*, 3rd ed. New York: St Martin's.

Ware, Alan. 1996. *Political Parties and Party Systems*. Oxford: Oxford University Press.

Wasserman, D.P. 1999. "The Local Contours of Campaign Coverage: State Newspapers and the 1988 Super Tuesday Campaign." *Communication Research* 26: 701–25.

Watanuki, Joji. 2001. "Japan—From Emerging to Stable Party System?" In *Party Systems and Voter Alignments Revisited*, ed. Lauri Karvonen and Stein Kuhnle. London: Routledge.

Wattenberg, Martin P. 1991. *The Rise of Candidate-Centered Politics: Presidential Elections of the 1980s*. Cambridge, MA: Harvard University Press.

Wattenberg, Martin P. 1998. *The Decline of American Political Parties, 1952–1996*. Cambridge, MA: Harvard University Press.

Wattenberg, Martin P. 2001. "The Decline of Party Mobilization." In *Parties without Partisans*, ed. Russell Dalton and Martin Wattenberg. New York: Oxford University Press.

Wattenberg, Martin P., and Matthew Shugart. 2000. *Mixed-member Electoral Systems: The Best of Both Worlds?* Oxford: Oxford University Press.

Weaver, David H. 1998. *The Global Journalist: News People Around the World*. Cresskill, NJ: Hampton Press.

Weingast, Barry. 1997. "The Political Foundations of Democracy and the Rule of Law." *American Political Science Review* 91: 245–63.

Welch, Susan, and Rebecca Herrick. 1992. "The Impact of At-Large Elections on the Representation of Minority Women." In *United States Electoral Systems: Their Impact on Women and Minorities*, ed. Wilma Rule and Joseph F. Zimmerman. New York: Praeger.

Wertman, Douglas A. 1988. "Italy: Local Involvement, Central Control." In *Candidate Selection in Comparative Perspective: The Secret Garden of Politics*, ed. Michael Gallagher and Michael Marsh. London: Sage.

West, Darrell M. 1997. *Air Wars: Television Advertising in Election Campaigns, 1952–1996*. Washington, DC: CQ Press.

Weymouth, Tony, and Bernard Lamizet. 1996. *Markets & Myth: Forces for Change in the European Media*. London: Longman.

White, Stephen. 2000. *Russia's New Politics: The Management of a Postcommunist Society*. Cambridge: Cambridge University Press.

White, Stephen, Richard Rose, and Ian McAllister. 1997. *How Russia Votes*. Chatham, NJ: Chatham House.

Whitehead, Laurence. 1989. "The Consolidation of Fragile Democracies: A Discussion with Illustrations." In *Democracy in the Americas: Stopping the Pendulum*, ed. Robert A. Pastor. New York: Holmes and Meier.

Whitten, Guy D., and Harvey D. Palmer. 1999. "Cross-National Analyses of Economic Voting." *Electoral Studies* 18: 49–67.

Widfeldt, Anders. 1995. "Party Membership and Party Representatives." In *Citizens and the State*, ed. Hans-Dieter Klingemann and Dieter Fuchs. Oxford: Oxford University Press.

Wilcox, Clyde. 2000. *Onward Christian Soldiers?*, 2nd ed. Boulder, CO: Westview.

Wilkin, Sam, Brandon Haller, and Helmut Norpoth. 1997. "From Argentina to Zambia: A World-Wide Test of Economic Voting." *Electoral Studies* 16: 301–16.

Wlezien, Christopher, and Mark Franklin, eds. 2002. "The Future of Election Studies." Special issue of *Electoral Studies* vol. 20.

Wolfinger, Raymond, and Steven Rosenstone. 1980. *Who Votes?* New Haven, CT: Yale University Press.

World Bank. 2000. *World Development Report 1999/2000*. Washington, DC: World Bank.

Wu, Chung-li. 2001. "The Transformation of the Kuomintang's Candidate Selection System." *Party Politics* 7: 103–18.

Zaller, John, R. 1992. *The Nature and Origins of Mass Opinion*. Cambridge: Cambridge University Press.

Zaller, John, R. 1996. "The Myth of Massive Media Impact Revisited: New Support for a Discredited Idea." In *Political Persuasion and Attitude Change*, ed. Diana C. Mutz, Paul M. Sniderman, and Richard A. Brody. Ann Arbor, MI: University of Michigan Press.

Zuckerman, Alan S. 1982. "New Approaches to Political Cleavage." *Comparative Politics* 15: 131–44.

Zuckerman, Alan S., Lawrence A. Kotler-Berkowitz, and Lucas A. Swaine. 1998. "Anchoring Political Preferences: The Structural Bases of Stable Electoral Decisions and Political Attitudes in Britain." *European Journal of Political Research* 33: 285–321.

About the Contributors

André Blais is Professor in the Department of Political Science and Associate Fellow at the Centre de Recherche et de Développement en Économique at the Unversité de Montréal. He was the co-principal investigator of the 2000 Canadian Election Study and has a Canada Research Chair in Electoral Studies. He has published *To Vote Or Not To Vote? The Merits and Limits of Rational Choice* (2000), *An Unsteady State: The 1997 Canadian Federal Election* (2000), *A Question of Ethics: Canadians Speak Out* (1998), *Governments, Parties and Public Sector Employees: Canada, United States, Britain, and France* (1997), and *The Challenge of Direct Democracy: The 1992 Canadian Referendum* (1996). He was on the editorial board of the *International Encyclopedia of Elections*.

Russell J. Dalton is Professor of Political Science and Director of the Center for the Study of Democracy at the University of California, Irvine. He has been a Fulbright Professor at the University of Mannheim and held a German Marshall Fund Fellowship. He has written *The Green Rainbow: Environmental Interest Groups in Western Europe* (1994), *Citizen Politics* (2002), and *Politics in Germany* (1993); co-authored *Critical Masses: Citizens, Environmental Destruction, and Nuclear Weapons Production in Russia and the United States* (1999); and edited *Parties without Partisans* (2001), *Germans Divided* (1996), *The New Germany Votes* (1993), and *Challenging the Political Order* (1990). He is now working on a comparative study of political support in advanced industrial democracies.

Larry Diamond is a Senior Fellow at the Hoover Institution, Stanford University, co-editor of the *Journal of Democracy*, and co-director of the National Endowment for Democracy's International Forum for Democratic Studies. He is the author of *Developing Democracy: Toward Consolidation* (1999), and *Promoting Democracy in the 1990s* (1995). Among his recent edited books are *Political Parties and Democracy* (with Richard Gunther, 2001), *Consolidating Democracy in South Korea* (with Byung-Kook Kim, 2000), *Institutional Reform and Democratic Consolidation in Korea* (with Doh Chull Shin, 2000), *The Self-Restraining State: Power and Accountability in New Democracies* (with Andreas Schedler and Marc F. Plattner), and (with Marc F. Plattner) *Democracy in East Asia* (1998), *Democratization in Africa* (1999), and *The Global Divergence of Democracies* (2001). He is currently researching democratic consolidation in Taiwan and is part of a collaborative research project on public opinion in East Asian democracies.

Mark N. Franklin is the John R. Reitemeyer Professor of International Politics at Trinity College, Hartford, Connecticut, and Associated Professor in the Amsterdam School of Communications Research. He is also a director of the European Elections Studies project. He is the author or co-author of seven books, including *The Decline of Class Voting in Britain* (1985), *Electoral Change* (1992), and *Choosing Europe? The European Electorate and National Politics in the Face of Union* (1996). He is also editor or co-editor of four volumes including a Special Issue on "The Future of Election Studies," *Electoral Studies* (2002).

Reuven Y. Hazan is a senior Lecturer in the Department of Political Science at the Hebrew University of Jerusalem. His research interests include parties and party systems, electoral systems, and legislative studies. His articles have appeared in *Comparative Political Studies, Electoral Studies, Journal of Legislative Studies, Journal of Theoretical Politics, Legislative Studies Quarterly, Party Politics, Political Geography*, and various other journals. He is the author of *Centre Parties: Polarization and Competition in European Parliamentary Democracies* (2000), and *Reforming Parliamentary Committees: Israel in Comparative Perspective* (2001).

Lawrence LeDuc is Professor of Political Science at the University of Toronto. His publications include *Absent Mandate: Canadian Electoral Politics in an Era of Restructuring* (1996), *How Voters Change* (1990), and *Political Choice in Canada* (1980), as well as articles on voting and elections in a number of North American and European political science journals. His most recent book is *Understanding Referendums: Direct Democracy in Theory and Practice* (2002).

Peter Mair is Professor of Comparative Politics in Leiden University in the Netherlands and previously taught at the University of Limerick, the University of Strathclyde, the University of Manchester, and the European University Institute, Florence. He is co-editor of the journal *West European Politics*, and among his recent books are *Party System Change: Approaches and Interpretations* (1997), and *Representative Government in Modern Europe: Institutions, Parties and Governments* (with Michael Gallagher and Michael Laver, 3rd edn, 2000).

Louis Massicotte is Associate Professor of Political Science at the Université de Montréal. His publications include two books *Le Scrutin au Québec: Un Miroir Déformant* (1985), and *Responsible Government in Canada* (1999). His articles on electoral systems, legislatures, party discipline, federalism, and by-elections have been published in the *European Journal of Political Research, Electoral Studies*, the *Journal of Legislative Studies, Commonwealth and Comparative Politics*, the *Canadian Journal of Political Science*, and the *Review of Constitutional Studies*. He contributed numerous articles to the *International Encyclopedia of Elections*. Formerly with Elections Canada, he has been active in the field of democratic development in 13 countries.

William L. Miller is Edward Caird Professor of Politics at Glasgow University, Scotland and a Fellow of the British Academy. Among his recent books are *Political Culture in Contemporary Britain: People and Politicians, Principles and Practice* (with Annis May Timpson and Michael Lessnoff, 1996), *Values and Political Change in Postcommunist Europe* (with Stephen White and Paul Heywood, 1998), *Models of Local Governance: Political Theory and Public Opinion in Britain* (with Malcolm Dickson and Gerry Stoker, 2000), and *A Culture of Corruption? Coping with Government in Postcommunist Europe* (with Åse B. Grødeland and Tatyana Y. Koshechkina, 2001).

Richard G. Niemi is Don Alonzo Watson Professor of Political Science at the University of Rochester. He is co-author or co-editor of *Vital Statistics on American Politics 2001–2002* (2001), *Controversies in Voting Behavior*, 4th edition (2001), *Term Limits in the State Legislatures* (2000), *Civic Education: What Makes Students Learn* (1998), and other books. He has written numerous articles on political socialization, voting, and legislative districting. His current research includes topics on public opinion and on civic education.

Pippa Norris is Associate Director (Research) at the Joan Shorenstein Center on the Press, Politics, and Public Policy at the John F. Kennedy School of Government, Harvard University. She has published more than two-dozen books; the most recent include *A Virtuous Circle: Political Communications in Post-Industrial Societies* (2000), *Digital Divide: Information Poverty, Civic Engagement and the Internet Worldwide* (2001), *Britain Votes 2001* (2001), and *Democratic Phoenix: Political Activism Worldwide* (2002). Her interests focus on comparative political behavior, political communications, and gender politics.

Author Index

Subject Index